BARRON'S

GRE

MATH WORKBOOK

BARRON'S
GRE
MATH WORKBOOK

Blair Madore, Ph.D.
Associate Professor of Mathematics
State University of New York (SUNY) at Potsdam

About the Author

Blair Madore is a native of Newfoundland who earned a BMATH from the University of Waterloo and an MSc and Ph.D. from the University of Toronto. He has been happily residing and teaching college math for the past ten years in Potsdam, New York. This is his first book for Barron's.

Acknowledgments

Many thanks to my wife, Magaret, and SUNY Potsdam for their support while working on this project. Special thanks to Harold Ellingsen and Andrew Brouwer for their review of the math in this book.

All inquiries should be addressed to:
Barron's Educational Series, Inc.
250 Wireless Boulevard
Hauppauge, NY 11788
www.barronseduc.com

Library of Congress Catalog Card No. 2009002102

ISBN-13: 978-0-7641-4174-4
ISBN-10: 0-7641-4174-0

Library of Congress Cataloging-in-Publication Data

Madore, Blair.
   GRE math workbook / Blair Madore.
      p. cm.
   ISBN–13: 978–0–7641–4174–4
   ISBN–10: 0–7641–4174–0
   1.   Mathematics—Examinations, questions, etc.   2.   Mathematics—Examinations—Study guides.
   3.   Graduate Record Examination—Study guides.   I. Title.

   QA43.M228 2009
   510.76—dc22   2009002102

PRINTED IN THE UNITED STATES OF AMERICA

9 8 7 6 5 4 3 2 1

Contents

4 ALGEBRA 99

5 DATA ANALYSIS 135

6 GEOMETRY 173

To the Student

Dear Student,

You're at a very exciting point in your life! You've completed or will soon complete your undergraduate degree and you're planning to enter the most demanding, stimulating, and rewarding of educational experiences—graduate school.

Although no one likes to take another exam, your GRE score is one of several tools your future school will use to determine your admission or even more importantly, the funding you may receive while attending graduate school. A small investment of time preparing for this exam could pay off very well.

I encourage you to take the GRE seriously and allocate regular time to study and preparation. A few hours each week would be preferable to 20 hours just before you take the test. If you need motivation or extra help, look for a GRE prep course in your area. It can be much easier to study when you have a teacher to consult and a group of other students to work with.

Every student is in a different situation. You may be a physics whiz who needs to polish her math skills so you can score the 750 your dream graduate school expects. You may be a psychology major who hasn't formally studied math since high school and needs to improve his math skills so you can score the 550 your dream graduate school requires. To avoid disappointment and set clear expectations for yourself, I suggest you contact graduate schools you intend to apply to and ask them what score is needed (or even what score would earn you a top scholarship).

This workbook is designed to help you review the mathematics typically needed on the GRE general math exam. Since virtually all high school mathematics *could* be covered, this book cannot attempt to be a complete replacement for your high school texts. Don't worry though; even if you feel uncertain of your math skills, I know that you will recall most rudimentary ideas when reminded of them. Thus this book reminds you of basics and focuses on the topics that appear most frequently in the exam and that most students have difficulty with. We provide references for further study if needed.

Good luck and good studying!

Guide to Using This Book

Chapter 1 introduces the format of the test, while Chapter 2 discusses strategies for different types of questions. Both chapters have GRE-style problems and solutions for you to test your newfound skills.

Chapters 3–6 review the all the mathematics relevant to the GRE quantitative test. Each section of these chapters concludes with Basic problems and GRE problems. The Basic problems test the knowledge from that section. In some cases, they are less likely to appear as an actual GRE problem. GRE problems are more challenging and are similar to problems that actually appear on the GRE. They can test more than just the skills of that section. Detailed solutions for all problems are at the end of each chapter.

Chapter 7 contains two sample tests and full solutions for those problems. The Appendix is a list of suggested information to memorize.

If you are confident of your math skills,

- Read Chapters 1 and 2 and concentrate on problem-solving strategies. These can improve your speed and help you with problems you don't immediately know how to solve.

- Read through Chapters 3–6, concentrating on the tips and more challenging examples. Work all the GRE problems, returning to the chapter for more information as needed.

- Consider the Appendix and memorize the facts there, if you don't know them already.

- Try the sample tests in Chapter 7. Return to earlier sections of the book as needed to review any topics that caused you trouble on the sample test.

If you are less certain of your math skills,

- Read Chapter 1 to familiarize yourself with the style of the test.

- Read through Chapters 3–6 concentrating on basic skills and examples. Work all the Basic problems, returning to the chapter for more information as needed.

- Read Chapter 2 and concentrate on problem-solving strategies. These can improve your speed and help you with problems you don't immediately know how to solve.

- Reread Chapters 3–6, concentrating on the tips and more challenging examples. Work all the GRE problems.

- Consider the Appendix and memorize the facts there, if you don't know them already.

- Try the sample tests in Chapter 7. Return to earlier sections of the book as needed to review any topics that caused you trouble on the sample tests.

The GRE General Math Exam

The GRE general test includes sections called quantitative, verbal, and analytical. This book focuses on the quantitative sections where your mathematical abilities are tested.

For more general information about taking the GRE, consult *www.ets.org* or your local testing center. This will answer questions like

- Do I have to register or can I just show up?

- How do I register for the test?

- What should I bring with me to the testing center?

- What aids can I bring into the test?

- What does it cost?

The quantitative section tests your knowledge of arithmetic, elementary algebra, some geometry, and very elementary probability and statistics. This is material that you studied in elementary, middle, and high school. It does not cover any calculus or advanced mathematics. It mainly tests your ability to reason logically.

Even though the material covered is pre-college, this test expects you to demonstrate the sophisticated reasoning skills of a (soon-to-be) college graduate. Math and science majors should not underestimate this test—there is challenge here for everyone. Students who have not studied mathematics in a number of years should not overestimate this test—with practice a good score is possible for every reasonably good thinker.

EXAM STRUCTURE

In the *written* GRE general test you will be given two[1] quantitative sections to solve. Each section consists of 30 questions and you have 30 minutes to solve them. Once your 30 minutes are up, you are done with that section and cannot return to those questions or change those answers.

---

[1] *You may be given additional sections that are not scored or are used for research purposes.*

In the *computer-based* GRE general test you will be given one[2] section of quantitative questions to solve. This consists of 28 questions and you have 45 minutes to solve them. Unlike the written exam, only one question is presented at a time, and after you submit an answer you may not return to that question or change that answer.

QUESTION TYPES

There are three types of questions on the GRE quantitative test. Approximately half of the questions are multiple choice and the rest are two column. On the *computer-based* GRE general test, there may be one numeric entry question or possibly none.

Multiple-choice questions are very familiar to most people. A question and five answers (A, B, C, D, or E) are given, and you must choose the *best* answer.

EXAMPLE 1

You are given two circles with radii *r* and *R*, respectively. The second circle has twice the area of the first. What is the relationship between the radii?

(A) $2r = R$
(B) $r = 2R$
(C) $r^2 = 2R^2$
(D) $2r^2 = R^2$
(E) $r = \sqrt{2}\ R$

Solution: The area of the first is πr^2 and the area of the second is πR^2. Since the area of the second is twice the first, $\pi R^2 = 2\pi r^2$. We cancel π from each side and see that $R^2 = 2r^2$. Choose **D**. If we take the square root of both sides, we see that $R = \sqrt{2}\ r$, an alternate solution, but not one of the choices.

I say you should choose the *best* answer because it is not uncommon to work a problem and determine an answer that is not exactly equal to any of the given answers. This can happen when you make a mistake and you're wrong. This can also happen when you're right but some rounding in the calculation can lead your answer and the given answer to not match exactly. If your answer is close to a given answer but not exactly the same, it's probably the right answer. If your answer lies halfway between two given answers, it's time to go back and check things over (unless you're in a time rush, when you'd guess one of those two choices).

EXAMPLE 2

Which number is closest to $\sqrt{139}$?

(A) 11
(B) 12
(C) 13
(D) 14
(E) 15

---

[2]*An additional unscored section will be given and may consist of quantitative questions.*

Solution: First we know that $11^2 = 121$ and $12^2 = 144$ so $\sqrt{121} = 11$ and $\sqrt{144} = 12$. As 139 is between 121 and 144, $\sqrt{139}$ is between 11 and 12. But is it closer to 11 or 12? Since 139 is much closer to 144 than 121, we can be certain that $\sqrt{139}$ is much closer to 12 than 11. Choose **B**.

Be careful to not overextend this kind of reasoning. 132.5 is exactly halfway between 121 and 144 but $\sqrt{132.5}$ is not exactly halfway between 11 and 12. In fact $\sqrt{132.5} = 11.510\ldots$, close to halfway but not exactly.

Note that using a calculator (or some other sort of calculating device) we could determine that $\sqrt{139}$ is approximately 11.7898. But you cannot use any aids on the GRE so we are forced to use other techniques. Some people think this means the GRE is not practical or realistic—wouldn't anyone have access to a calculator, in their career? I would counter that, yes, most people always have access to a calculator, but they might not have the time or inclination to use it. A sharp business executive might make any number of quick calculations in her mind during a business negotiation, but she might not want to show publicly what she was doing. The kind of reasoning skills that the GRE assesses can be a real asset in any career.

Two column questions are usually found only on the GRE tests (or some other standardized tests). For that reason it is most important to familiarize yourself with this type of question and any strategies that are appropriate for them. You are given two quantities, one in Column A and one in Column B. You must determine the relationship between the quantities. You may give four possible answers:

Choose **A** if Column A is greater than Column B.
Choose **B** if Column B is greater than Column A.
Choose **C** if they are equal.
Choose **D** if it cannot be determined.

EXAMPLE 3

Column A	Column B
$\left(3 + \dfrac{1}{5}\right)\left(3 - \dfrac{1}{5}\right)$	$\left(3 + \dfrac{1}{4}\right)\left(3 - \dfrac{1}{4}\right)$

Solution: You could just calculate both quantities as fractions and compare but this is tedious at best. If you remember your rule for difference of squares, then Column A is $3^2 - \left(\dfrac{1}{5}\right)^2 = 9 - \dfrac{1}{25}$ while Column B is $3^2 - \left(\dfrac{1}{4}\right)^2 = 9 - \dfrac{1}{16}$. Since $\dfrac{1}{25} < \dfrac{1}{16}$, $9 - \dfrac{1}{25} > 9 - \dfrac{1}{16}$. Choose **A**, since Column A is larger than Column B.

EXAMPLE 4

Column A	Column B
$(3 + x)(3 - x)$	$(x + 3)(x - 3)$

Solution: Using difference of squares (see Chapter 4) to expand, we discover that Column A is $9 - x^2$ while Column B is $x^2 - 9$. Which is larger? It will depend on the value of x. When $x = 0$, Column A is 9, and Column B is -9. When $x = 4$, Column A is -7, and Column B is 7. So sometimes Column A is larger and sometimes Column B is larger. Choose **D**, it cannot be determined (without knowing more about x).

Numeric entry questions ask you to give a decimal or fraction as the answer to a question. If it is a fraction, you will be asked to enter the numerator and denominator separately. This type of question tests your ability to work directly to an answer.

EXAMPLE 5

The town council charges each residence for services including $2 each week for trash pickup, $10 a month for water hookup plus $0.002 per gallon of water used, and $25 each fall for leaf removal. Bills are calculated annually but paid in quarterly installments. Kareem's family used 125,000 gallons of water last year. What did they pay each quarter?

Solution: They paid

52 weeks × $2/week	= $104 for trash
12 months × $10/month	= $120 for water hookup
125,000 gallons × $0.002/gallon	= $250 for water used
	$25 for leaf collection
Total	$499

So each quarter they paid $499/4 = $124.75.

TOPICS AND SCORING

The quantitative test covers many kinds of quantitative reasoning. This includes working with integers, fractions, rates of change, proportions, measurement, decimals, radicals, exponents, GCDs, LCMs, primes, factoring, polynomials, solving equations and inequalities, functions, percentages, averages, charts and graphs, probability, counting, triangles, quadrilaterals, circles, Pythagorean theorem perimeter, area, surface area, and volume. Most questions cover more than one topic. In any given GRE test, almost every one of these topics will be covered. None of them appear very frequently so all topics need attention. Yes, it is important to know the basics of each topic, but the test wants you to show you can reason—not just recite a mathematical fact or formula. Above all else, developing and improving your reasoning skill is very important.

TIP

Since every question has equal weight and you can do questions in any order, do the easiest ones first. What is easy for you may not be easy for other students. Still most students find the Data Analysis questions challenging. You would be wise to leave them until last.

In the *written* GRE general test all questions are weighted equally. Your total number of correct questions becomes your raw score (out of 30) which is then scaled to give a score out of 800. Scores are scaled to account for variations in the difficulty of some exams.

In the *computer-based* GRE general test, you answer one problem at a time and there is no backtracking to change your answers. The computer will start by asking you an average difficulty question. If you get it right you will be asked a harder question. If you get it wrong you will be asked an easier question. By the end of the test you may be alternately answering correctly and incorrectly questions of about the same difficulty. That difficulty determines your score.

Usually, the first few questions determine the approximate range of your score. The remaining questions, chosen from your approximate range of difficulty, are used to fine-tune your score.

NO CALCULATORS?!

No calculators are allowed on the GRE quantitative test. Since most people taking the test have grown up with a calculator handy, this seems like a real hindrance. Why are calculators not allowed? You may think it is to reward those who can calculate quickly without a calculator. In my opinion, it's the exact opposite. It's to reward those who can *reason quickly without calculating.* Many questions can be answered with minimal calculation if you use the right kind of reasoning. Our leaders of tomorrow will always have access to calculation equipment or even someone to run the computer or calculator for them. But they have to know the right questions to ask and the right line of reasoning to investigate. The GRE searches for that kind of higher quantitative reasoning.

We could speculate further about why calculators are not allowed, but that will not help you with the GRE. Here are some practical suggestions that will help you.

- *Practice without a calculator.* If you can't use a calculator on the test, why would you use one while practicing for it? You don't prepare for a foot race with a bicycle. Start working without a calculator immediately. Don't use a calculator while studying from this book, taking a GRE prep class, or during other times in your life. You can survive without one, and the sooner you get used to that the better you will be able to work without one on the GRE.

- *Reason. Don't calculate.* Part of the reason you can do well without a calculator is that many situations do not actually require one. Multiple-choice questions like "In which year was the percentage of blank highest?" or "Which has the largest area?" may not require you to calculate anything. Try to determine answers with comparisons and not calculation. Many two column questions can be approached this way.

EXAMPLE 6

Which of the five following figures has the largest shaded area?

(A) (B) (C) (D) (E)

Solution: You do not need to calculate the area of any of these figures to solve the problem. If we divide C with a vertical line you'll see it is made of two shapes congruent to B. If you flip one of the triangles vertically, those two triangles could be combined to form the rectangle in E. Hence B, C, and E all have the same area. If you think of D as a square and two small triangles, you can rotate and move the bottom left small triangle beside the top one to make a 2 × 1 rectangle. So D and E have the same area. Finally, A is comprised of 1 small square and three small triangles, while D has one square and two small triangles. A has more area than D. So B, C, D, and E have the same area while A has more. Choose **A**.

- *Memorize some basic facts that help make calculations quicker and easier.* We presume you know your times tables. It is also helpful to know the perfect squares like $12^2 = 144$, $13^2 = 169$, . . . , $20^2 = 400$ (or even more). The most common fractions that appear are $\frac{1}{2}, \frac{1}{3}$, and $\frac{2}{3}$. It is helpful to know that $\frac{2}{3} - \frac{1}{2} = \frac{1}{6}$ and other related facts like $\frac{1}{2} + \frac{1}{6} = \frac{2}{3}, \frac{1}{2} - \frac{1}{3} = \frac{1}{6}$, and $\frac{1}{2} + \frac{1}{3} = \frac{5}{6}$. The appendix gives a list of facts to memorize.

- *Learn tricks for calculating without a calculator.* There are many books available to help you with this skill. I recommend Arthur Benjamin's book, *Secrets of Mental Math*, but there are many available with titles that include terms like *Shortcut Math, Speed Math*, and *Rapid Math*. Just to be clear, although it would help, mastering one of these books is not necessary to succeed on the GRE. We'll point out just a few ideas here. Others, how to calculate percentages for instance, appear throughout the book.

- *Use the distributive property.* Instead of multiplying 42×30, we can use the distributive property to break this into pieces you can multiply in your head.

$$42 \times 30 = (40 + 2) \times 30 = 40 \times 30 + 2 \times 30 = 1{,}200 + 60 = 1{,}260$$

This also works well with subtraction.

$$38 \times 25 = (40 - 2) \times 25 = (40 \times 25) - (2 \times 25) = 1{,}000 - 50 = 950$$

In theory, you can do this with any pair of numbers.

$$37 \times 24 = (40 - 3) \times (20 + 4) = 40 \times 20 - 3 \times 20 + 4 \times 40 - 3 \times 4$$
$$= 800 - 60 + 160 - 12 = 888$$

This example would have been easier to multiply the standard way. This method works best when one of the numbers ends in 5 or 0 and the other is close to a multiple of 10.

- *Find the difference of squares.* You may know this as a rule of algebra, $A^2 - B^2 = (A - B)(A + B)$, but it can be useful for some calculations. To find $77^2 - 23^2$, instead of calculating each square, we find $(77 - 23)(77 + 23)$. The first factor is easy to subtract $77 - 23 = 54$, and the second factor is easy to add $77 + 23 = 100$. Their product $54 \times 100 = 5{,}400$ is also easy. This whole computation could even be done in your head and quickly!

- *Cancel before you calculate.* Always try to cancel factors before you calculate. This reduces the size of the numbers you have to work with. To simplify

$\dfrac{3}{7} \times \dfrac{10}{33} \times \dfrac{14}{26}$, we factor the terms first and then use cancellation

$\dfrac{\cancel{3}}{\cancel{7}} \times \dfrac{\cancel{2} \times 5}{\cancel{3} \times 11} \times \dfrac{2 \times \cancel{7}}{\cancel{2} \times 13}$. Now it is easy to see the answer is $\dfrac{5 \times 2}{13 \times 11}$, which

equals 10/143. The toughest part of this problem was multiplying 13 by 11, which is not so tough if you do $13 \times 10 + 13 \times 1 = 130 + 13 = 143$.

- *Estimate, don't calculate.* Which is larger $137 \times 2,185$ or $89 \times 5,856$? It would be painful to calculate these but even a rough estimate will give us the answer. We approximate $137 \times 2,185$ as $100 \times 2,000$, which equals 200,000. We approximate $89 \times 5,856$ as $90 \times 5,000$, which equals 450,000. Even allowing for some serious error in our approximation, we can be certain the second product is larger than the first.

Problems

Remember, for two column questions:
Choose **A** if Column A is greater than Column B.
Choose **B** if Column B is greater than Column A.
Choose **C** if they are equal.
Choose **D** if it cannot be determined.

	Column A	Column B
1.	$20^2 - 10^2$	$11^2 + 13^2$
2.	$x^2 - y^3$	$x^2 + y^3$
3.	$48 \times 37 \times 25$	$35 \times 44 \times 21$
4.	52×48	51×49
5.	$\dfrac{20 \times 18 \times 16}{9 \times 8 \times 7}$	$\dfrac{12 \times 10 \times 8}{4 \times 3 \times 2}$

$$x \neq 5$$

	Column A	Column B
6.	$\dfrac{1}{x - 5}$	$x + 5$
7.	$5^{-5}(9 \times 7 \times 5 \times 3 \times 1)$	$6^{-5}(10 \times 8 \times 6 \times 4 \times 2)$

8. Which of the following values is closest to $\sqrt{85}$?

    (A) 7
    (B) 8
    (C) 9
    (D) 10
    (E) 11

9. Which of the following values is closest to $\sqrt[3]{40}$?

    (A) 2
    (B) 3
    (C) 3.5
    (D) 4
    (E) 11

10. Cole Corporation earned $3.6 million in profits in 2008. They pay 10% taxes on the first million, 15% on the second million, and 18% on any further profits. Approximately how much tax do they owe (in thousands of dollars)?

    (A) 360
    (B) 400
    (C) 500
    (D) 600
    (E) 700

11. In 2007 Cole Corporation paid $220,000 in tax on $1.4 million in profits. What was their *average* tax rate?

    (A) 10%
    (B) 14%
    (C) 16%
    (D) 18%
    (E) 20%

12. Sammi has 36 marbles. Some are red, some are blue, and some are both red and blue. Twenty have red on them and 30 have blue on them. What fraction of her marbles are both red and blue?

    Give your answer as a fraction: ☐
    ☐

13. What is $\frac{1}{3}$ of 2% of $\frac{4}{5}$ of 9? Express your answer as a decimal.

    ☐

SOLUTIONS

1. **(A)** Do not make the classic mistake of thinking that $20^2 - 10^2 = 10^2$. Using difference of squares you can see that $20^2 - 10^2 = (20 - 10)(20 + 10) = 10 \times 30 = 300$. If you know your perfect squares, then you know that $11^2 = 121$ and $13^2 = 169$. Adding, 121 plus 169 equals 290. That is less than 300. Choose **A**.

2. **(D)** Since both sides have x^2, and x^2 is always nonnegative, it has no impact on the question. We focus on y^3. Isn't y^3 always larger than $-y^3$? No. When $y = -1$, $y^3 = -1$ and $-y^3 = -(-1) = 1$. When $y = 1$, $y^3 = 1$ and $-y^3 = -1$. So sometimes the first is larger and sometimes the second is larger. It depends on the value of y. Choose **D**.

3. **(A)** This looks like an ugly computation at first. But notice that $48 > 44$, $37 > 35$, and $25 > 21$. So $48 \times 37 \times 25 > 44 \times 35 \times 21$. Choose **A**.

4. **(B)** The technique from question 3 does not work here as $52 > 51$ but $48 < 49$. Estimation isn't much help either as both products are close to 50×50. We can use difference of squares in reverse for this problem. Notice that $52 \times 48 = (50 + 2)(50 - 2) = 50^2 - 2^2 = 2,500 - 4$ and $51 \times 49 = (50 + 1)(50 - 1) = 50^2 - 1^2 = 2,500 - 1$. Choose **B**.

5. **(B)** Cancellation helps a lot here. In Column A, 9 divides into 18 twice and 8 divides into 16 twice leaving $\dfrac{20 \times \cancel{18}^{\,2} \times \cancel{16}^{\,2}}{\cancel{9} \times \cancel{8} \times 7} = \dfrac{20 \times 2 \times 2}{7} = \dfrac{80}{7}$. In Column B, 3×4 cancels with 12 and 2 divides into 8 four times leaving

$$\dfrac{\cancel{12} \times 10 \times \cancel{8}^{\,4}}{\cancel{4 \times 3} \times \cancel{2}} = 4 \times 10 = 40.$$ Notice that $40 = 80/2$ which is larger than 80/7. Choose **B**.

6. **(D)** If you only consider positive integers $x + 5$ will always be larger than $1/(x - 5)$. For instance $(10) + 5 = 15$, which is larger than $1/(10 - 5) = 1/5$. But, when x is a number very close to 5, like $x = 5.01$, then $1/(x - 5) = 1/(5.01 - 5) = 1/(0.01) = 100$. At the same time, $x + 5 = 5.01 + 5 = 10.01$. Hence, it depends on the value of x. Choose **D**.

7. **(B)** First we cancelled as many factors as possible and then multiplied out.

$$5^{-5}(9 \times 7 \times 5 \times 3 \times 1) = \dfrac{9 \times 7 \times \cancel{5} \times 3 \times 1}{5 \times 5 \times \cancel{5} \times 5 \times 5} = \dfrac{63 \times 3}{25 \times 25} = \dfrac{189}{625}.$$ We

knew our perfect squares ($25^2 = 625$), and we used distribution to find $63 \times 3 = (60 + 3) \times 3 = 60 \times 3 + 3 \times 3 = 180 + 9$. Then a very rough approximation shows that $\dfrac{189}{625} \cong \dfrac{200}{600} = 1/3$. In Column B, $6^{-5}(10 \times 8 \times 6 \times 4 \times 2) =$

$$\dfrac{10 \times \cancel{8} \times \cancel{6} \times 4 \times \cancel{2}}{\cancel{6} \times \cancel{6}_{3} \times \cancel{6}_{3} \times \cancel{6}_{3} \times \cancel{6}_{3}} = \dfrac{40}{3^4} = 40/81$$ which is approximately 1/2.

Choose **B**.

8. **(C)** To approximate $\sqrt{85}$, we note that $9^2 = 81$ and $10^2 = 100$ and thus $9 < 10$. Since 85 is much closer to 81 than 100, we know $\sqrt{85}$ is closer to 9 than 10. Choose **C**.

9. **(C)** To approximate $\sqrt[3]{40}$, we note that $3^3 = 27$ and $4^3 = 64$. Since 40 is much closer to 27 than 64, we know $\sqrt[3]{40}$ is closer to 3 than 4. Is it closer to 3 or 3.5? We check 3.5 as a possible answer by multiplication. First $35 \times 35 = (30 + 5) \times 35 = 1,050 + 165 = 1,215$. Then $35^3 = 1,215 \times 35$, which is approximately $1,200 \times 35 = 1,200 \times 30 + 1,200 \times 5 = 36,000 + 6,000 = 42,000$. So 3.5^3 is approximately 42. Since 40 is much closer to 42 than 27, we expect $\sqrt[3]{40}$ to be closer to 3.5 than 3. Choose **C**.

10. **(C)** 10% on the first million is 100,000. 15% on the second million is 150,000. 18% on the next million is 180,000. 18% on the next half million would be half of 180,000 or 90,000. That makes a total of at least 100K + 150K + 180K + 90K = 520K. The actual tax will only be slightly larger than this. Choose **C**.

11. **(C)** We need to find a percentage $\dfrac{\$220,000}{\$1,400,000} \times 100\%$. We use cancellation to simplify $\dfrac{\$220,\cancel{000}}{\$1,4\cancel{00},\cancel{000}} \times 1\cancel{00}\% = \dfrac{220}{14}\%$. If we approximate this by $\dfrac{210}{14}$, we can cancel 7s, $\dfrac{\overset{30}{\cancel{210}}}{\underset{2}{\cancel{14}}} = \dfrac{30}{2}$ and get 15%. Hence the average tax rate was a bit more than 15%. Choose **C**.

12. **(7/18)** Since Sammi has 36 marbles and 20 of then have red, at most 16 (= 36 − 20) have just blue on them. If 16 have just blue on them but 30 have blue on them then 14 (= 30 − 16) must have red and blue on them. As a fraction, $14/36 = 7/18$ of her marbles are both red and blue. You can enter $\boxed{\dfrac{7}{18}}$, $\boxed{\dfrac{14}{36}}$, or any equivalent fraction. The numeric entry questions do not require fractions to be in lowest form.

13. **(.048)** Remembering that *of* means multiplication, $\dfrac{1}{3}$ of 2% of $\dfrac{4}{5}$ of 9 = $\dfrac{1}{\cancel{3}} \times \dfrac{2}{\cancel{100}_{25}} \times \dfrac{\cancel{4}}{5} \times \cancel{9}^3 = \dfrac{2 \times 3}{25 \times 5} = \dfrac{6}{125}$. Now you may recall $125 \times 8 = 1,000$ (since $1/8 = 0.125$), hence $\dfrac{6}{125} \times \dfrac{8}{8} = \dfrac{48}{1,000} = 0.048$. You should enter $\boxed{0.048}$ or $\boxed{.048}$. Either will be accepted.

Strategies and Problem Solving

TEST-TAKING STRATEGIES

Strategies for individual questions are addressed throughout the book. In addition to typical test-taking strategies (get a good night's rest, monitor your time, etc.), there are specific general strategies for the GRE quantitative tests.

In the paper-based test, you have the option to return to questions so it is a good idea to start by quickly answering all questions that you know how to do. Of course you should watch the clock and ensure you have sufficient time to attempt every problem. Do not spend too much time on any one question (no matter how fascinating it is) as all questions count equally. Return to the unanswered questions, and use your best strategies to eliminate wrong answers, and then, if necessary, guess. At regular intervals make sure your answers are recorded on the answer sheet; you will not be given extra time to record them. Record an answer for every question—even if you have to guess. There is no penalty for guessing!

> **TIP**
>
> If you complete all the questions, be sure to review your answers! When I took the GRE general written exam, I completed my quantitative sections with plenty of time to spare so I put my head down and rested. I had to take the exam at 7 a.m. on a Sunday morning so I was tired! In the end, I received 790 because I got two fairly easy questions wrong. If I had been better rested and checked over my answers, I might have gotten that perfect 800 and a better scholarship in graduate school.

In the computer-based test, you cannot return to previously answered questions. Thus it is very important to watch your time carefully and spend sufficient but not too much time with each question. It is very hard to score well if you don't finish the test! Through practice you will become familiar with the appropriate pace for solving 28 questions in 45 minutes (roughly 90 seconds for each question). A clock will always be on the screen counting down the time remaining. Use this clock to keep on pace. If you have 12 questions left and only 15 minutes, you are behind schedule. If you have 12 questions left and 30 minutes left, you are ahead of schedule and can now afford to spend 2.5 minutes with each question. Sometimes, to keep on pace, you will have to guess and move on. Try to avoid wild random guessing. When you're behind, resist the urge to "just pick C and go on" to catch up. It will likely not help you. Always take a few seconds to read a question and eliminate wrong answers before guessing.

PROBLEM SOLVING

George Polya was famous for being an excellent problem solver. He is even more famous for teaching many other people to become excellent problem solvers. Practicing for the GRE will make you a better problem solver—especially if you try some of Polya's ideas.

Polya emphasizes four steps to problem solving:

P1. Understand the problem
P2. Make a plan for solving the problem
P3. Carry out the plan
P4. Look back

You don't have to follow these four steps with every problem you solve, but if you're not sure how to solve a problem, these steps will help.

We illustrate the meaning of the steps with the following example.

TIP

Do not make the mistake of thinking you *have* to use Polya's Four Steps and the strategies presented in this chapter to solve GRE problems. When you already know how to solve a problem—just go ahead and do it. The material in this chapter is meant to help you know what to do when you *don't* immediately know how to solve a problem.

EXAMPLE 1

If H hot dogs cost D dollars and S sodas cost C cents, how much will it cost to feed K kids 2 hot dogs and one soda each?

Solution:

Step	Meaning	Example
P1. Understand the problem	Read the problem one or two times. Sometimes you might have to plug in a number for a variable and do a few computations to understand what it really means. Or sometimes you might have to draw a diagram to help understand the relationships involved.	After reading the problem twice, I'm still uncertain so I decided to put numbers into the question. "If 5 hot dogs cost 10 dollars and two sodas cost 150 cents how much will it cost to feed 7 kids." OK—now I get it.
P2. Make a plan	If you already know how to solve this problem, your plan is just solve it. Otherwise, your plan might be to employ a specific strategy that we talk about in this chapter—or maybe an idea of your own.	Find the price for each hot dog and each soda. Use numbers first instead of letters to understand what to do.

Step	Meaning	Example
P3. Carry out the plan	Follow the steps needed to complete your plan. Usually this means solving the problem—though sometimes you'll get stuck. Then you can return to Step 2.	If 5 hot dogs cost 10 dollars then each hot dog costs $2 = \$10/5$. So if H hotdogs cost D dollars then each hot dog costs D/H dollars. Similarly each soda cost C/S cents. To convert to dollars we divide by 100. So each soda costs $C/100S$. Each kid gets 2 hot dogs and one soda so that would cost $2D/H$ plus $C/100S$. And we have K kids so that is $K(2D/H + C/100S)$ or $2DK/H + KC/100S$ dollars.
P4. Look back	Check your answer. This can also mean to look for patterns that would enable you to solve other (similar) problems.	One way to check would be to plug numbers into our final answer $K = 7$, $H = 5$, $D = 10$, $S = 2$, $C = 150$. $2DK/H + KC/100S = 2 \times 10 \times 7/5 + 7 \times 150/(100 \times 2) = 28 + 5.25 = \$33.25$. At $2 per hot dog and 75 cents per drink that makes sense (since $4.75 \times 7 = 33.25$)!

EXAMPLE 2

If there are 37 people at a party, and everyone greets everyone else with a handshake, how many handshakes take place?

(A) 37^2
(B) 36×37
(C) 18×37
(D) 19×37
(E) 36^2

Solution: Step 1—After reading the problem several times, you understand that you must count the total number of handshakes at the party.

Step 2—Having no idea how to proceed, you decide to try the strategy of solving an easier problem. For a small party, you could actually count handshakes.

Step 3—What if there were only 4 people at the party? Call them K, L, M and N. First K shakes hands with L, then K shakes hands with M, and then K shakes hands with N. Then L shakes hands with M, and L shakes hands with N. L doesn't need to shake hands with K, because K already shook her hand! M shakes hands with N. N has already shaken hands with everyone else. That makes a total of $3 + 2 + 1 = 6$ handshakes.

What if there were five people at the party? Call them K, L, M, N and O. K would do 4 shakes, L would do 3, M would do 2 and N, 1. O would have already shaken everyone's hands. That would be $4 + 3 + 2 + 1 = 10$ handshakes.

Now you can see that at a party of 37 people there would be $36 + 35 + \ldots + 2 + 1$ handshakes. How much is that? You may recall that the sum of the first n numbers is $\frac{1}{2}n$ $(n + 1)$. So $1 + 2 + \ldots + 35 + 36 = 1/2\,(36 \times 37) = 18 \times 37$.

Step 4—You notice that from the point of view of each person they shook 36 other hands. Why isn't the answer 37×36? If we did that each handshake would be counted twice, once for each person shaking. So another approach is $(37 \times 36) \div 2$, which leads to the same answer. Choose **C**.

GENERAL STRATEGIES

There are many strategies developed throughout this book. The most important strategy to remember is—if you already know how to solve it then just do it! Strategies are what you use when you aren't sure how to solve the problem. We outline four strategies that work for many different problems.

TIP

Draw a diagram while rereading the problem.

Use a Diagram

Many questions can be solved more easily using a diagram. If one is not given, then draw one! A diagram allows you to see relationships you might not notice just by reading the problem.

EXAMPLE 3

If A is the point $(1, 0)$ and B is the point $(2, 2)$, what is the area of the circle that has AB as its radius?

(A) π
(B) $\sqrt{3}\,\pi$
(C) 2π
(D) $\sqrt{5}\,\pi$
(E) 5π

Solution: While reading the question for the second time, draw a diagram with points A and B labeled on it. AB is the radius of the circle but what is the center of the circle? It doesn't matter, the circle will have the same area no matter where the center is so let's conveniently choose A. Sketch the circle.

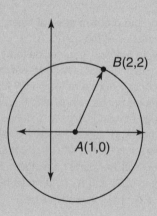

You should now realize the key to this question is determining the length of *AB*—the radius. Use the given points to find the lengths of the legs of the triangle, and use the Pythagorean theorem.

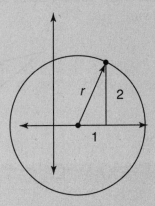

Then $r^2 = 2^2 + 1^2 = 5$. We need the area of the circle $A = \pi r^2$, so $A = \pi \times 5$. The area is 5π square units. Choose **E**. Notice we did not bother to find r. We did not need to know r if we knew r^2.

TIP

Add to a given diagram.

Diagrams are often given, but embellishing the diagram may be necessary to express other information given in the question or information needed to solve the problem.

EXAMPLE 4

Find the area of trapezoid *ABCD*.

(A) 2
(B) 2.5
(C) 3
(D) 3.5
(E) 6

Solution: One of the easiest ways to solve this problem is to divide the trapezoid into shapes that have easy to calculate areas. We add lines to do this.

You should now to be able to see our trapezoid is composed of one unit square and four triangles, each half of a unit square. Hence the area of *ABCD* is $1 + 4 \times \frac{1}{2} = 3$ square units. Choose **C**.

TIP

Trust a diagram and estimate, when you can.

The instructions for the quantitative exam cautions you that diagrams are not necessarily drawn to scale. Can you trust given diagrams? Sometimes you cannot. A triangle with two equal sides could appear with three acute angles, but it is possible for such a triangle to have an obtuse angle. You should be careful not to assume all angles in a triangle are exactly as drawn.

EXAMPLE 5

Column A   Column B

A triangle has two sides 5 cm long

| Perimeter of the triangle | 16 cm |

Incorrect Answer: If we trust that the triangle is similar to what is drawn, then the third side must be close to 5 cm in length. There's no way it could be more than 5 cm. So the perimeter is less than 5 cm + 5 cm + 5 cm = 15 cm. Choose **B**.

Solution: The angle between the two 5-cm long sides could be anywhere between 0 and 180°.

If the angle is near 0° then the third side is near 0 cm in length so the perimeter is a little more than 10 cm. If the angle is near 180° the third side is nearly 10 cm long. Then the perimeter is nearly 20 cm. Choose **D**. The perimeter could be more or less than 16 cm.

Alternate Solution: The triangle inequality tells us that a triangle with lengths a, b, and c exists if and only if the sum of any two sides is more than the third. If $a = 5$ and $b = 5$, this means we need $5 + 5 > c$, $5 + c > 5$, and $c + 5 > 5$. The second two inequalities guarantee that $c > 0$ while the first guarantees that $c < 10$. So for any c between 0 and 10, a triangle with side lengths 5, 5, and c exists. Hence any perimeter between 10 and 20 is possible. Choose **D**

Sometimes you can trust a diagram to be accurate. If the question says it is a square and it looks like a square (4 equal sides and 4 right angles), then it is one.

EXAMPLE 6

<u>Column A</u>   <u>Column B</u>

This is a unit square with circular arcs that are centered at opposite corners of the square.

| The area of the shaded region | 1/3 |

Solution: It is fair to trust this diagram—it is a square and the circular arcs could not be drawn another way. The square is divided into three pieces and the shaded piece is clearly larger than each of the other pieces. Hence, the shaded area is more than 1/3 the area of the square and 1/3 of 1^2 is 1/3. Choose **A**.

TIP

Subtract to find shaded areas.

Most GRE tests ask you to find the area of figures. They are usually nonstandard—you can't just apply a formula like you might with a triangle or rectangle. A good tip is to decompose figures and find areas by subtracting (or adding) the areas of standard figures. We illustrate with two different solutions for Example 6.

ALTERNATE SOLUTION TO EXAMPLE 6

Label the regions in the square ①, ②, and ③.

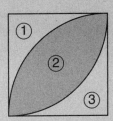

Then notice that the area of region ③ is equal to the area of the square minus a quarter circle.

 = −

Hence region ③ has area $1^2 - \frac{1}{4}\pi 1^2 = 1 - \frac{\pi}{4}$. But region ① is congruent to and thus equal in area to region ③. Hence, the shaded region is equal to a square minus two times region ③.

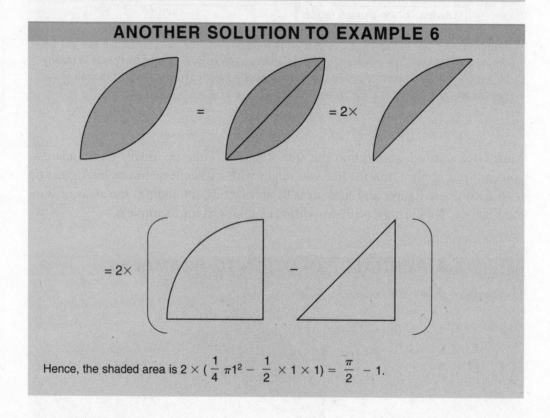

That is $1^2 - (1 - \frac{\pi}{4}) - (1 - \frac{\pi}{4}) = \frac{\pi}{2} - 1$ or approximately 0.57 square units in area. Clearly that is much more than 1/3.

ANOTHER SOLUTION TO EXAMPLE 6

Hence, the shaded area is $2 \times (\frac{1}{4}\pi 1^2 - \frac{1}{2} \times 1 \times 1) = \frac{\pi}{2} - 1$.

Pay Attention to Units

You may encounter several different units of measure in the same question. Be careful to convert appropriately.

EXAMPLE 7

If an ant can walk 7 inches per minute and the road is 28 feet wide, how many seconds will it take him to cross?

(A) 4
(B) 48
(C) 2,352
(D) 2,880
(E) 4,560

Incorrect Solution: It is very tempting to divide 28 by 7, get 4 and choose answer **A**. That would be very incorrect! The road is measured in feet and the ant's rate of speed is in inches per minute. And your answer must be reported in seconds not minutes!

Solution: 28 feet × (12 inches/foot) = 28 × 12 inches. Notice we didn't multiply this out. Some things are going to cancel before we get the final answer saving us a lot of computation. 28 × 12 inches × $\frac{1 \text{ minute}}{7 \text{ inches}}$ = 4 × 12 minutes = 48 minutes. And to convert to seconds, 48 minutes × (60 seconds/minute). That computation is tedious so I'll estimate 50 × 60 = 3,000 seconds. If you want to calculate it exactly, try 48 × 60 = (50 − 2) × 60 = 50 × 60 − 2 × 60 = 3,000 − 120 = 2,880. These are steps you can do in your head and without a calculator! Choose **D**.

Use Numbers Instead of Variables

Some questions appear difficult because they have so many different variables in them. It can be easier to understand these problems when you replace each variable with a number, and reread the question. Often you can then proceed to solve the problem, even with variables.

EXAMPLE 8

A math professor has $x + 2$ students in her class. They each answer $x - 2$ problems on an assignment. If a quarter of their problems are solved incorrectly, what is the total number of incorrectly solved problems the professor must grade?

(A) $\dfrac{x}{2}$

(B) $\dfrac{x^2 - 2}{4}$

(C) $x^2 - 4$

(D) $\dfrac{x^2}{4} - 1$

(E) $\dfrac{x^2}{4}$

Solution: We replace x with 18 and try to solve the problem. We chose 18 because 18 + 2 and 18 − 2 are easy numbers to work with. There are 18 + 2 = 20 students in class. Each answers 18 − 2 = 16 problems. A quarter of their problems are answered incorrectly, so ¼ × 16 = 4 problems are incorrect for each student. Thus the professor grades 4 incorrect problems for each student or 20 × 4 = 80 incorrect problems in total.

Now we follow the same steps with the variables in place. There are $x + 2$ students in class. Each answers $x - 2$, a quarter of which, $1/4 \times (x - 2)$, are incorrect. Thus the professor grades $(x + 2) \times ¼ \times (x - 2)$ incorrect problems, in total. Now we simplify the algebra $(x + 2) \times 1/4 \times (x - 2) = \dfrac{(x + 2)(x - 2)}{4} = \dfrac{x^2 - 4}{4} = \dfrac{x^2}{4} - \dfrac{4}{4} = \dfrac{x^2}{4} - 1$. Choose **D**.

What numbers are best to choose for your variables? I try to choose numbers that are easy to compute with like 10, 20, or 100. You can also use simple numbers like 0 or 1 though they may not make sense for all problems.

STRATEGIES FOR MULTIPLE-CHOICE QUESTIONS

Multiple-choice questions are very familiar to most people. A question and five answers (A, B, C, D, or E) are given, and you must choose the *best* answer. We will describe three helpful strategies that apply specifically to multiple-choice questions.

Test Answers Starting with C

EXAMPLE 9

Kirk starts a new business making fly fishing rods. It costs, in dollars, $1,500 + 65x$ to make x rods. Kirk can sell this lot of x rods to a retailer for $125x$ dollars. The retailer insists on receiving the fishing rods in multiples of 10. What is the least number of rods Kirk can manufacture, without losing money?

   (A) 10
   (B) 20
   (C) 30
   (D) 50
   (E) 100

Solution: Rather than trying to solve the problem, we use the answers to check and see if they are valid solutions. We start with C and then work left or right to find the correct answer. (A) If Kirk makes 30 rods it will cost $1,500 + 65(30) = 1,500 + 1,950 = 3,450$ dollars. He will receive $\$125(30) = \$3,750$ for a net profit of $300. So he will not lose money making 30 (or more) rods, but he could still potentially manufacture 20 rods and still be profitable. Let's check B. Then 20 rods cost $1,500 + 65(20) = 1,500 + 1,300 = 2,800$ dollars to make. He will receive only $\$125(20) = \$2,500$ and lose money. Choose **C**.

Use Numbers Instead of Variables

ALTERNATE SOLUTION TO EXAMPLE 8

After solving the problem with $x = 18$, we know the answer is 80. Plug $x = 18$ into each of the answers and see which ones equal 80.

   (A) $\dfrac{x}{2} = \dfrac{18}{2} = 9$

   (B) $\dfrac{x^2 - 2}{4} = \dfrac{18^2 - 2}{4} = \dfrac{324 - 2}{4} = \dfrac{322}{4} = 80.5$

   (C) $x^2 - 4 = 18^2 - 4 = 324 - 4 = 320$

   (D) $\dfrac{x^2}{4} - 1 = \dfrac{18^2}{4} - 1 = \dfrac{324}{4} - 1 = 81 - 1 = 80$

   (E) $\dfrac{x^2}{4} = \dfrac{18^2}{4} = \dfrac{324}{4} = 81$

Clearly the answer is **D**.

In the alternate solution we tested E even after we found the correct solution D. Why? Depending on the numbers you choose for variables, you may get more than one solution that gives the correct answer. If this happens, try other values for your variables.

EXAMPLE 10

Marty is having lunch with *n* of his friends. A sandwich uses two slices of bread, and they usually eat *m* sandwiches each. If there are *s* slices of bread in a loaf, how many loaves of bread should Marty buy?

    (A) $2nm/s$
    (B) $2nm/s + 2m/s$
    (C) $(2n + 1)m/s$
    (D) $2ns/m$
    (E) $2(n + 1)s/m$

Solution: We try $n = 2$, $m = 2$, $s = 2$. Although this does not make a lot of sense, the algebra should be easy! There are three people at lunch, and they each eat 2 sandwiches. That is 6 sandwiches, so we need 12 slices of bread. If there are 2 slices in each loaf that means 6 loaves are needed. Now we substitute into the given solutions and look for 6.

    (A) $2nm/s = 2 \times 2 \times 2/2 = 4$
    (B) $2nm/s + 2m/s = 2 \times 2 \times 2/2 + 2 \times 2/2 = 4 + 2 = 6$
    (C) $(2n + 1)m/s = (2(2) + 1) \times 2/2 = 5$
    (D) $2ns/m = 2 \times 2 \times 2/2 = 4$
    (E) $2(n + 1)s/m = 2(2 + 1) \times 2/2 = 6$

So which is the correct answer—B or E? We don't know. We'll try again with $n = 3$, $m = 4$ and $s = 8$. So we have 4 people in total eating 4 sandwiches each. Marty needs $4 \times 4 \times 2 = 32$ pieces of bread and at 8 slices per loaf that is $32/8 = 4$ loaves. Now we try our numbers but only in the answers for B and E (we already know A, C and D are incorrect).
(B) $2nm/s + 2m/s = 2(3)(4)/(8) + 2(4)/8 = 24/8 + 8/8 = 3 + 1 = 4$.
(E) $2(n + 1)s/m = 2(3 + 1)(8)/(4) = 16$.
Choose **B**.

Eliminate Choices, then Guess

EXAMPLE 11

If $1 < xy < 2$, which of the following could be true?

    (A) $x < 0$ and $y < 0$
    (B) $x < -1$ and $y < -2$
    (C) $x < -1$ and $y < 2$
    (D) $0 < x < 1$ and $1 < y < 2$
    (E) $\frac{1}{2} < x < 1$ and $4 < y$

Partial Solution: You know that the product of a positive and negative number is negative. That means that A and C can be eliminated. You thought that you could multiply inequalities, part by part. In B that would mean that $xy < (-1)(-2) = 2$. But this doesn't seem right; if $x = -3$ and $y = -3$, then $x < -1$ and $y < -2$, but $xy = 9$, which is not less than 2. You are confused but your gut says B is not correct. Not wanting to waste any more time you guess between D and E. Choose **E**.

Actual Solution: The product of two negatives is always positive so in B $x < -1$ and $y < -2$ implies that $xy > (-1)(-2) = 2$. So you were correct—B is not the answer. With positive numbers, you can multiply inequalities so $x < 1$ and $y < 2$ implies $xy < 1 \times 2 = 2$. And $x > 0$ and $y < 1$ implies that $xy < 0 \times 1 = 0$. So D might be the answer. In E, we are again dealing with only positive numbers so $1/2 < x$ and $4 < y$ means $4 \times 1/2 < xy$ or $2 < xy$. This shows E is not the answer. Choose **D**. In fact if you take $x = 0.9$ and $y = 1.9$, we get $xy = 0.9 \times 1.9 = 1.71$.

You may think the partial solution is not very satisfying. Nobody likes to leave a question without knowing the answer. But time is limited and guessing wisely can be an important part of earning a good score. Statistics support this, guessing randomly you have only a 20% chance of getting a problem correct. If you eliminate three incorrect solutions first, you now have a 50% chance of being correct! Spread over 28 questions that is the difference between having less than 0.04% chance of getting 14 or more right versus a 57% chance of getting 14 or more right!

STRATEGIES FOR DATA INTERPRETATION QUESTIONS

TIP

Study your charts first.

Most people begin by reading the question and then looking at the data charts. If you do so, your mind is consumed by the question, and you may not notice all the important details in the chart. Some charts are complicated or have subtle details. You should always start by reviewing the chart and then reading the question.

Examples 12–13 are concerned with the following charts.

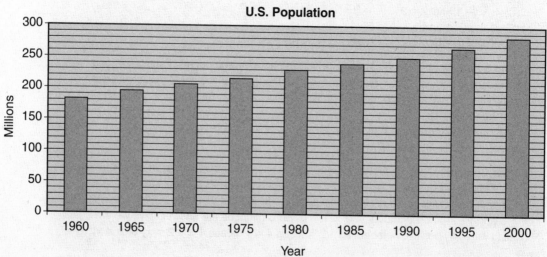

If you look carefully at these charts you should notice:

- The carrots sold are measured in millions of pounds.

- The price is measured in dollars but the unit of weight is not mentioned. We have to look in the legend to see it is dollars per hundred pounds.

- Data is given for each five years—the lines in between just join the data points. They do not represent what may have happened then.

Estimate Don't Calculate

Calculating exact values can be tedious or even difficult. Try to avoid tricky calculations by estimating.

EXAMPLE 12

The average consumption peaked at 11 pounds annually per person in what year?

(A) 1965
(B) 1975
(C) 1985
(D) 1995
(E) 2000

Solution: To calculate this precisely for each year we must divide the pounds sold by the population. Reading from the charts we see that in millions of pounds per million people we have 1,400/190 for 1965, 1,500/220 for 1975, 1,700/240 for 1985, 3,200/268 for 1995, and 2,900/280 for 2000. In 1965, 1975, and 1985, the numerator is less than 10 times the denominator so they are not the answer. For the year 2000, 2,900/280 is approximately 10 and in 1995, 3,200/268 is considerably more than 10 (as 3,200 > 2,680). Choose **D**.

Try to Visualize Rather than Calculate

In Example 12 you didn't need to know the actual average consumption for each year; just the approximate value and how it compared to the other was sufficient. Sometimes these comparisons can be done just by looking at relative sizes on graphs.

EXAMPLE 13

The net value of the fresh carrot sales increased most in what period?

(A) 1960–1965
(B) 1970–1975
(C) 1980–1985
(D) 1990–1995
(E) 1995–2000

Solution: To actually calculate the increase in value, we would have to calculate a net (price multiplied by weight sold) for each year and subtract. It is much easier to look at where things change and how much. Common sense tells us that net value changes the most when the price or the weight (or both) increase considerably. By observation we can see that the price increased the most in 1970–1975 or 1990–1995. But in 1990–1995 the weight sold increased more than in 1970–1975. Choose **D**.

STRATEGIES FOR QUANTITATIVE COMPARISON QUESTIONS

Probably the most unusual part of the exam for you will be the quantitative comparison or two-column question. Thus it's very important to become accustomed to them through practice and to learn some strategies for answering them.

Do the Same Thing to Each Column

You can treat the two columns as if they are two sides of an equality (or inequality). If you do the same to each side, you will preserve the equality (inequality). The resulting quantities may be easier to compare. Of course you must use only operations that would not change the inequality! It is safe to add (subtract) the same value to (from) both columns, multiply (divide) both columns by a positive number, and take the square root of both columns if both are nonnegative. It may not be safe to square both sides or multiply (divide) both sides by a negative.

EXAMPLE 14

Column A   Column B
$x > 12$

$2x + 5$ $3x - 7$

Solution: At first glance you may think that $3x$ is bigger than $2x$ so B would be larger. But subtracting 7 from B may erase that advantage, especially as 5 is added to A. You can proceed as follows:

Add 7	$2x + 12$	$3x$
Subtract $2x$	12	x

Clearly $x > 12$ so choose **B**.

EXAMPLE 15

Column A   Column B

$2x + 5$ $3x - 7$

Solution: If we are given no condition on x, we can still solve this problem.

Add 7	$2x + 12$	$3x$
Subtract $2x$	12	x

Since we do not know what x is, it may be greater than, less than, or equal to 12. Choose **D**.

Compare, Don't Calculate

Many times you can compare quantities without doing calculations. This is especially useful when given two numeric quantities.

EXAMPLE 16

Column A	Column B
$(0.07)^2 (0.07)^4$	$(0.07)^7$

Solution: It would be quite tedious to calculate all these powers of decimals. First we should notice that in Column A we can keep the base and add the exponents to get $(0.07)^6$. Now how does this compare with $(0.07)^7$? Most people expect $(0.07)^7$ to be larger but that is not the case. You may recall that for numbers between 0 and 1, raising it to a higher power decreases the value. Another way to look at this is that $(0.07)^7 = (0.07)(0.07)^6 = 7\%$ of $(0.07)^6$. Clearly 7% of a positive number is less than the number.

Alternate Solution:
First divide both columns by $(0.07)^2$. That leaves
$(0.07)^4$ $(0.07)^5$
Then divide both columns by $(0.07)^4$ to leave
1   (0.07)

Clearly $1 > 0.07$. Choose **A**.

Replace Variables with Numbers

This is one of the most important techniques for two column questions. It is easy to do this and even if it doesn't give you an immediate answer—it will often stimulate the right idea to lead you to an answer.

What values should you try? This can depend on the question, but here are some good suggestions.

- Try a positive and a negative number.

- Try zero.

- Try a number between 0 and 1 and a number greater than one.

- Try a very small number (like 0.001) and a very large number like 1,000.

- Try a prime number and a composite number.

EXAMPLE 17

Column A	Column B
a and c are nonzero.	
$\dfrac{a + c}{c}$	$1 + (c \div a)^{-1}$

Solution: Try $a = c = 1$. Then Column A is 2/1 = 2 and Column B is $1 + (1 \div 1)^{-1} = 1 + (1)^{-1} = 1 + 1 = 2$. They have the same value! We try some other values, $a = 10$ and $c = 1/2$. Then Column A is 10.5/0.5 = 21. Column B is $1 + (1/2 \div 10)^{-1} = 1 + (1/2 \times 1/10)^{-1} = 1 + (1/20)^{-1} = 1 + 20 = 21$. Again they are equal! Now you should suspect they might always be equal. We try simplifying Column B.

$$1 + (c \div a)^{-1} = 1 + \left(\frac{c}{a}\right)^{-1} = 1 + \frac{a}{c} = \frac{c}{c} + \frac{a}{c} = \frac{c + a}{c},$$ which is equal to Column A.

Choose **C**.

Trying values will convince you that one column is larger than the other or that the columns are equal. But it cannot prove that fact. Trying values can prove that the answer is D—it cannot be determined. If for one value of the variables, A is larger than B and for another value B is larger than or equal to A, then the answer cannot be determined. This is the best technique to determine if the answer is D.

Solution: You may notice that the left-hand side can be factored, and then some cancellation

will occur: $\dfrac{r-s}{r^2-s^2} = \dfrac{\cancel{r-s}}{(\cancel{r-s})(r+s)} = \dfrac{1}{r+s}$. So now we have to compare $1/(r+s)$ with

$r+s$. If we try $r = 5$ and $s = 4$, we get $1/9 < 9$. But if we try $r = 1/2$ and $s = 1/4$, we get

$\dfrac{1}{\frac{1}{2}+\frac{1}{4}} = \dfrac{1}{\frac{3}{4}} = \dfrac{4}{3}$ in Column A and $\frac{1}{2} + \frac{1}{4} = \dfrac{3}{4}$ in Column B. Since Column B is larger

in the first case and smaller in the second, we conclude the answer is **D**.

Choose a Good Number for the Whole

Some problems refer to an unnamed quantity, for example, "37% of a number" or

" $\dfrac{1}{5}$ of the class." In these problems it can often be useful to work with a specific

value. 100 is a common choice but 60 can be a better choice when you have to divide because it is divisible by 2, 3, 4, 5, 6, 10, 15, 20, and 30. Choosing a number that works best will make solving the problem much easier.

Solution 1: Assume $x = 100$. One-third of 100 is $33\frac{1}{3}$. Half of 100 is 50, and 20% of 50 is

10 (2 out of 10 for each of five tens). Thus Column A is $33\frac{1}{3} + 10 = 43\frac{1}{3}$. Two-fifths of 100

is 40. 10% of 50 (half of 100) is 5. So Column B is 45. Choose **B**.

Solution 2: Assume $x = 60$. One-third of 60 is 20. Half of 60 is 30, and 20% of 30 is 6 (2 out of 10 for each of three tens). Thus Column A is $20 + 6 = 26$. Two-fifths of 60 is 24. Ten percent of 30 (half of 60) is 3. So Column B is $24 + 3 = 27$. Choose **B**.

Neither solution is easy, but I like avoiding the fractions in the second solution.

Guess

As in multiple-choice questions, sometimes you have no choice but to guess. Even in this case, be sure to eliminate impossible choices before guessing. Here are some tips to improve your guessing:

- Never answer E for a two column question. Even though it may be on your answer sheet (on the paper version) it is not a choice for two column questions. Don't waste your guess!

- If the columns have only numbers don't choose D. Given two numbers they are either equal or one of them is larger. Even if you can't tell what the answer is, it is determinable by someone.

- If the question involves just switching order in a computation guess C. Many such questions are designed to test if you know when you can and can't switch order. As such it's probably a fifty-fifty chance that C is correct.

EXAMPLE 20

Column A   Column B

$2^{(3^4)}$ $\left(2^3\right)^4$

Solution: Both quantities are numbers so do not choose D. This question is really about determining the right order for evaluating exponents. As such, if you don't know what to do, it would be a reasonable guess that it may not make any difference and choose C. You would be wrong, but it's a reasonable guess. $3^4 = 3 \times 3 \times 3 \times 3 = 81$ so Column A is 2^{81}. $2^3 = 2 \times 2 \times 2 = 8$ so Column B is 8^4. Instinct tells me that 81 factors of 2 will be larger than four factors of 8. If you remember your rule for exponents, $\left(2^3\right)^4 = 2^{3 \times 4} = 2^{12}$ which is clearly less than 2^{81}. Choose **A**.

EXAMPLE 21

Column A   Column B

2% of 3% of 4   4% of 3% of 2

Solution: Both quantities are numbers so do not choose D. This question uses the same values in different orders. As such, if you don't know what to do, it would be a reasonable guess that it may not make any difference and choose C. In this case you would be right. In fact 2% of 3% of 4 = $2/100 \times 3/100 \times 4 = (2 \times 3 \times 4)/100^2$. Also 4% of 3% of 2 = $4/100 \times 3/100 \times 2 = (4 \times 3 \times 2)/100^2$. Choose **C**.

STRATEGIES FOR NUMERIC ENTRY QUESTIONS

This is a new type of question, and we do not have a lot of examples from which to formulate strategies. We can make two observations though.

Difficult to Guess

There is really no good way to guess on these problems. When faced with a problem you can't solve, don't waste precious time. You may choose to make a wild guess of 0 or 1 or to perform some computation with the numbers in the problem, like an average or product. Whatever you choose to do, do not waste too much time on the question.

Don't Simplify Fractions

You should take careful note that you do not need to simplify fractions. This can save you valuable time.

EXAMPLE 22

To find the sale price of a bottle of liquor, the owner starts with the wholesale price and then adds 50%. He then reduces the price by 30% for a sale. Finally he adds 10% for taxes. The sale price is what fraction of the wholesale price?

Give your answer as a fraction: ▭

Solution: Assume the wholesale price is $10. To add 50% multiply by $\frac{3}{2}$, to reduce by 30% multiply by $\frac{7}{10}$, and to add 10% multiply by $\frac{11}{10}$. That means the sales price is $\$10 \times \frac{3}{2} \times \frac{7}{10} \times \frac{11}{10}$. As a fraction of the wholesale price that is $(\$10 \times \frac{3}{2} \times \frac{7}{10} \times \frac{11}{10}) \div \$10 = \frac{3 \times 7 \times 11}{2 \times 10 \times 10}$. That is $\frac{231}{200}$. Don't try to reduce the fraction to lowest terms. Just enter $\frac{231}{200}$.

Problems

Column A		Column B
1. 1/3 of the price after a 40% discount.		1/4 of the price after a 25% discount.

$x > 1$

Column A		Column B
2. $3x^2 + 47$		$5x^3 - 56$

$x + 3 < 0$

Column A		Column B
3. $(x - 3)^2$		$(x + 2)^2$

$x > 1$

Column A		Column B
4. $\dfrac{x}{x - 1}$		$\dfrac{x}{x + 1}$

5.	$8^3 \times 25^4$	10,000,000

6.	$p^2 - q^2$	$(p - q)^2$

$$x > y > 0$$

7.	$(x - y)^2$	$x^2 - y^2$

8.	# of mushrooms after 28% die and 35% reproduce	# of mushrooms after 38% die and 25% reproduce

9. On November 7, $\dfrac{1}{7}$ of the school is absent due to a virus. Of those present, $\dfrac{3}{4}$ remain in school while the rest go on a field trip. Only $\dfrac{2}{3}$ of those in school eat the lunch special. What fraction of the total school population did not eat the lunch special that day?

Give your answer as a fraction:

Problems 10 and 11 are concerned with the following two charts:

Area
- 4%
- 10%
- 4%
- 21%
- 21%
- 25%
- 15%

Population
- 8% 1% 10%
- 17%
- 14%
- 18%
- 32%

Legend		
■ Belize	▦ Costa Rica	▨ El Salvador
⊞ Guatemala	⊟ Honduras	Nicaragua
Panama		

10. Which country has the highest population density (average population per square mile)?

(A) Guatemala
(B) Nicaragua
(C) El Salvador
(D) Belize
(E) Honduras

11. Approximately 70% of Central Americans identify their ethnicity as Mestizo. The Mestizo would have to be at least what portion of the population of Guatemala?

    (A) 70%
    (B) 45%
    (C) 6%
    (D) 2%
    (E) 1%

    Problem 12 is based on the charts about carrot consumption on page 22.

12. Which carrot purchase would cost the most?

    (A) 100 lb in 1960
    (B) 50 lb in 1975
    (C) 50 lb in 1980
    (D) 25 lb in 1990
    (E) 20 lb in 1995

13. A bus was full (48 people) when leaving the subway station. At the first stop, $\frac{1}{3}$ of the people on the bus left. Four got on. At the second stop, $\frac{1}{4}$ of the people on the bus left and 8 got on. At the third stop no one left but 1 got on. What fraction of the bus is empty?

    Give your answer as a fraction:

14. If $-1 < xy < 1$, which of the following is not possibly true?

    (A) $x < 0$ and $y < 0$
    (B) $x < -1$ and $y < -2$
    (C) $-1 < x < 0$ and $y > 2$
    (D) $0 < x < 1$ and $1 < y < 2$
    (E) $0 < x < \frac{1}{2}$ and $4 < y$

SOLUTIONS

1. (**A**) Assume the price is $100. After a 40% discount ($40 off), the price is $60. One-third of $60 is $20. After a 25% discount ($25 off), the price is $75. One quarter of $75 is less than $20 since $20 is one quarter of $80. Choose **A**.

2. (**D**) Try $x = 2$. Then $3x^2 + 47 = 3(2^2) + 47 = 59$, while $5x^3 - 56 = 5(2^3) - 56 = -16$. When $x = 2$, A is larger. Now try a much larger value for x that is easy to compute with, say $x = 10$. Then $3x^2 + 47 = 3(10^2) + 47 = 347$ while $5x^3 - 56 = 5(10^3) - 56 = 5,000 - 56$. This time B is larger. Choose **D**.

3. **(A)** As $x + 3 < 0$, subtracting 6 from both sides we see that $x - 3 > -6$. As $x + 3 < 0$, subtracting one from both sides we see that $x + 2 < -1$. Take the square root of both columns but be careful to take the positive, not the negative root.

$$\sqrt{(x-3)^2} \qquad \sqrt{(x+2)^2}$$

$$-(x - 3) \qquad -(x + 2)$$

$$-x + 3 \qquad -x - 2$$

Add x to both columns.

$$3 \qquad\qquad -2$$

Choose **A**.

Alternatively, as $x - 3 < x + 2 < -1$, when we square all parts, the inequality is reversed.
So $(x - 3)^2 > (x + 2)^2 > 1$. Choose **A**.

4. **(A)** Multiply both columns by $(x - 1)(x + 1)$ to clear the denominators. Since $x > 1$ we are multiplying by a positive value and not changing the relationship between Column A and Column B.

$$\frac{x(x + 1)(x - 1)}{x - 1} \qquad\qquad \frac{x(x + 1)(x - 1)}{x + 1}$$

Simplify. $\qquad x^2 + x \qquad\qquad x^2 - x$

Subtract x^2. $\qquad x \qquad\qquad\qquad -x$

As $x > 1$ clearly $-x < x$. Choose **A**.

Alternate answer: Since $0 < x - 1 < x + 1$ and the numerators are the same, dividing by a smaller value, $(x - 1)$, gives a larger result.

5. **(A)** Notice that both columns have only 2 and 5 for prime factors. Let's express them in terms of their prime factorization.

$$8^3 \times 25^4 \qquad\qquad 10{,}000{,}000$$

$$(2^3)^3 (5^2)^4 \qquad\qquad (10)^6$$

$$2^9 5^8 \qquad\qquad\qquad (2 \times 5)^6$$

$$2^9 5^8 \qquad\qquad\qquad 2^6 5^6$$

It's clear that $2^9 > 2^6$ and $5^8 > 5^6$. Choose **A**.

6. **(D)** Many people (incorrectly) think these are equal. When $p = 0$ and q is not zero, A is $-q^2$, a negative number, while B is $(0 - q)^2 = q^2$, a positive number. When $p = q$, both columns are zero. Choose **D**.

7. **(B)** This is the same as question 6, but there are further restrictions on the variable, so our answer for question 6 is not valid here. First we factor both columns.

$$(x - y)(x - y) \qquad\qquad (x - y)(x + y)$$

Since $x > y$, $(x - y)$ is not zero. Divide both columns by $(x - y)$.

$(x - y)$ $(x + y)$

Subtract x from each column.

$-y$ y

Since $y > 0$, we know $y > -y$. Choose **B**.

8. **(A)** Notice 38% > 28% and 25% < 35%. Common sense tells us that when more die and fewer reproduce that there will be fewer mushrooms. Choose **A**.

Alternatively, assume each mushroom produces M offspring when they reproduce, and that we started with 100 mushrooms. Then in A we end up with $100(0.72) + 100(0.72)(0.35)M$ mushrooms. In B we will have $100(0.62) + 100(0.62)(0.25)M$. This is too tedious to calculate. Strictly comparing it is clear that $100(0.72) > 100(0.62)$ and $100(0.72)(0.35)M > 100(0.62)(0.25)M$. So **A** is larger.

9. It is much easier to calculate the fraction that did eat the lunch special; $\frac{6}{7}$ were in school. Of those, $\frac{3}{4}$ stayed. Of those, $\frac{2}{3}$ ate the special. So $\frac{6}{7} \times \frac{3}{4} \times \frac{2}{3}$ ate the special. We cancel 2 and 6 in the numerator with 3 and 4 in the denominator to see that $\frac{3}{7}$ of the school population ate the special that day. That means $\frac{4}{7}$ did not eat the special. Give your answer as a fraction: $\boxed{\dfrac{4}{7}}$

Alternatively, we did not have to reduce the fraction; we could have just multiplied across to get $\frac{6}{7} \times \frac{3}{4} \times \frac{2}{3} = \frac{36}{84}$. Then $\frac{48}{84}$ would have also been an acceptable answer.

10. **(C)** Population density is given by population per unit area. If the total area of Central America is R and the population of Central America is P, we could calculate the population density for Belize as $\frac{0.01P}{0.04R}$. As we only need to compare, it suffices to just look at the ratio of the percentage of the population to the percentage of the area. This can even be eyeballed rather than calculated. El Salvador and Guatemala are the only countries that have a greater percentage of the population than area. For Guatemala it is 32/21, and for El Salvador, 17/4. El Salvador has the greatest population density. Choose **C**.

11. **(C)** Assume there are 100 people in Central America. Where do the 70 Mestizo live? Even if everyone outside Guatemala is Mestizo that would be only

68 Mestizos. So at least 2 must live in Guatemala. Thus the minimum percentage of Guatemala that is Mestizo is $\dfrac{2}{32} \times 100\%$, which is approximately 6%.

Choose **C**.

12. **(C)** First we notice that the price per 100 lb in 1975 is more than double the price per 100 lb in 1960. So B > A. Also the price in 1980 is more than the price in 1975 so C > B. The price in 1990 is similar to the price in 1980 but ordering much less potatoes means D < C. That leaves E or C as the answer. Now we need to calculate. 100 lb in 1995 is about $16 so 20 lb is about $16/5 or $5.33. 100 lb in 1980 is at least $11, so 50 lb would be $5.50. Choose **C**.

13. Start with 48 people. $\dfrac{1}{3}$ of 48, or 16, leave and then 4 got on. Now there are 36 people on the bus. $\dfrac{1}{4}$ of 36, or 9, leave. Thus 25 are on the bus, 8 more get on, and then one more gets on. That makes $25 + 8 + 1 = 36$ people on the bus. So $48 - 36 = 12$ seats are empty. $\dfrac{12}{48}$ of the bus is empty. This is $\dfrac{1}{4}$ but you do not need to reduce the fraction. Give your answer as a fraction: $\boxed{\dfrac{12}{48}}$

14. **(B)** I do not see an ideal strategy for this type of question. It can be time consuming but I recommend checking each answer to see if it is possible. Consider A, $x < 0$ and $y < 0$. If $x < 0$ and $y < 0$, then $xy > 0$. But could xy be less than 1? Not if you stick to integers, but if we use rational numbers like $x = -0.1$ and $y = -0.1$, then $xy = (-0.1)(-0.1) = 0.01$. So A could be true. Consider B, $x < -1$ and $y < -2$. Then xy is positive and greater than $(-1)(-2) = 2$. This is not possible. Choose **B**.

Numbers

The GRE uses the word *numbers* to mean real numbers—all numbers that you can find on the number line.

These include the integers (like -2, 0, and 137), rational numbers (like $\frac{5}{8}$, $\frac{-7}{13}$, or $\frac{2}{5}$), and irrational numbers (like $\sqrt{2}$ or π).

Numbers

$\frac{3}{4}$ $\frac{2}{-11}$ $\frac{-1}{5}$

Rational Numbers

$\sqrt{2}$ π

Irrational Numbers

-132 -5 $\frac{33}{7}$ e $\sqrt{7}$

1

Integers

-2 0

3 $-56\frac{1}{8}$ $1-\pi$

78

NUMBERS

Operations

There are two basic operations for numbers, addition (+) and multiplication (×). The numbers being added are called *summands*, and the result is called the *sum*. The numbers multiplied are called *factors*, and the result is called the *product*.

The opposite (inverse) of addition is subtraction (−), and the opposite of multiplication is division (÷). In a subtraction problem the result is called the *difference*. In a division problem the first number is called the *dividend*, the second is called the *divisor*, and the result is called the *quotient*.

You can always add, subtract or multiply two numbers. You can always divide a number by a nonzero number, but you can never divide by zero.

EXAMPLE 1

Column A	Column B

There are two positive integers whose difference is 2 and quotient is $\frac{4}{3}$

Sum of the numbers	Product of the numbers

Solution: As their quotient is $\frac{4}{3}$, the numbers must be multiples of 4 and 3 since

$$\frac{4}{3} = \frac{8}{6} = \frac{12}{9} = \frac{16}{12} = \dots$$

Because the difference between the numbers is 2 they must be 8 and 6. Their sum is $8 + 6 = 14$, and their product is $8 \times 6 = 48$ so the answer is **B**.

Basic Properties

Our number system has many properties.

- Both addition and multiplication are *commutative*; that means you get the same result no matter what order you perform the operation: $7 + 9 = 9 + 7$ and $5 \times 11 = 11 \times 5$.

- Subtraction and division are not commutative; as you can see, since $4 - 3 \neq 3 - 4$ and $8 \div 4 \neq 4 \div 8$.

- Every number a has an *opposite* (or additive inverse), which is $-a$ and $a + (-a) = 0 = (-a) + a$. The opposite of 3 is -3 and the opposite of -3 is $-(-3) = 3$. Subtracting a number is the same as adding its opposite, $8 - 5 = 8 + (-5) = 3$.

- Every nonzero number a has a *reciprocal* (or multiplicative inverse) which is $\dfrac{1}{a}$ and $a \times \dfrac{1}{a} = 1 = \dfrac{1}{a} \times a$. The reciprocal of 5 is $\dfrac{1}{5}$ and the reciprocal of $\dfrac{2}{3}$ is $\dfrac{1}{\frac{2}{3}} = \dfrac{1 \times 3}{\frac{2}{3} \times 3} = \dfrac{3}{2}$. The reciprocal of a/b is b/a. Dividing by a number is the same as multiplying by its reciprocal: $20 \div 5 = 20 \times \dfrac{1}{5} = \dfrac{20}{5} = 4$.

- Multiplication *distributes* over addition: $5 \times (6 + 7) = (5 \times 6) + (5 \times 7)$. Also $(5 + 6) \times 7 = (5 \times 7) + (6 \times 7)$.

- Multiply any number, a, by the number 1, and the product is that number: $a \times 1 = 1 \times a = a$. The number 1 is called the *multiplicative identity*.

- Add zero to any number, a, and the sum is that number: $a + 0 = 0 + a = a$. Zero is called the *additive identity*.

- Multiply any number by zero, and the product is zero. For example, $5 \times 0 = 0$, $\pi \times 0 = 0$, and even $0 \times 0 = 0$.

- If the product of two or more numbers is zero, one of them must be zero. If $a \times b = 0$ then $a = 0$ or $b = 0$.

EXAMPLE 2

Column A

Column B

$$\dfrac{5 \times (2 + 11)}{\frac{34}{7} + \frac{1}{9}} \times \dfrac{\frac{1}{9} + \frac{34}{7}}{(5 \times 2) + (5 \times 11)}$$

1

Solution: There is no need to do any long and difficult computation to solve this problem. The numerator of the first fraction equals the denominator of the second fraction because of the distributive property. The denominator of the first fraction equals the numerator of the second fraction because of the commutative property. Thus, the second fraction is the reciprocal of the first. The product of a number and its reciprocal is always 1. So the answer is **C**, they are equal.

EXAMPLE 3

Column A	Column B
$34 \times 71 \div 32 \times 0 \times 113$	$34 + 71 - 32 + 0 + 113$

Solution: Do not try to compute the results here. Column A has zero as a factor. Anything multiplied by zero will be zero. So Column A is zero. Without computing, it is still clear that Column B is greater than zero, as only 32 is subtracted and the other values clearly add up to more than 32. Hence the answer is **B**.

EXAMPLE 4

Column A	Column B

a is a nonzero number

Column A	Column B
The product of the opposite of *a* and the reciprocal of *a*.	The product of *a* and and the reciprocal of *a*.

Solution: A good strategy for this problem is to use a number for *a*, say 4. The opposite of 4 is -4 and the reciprocal of 4 is $\frac{1}{4}$. So Column A is $-4 \times \frac{1}{4} = -1$. In fact for any number *a*, Column A is $-a \times \frac{1}{a} = \frac{-a}{a} = -1$. Column B is 1, since the product of any number and its reciprocal is 1. So Column **B** is larger.

Absolute Value

The absolute value of a number is its distance from zero on the number line. For example $|3| = 3$ and $|-7| = 7$.

Of course the absolute value of zero is zero. If a number is positive, its absolute value is itself. If a number is negative, its absolute value is the number without the negative sign $|-7| = 7$. It is also the opposite of the negative number. For instance, $|-7| = -(-7) = 7$. This approach to absolute value can be very useful when dealing with expressions.

EXAMPLE 5

Column A	Column B
$|3 - \pi|$	$\pi - 3$

Solution: Recall that π is approximately 3.14. So $3 - \pi$ is negative, as 3 is less than π. Hence, the absolute value of $3 - \pi$ is its opposite: $-(3 - \pi) = -3 - (-\pi) = -3 + \pi$. Clearly this is equal to $\pi - 3$ so the answer is **C**.

EXAMPLE 6

Column A	Column B
$\left\lvert \dfrac{\pi - 4}{5^2 - 3^2} \right\rvert$	$\left\lvert \dfrac{4 - \pi}{5^2 - 3^2} \right\rvert$

Solution: There is no need to do any computations here. Notice that the only difference is the numerators and $-(\pi - 4) = 4 - \pi$. So the numbers inside the absolute value signs are opposites of each other (opposite of a/b is $-a/b$). Thus the answer is **C**.

TIP

The absolute value of a number and its opposite are always equal. $|23| = |-23| = 23$ and $|-7| = |-(-7)| = 7$.

Order of Operations: PEMDAS

When performing multiple operations there is a standard order in which they must be applied. In most cases parentheses make this clear, but when there is uncertainty follow these guidelines.

<u>P</u>arentheses—First do any operations in parentheses (. . .), using PEMDAS if necessary.

<u>E</u>xponents—Second, evaluate all powers a^b. If need be, evaluate the exponent before calculating the power.

<u>M</u>ultiplication and <u>D</u>ivision—Next multiply and divide in order from left to right. Multiplication and division have equal priority so do not do all multiplications and then all divisions.

<u>A</u>ddition and <u>S</u>ubtraction—Finally add and subtract in order from left to right. Addition and subtraction have equal priority so do not do all additions and then all subtractions.

The order of operations can easily be remembered using the mnemonic "<u>P</u>lease <u>E</u>xcuse <u>M</u>y <u>D</u>ear <u>A</u>unt <u>S</u>ally" or just PEMDAS. Here are some examples of PEMDAS being used:

$(9 - 6) \div 3$ *[Parentheses]*
$= 3 \div 3$ *[Divide]*
$= 1$

$9 - 6 \div 3$ *[Divide]*
$= 9 - 2$ *[Subtract]*
$= 7$

In the first example, parentheses force subtraction to take place before division.

$6 \div 3 \times 2 \div 4$ *[Divide]*
$= 2 \times 2 \div 4$ *[Multiply]*
$= 4 \div 4$ *[Divide]*
$= 1$

$6 \div (3 \times 2) \div 4$ *[Parentheses]*
$= 6 \div 6 \div 4$ *[Divide(LtoR)]*
$= 1 \div 4$ *[Divide]*
$= \dfrac{1}{4}$

Remember to proceed from left to right with multiplication and division doing whichever comes first. When multiplication is done before the division (the right example) again the result is very different.

$$\left(5 \times 2 - 3\right)^2 - 9 \quad [\textit{Parentheses Multiply}]$$
$$= \left(10 - 3\right)^2 - 9 \quad [\textit{Parentheses Subtract}]$$
$$= \left(7\right)^2 - 9 \quad [\textit{Exponents}]$$
$$= 49 - 9 \quad [\textit{Subtract}]$$
$$= 40$$

This example shows that PEMDAS applies inside the parentheses as well.

$$4^{5-3}$$
$$= 4^{(5-3)} \quad [\textit{Parentheses}]$$
$$= 4^2 \quad [\textit{Exponent}]$$
$$= 16$$

Finally we see that sometimes complicated expressions appear in the exponent. We should always evaluate the exponent $(5 - 3)$ before calculating the power (4^2). You might say that implicitly all exponents are parenthesized.

EXAMPLE 7

What is the difference between $(6 \times (2^3 + 24)) \div 3$ and $6 \times 2^3 + 24 \div 3$?

(A) 8
(B) 24
(C) 40
(D) 56
(E) 64

Solution: Well let's calculate. We start with the exponent inside the innermost parentheses $(6 \times (2^3 + 24)) \div 3$ [exponent] $= (6 \times (8 + 24)) \div 3$ [add] $= (6 \times 32) \div 3$ [multiply] $= 192 \div 3$ [divide] $= 64$. In the second expression, $6 \times 2^3 + 24 \div 3$ [exponents] $= 6 \times 8 + 24 \div 3$ [multiply] $= 48 + 24 \div 3$ [divide] $= 48 + 8$ [add] $= 56$. The answers are 64 and 56, which has a difference of 8. The answer is **A**.

EXAMPLE 8

$(100 - 2)^2 - 4 =$

(A) 964
(B) 9,600
(C) 9,604
(D) 9,996
(E) 9,992

Solution: If you apply PEMDAS, you would calculate $(100 - 2)^2 - 4 = 98^2 - 4 = 9,604 - 4 = 9,600$, which is rather tedious without a calculator. This is one situation where it might be easier to not apply PEMDAS immediately. (Don't break the rules. Just do some simplification first.) If you remember how to square a binomial $(100 - 2)^2 - 4 = (100^2 - 400 + 4) - 4 = 10,000 - 400 = 9,600$, and you've found the answer, **B**, without any tedious multiplications.

Problems

Basic Problems

1. If the dividend is 44 and the quotient is 11, what is the divisor?

   (A) 1/4
   (B) 4
   (C) 11
   (D) 44
   (E) 484

2. Which of the following is equal to the reciprocal of 2/5?

   I. 1/(5/2)
   II. 2.5
   III. 5 ÷ 2

   (A) I only
   (B) II only
   (C) III only
   (D) II and III only
   (E) I, II, and III

Column A	Column B
3. a	opposite of a

$$abc = 0, \text{ and } b > 1$$

Column A	Column B
4. a	c

5. $\left\| \dfrac{3,456 - 2,345}{34 \times 24 \div 14} \right\|$	-1
6. $2 + 8 \div 4 \times 3$	$((2 + 8) \div 4) \times 3$

GRE Problems

In questions 7 and 8, a, b, and c are positive different single digit integers, and $c \div b = a$.

Column A	Column B
7. c	9
8. 4	a

There are two positive integers, *a* and *b*, whose sum is 11 and product is 30

9. | $a - b$ | a/b |

a is a nonzero number

10. | The quotient of the opposite of *a* and the reciprocal of *a* | The quotient of *a* and and the reciprocal of *a* |

a is an integer, and |*a*| ≤ 2

11. | $(a + 2)(a + 1)a(a - 1)(a - 2)$ | 4 |

a ≠ *b*, and |*b* − *a*| = *a* − *b*

12. | *a* | *b* |

INTEGERS

The integers consist of zero and all positive and negative whole numbers.

$$\text{Integers} = \{\ldots, -3, -2, -1, 0, 1, 2, 3, \ldots\}$$

All integers are rational numbers but not all rational numbers are integers. For instance, $5 = \dfrac{10}{2}$ but $\dfrac{1}{2}$ cannot be expressed as an integer since it is not a whole number.

EXAMPLE 1

How many integer solutions are there to the equation $(x - 2)(2x - 1)(x + 3) = 0$?

(A) 0
(B) 1
(C) 2
(D) 3
(E) None of the above

Solution: A product can only be zero if one of the multiplicands are zero. So at least one of $(x - 2)$, $(2x - 1)$, and $(x + 3)$ must equal zero. We solve each

$$x - 2 = 0 \quad 2x - 1 = 0 \quad x + 3 = 0$$
$$x = 2 \quad\quad 2x = 1 \quad\quad x = -3$$
$$x = \frac{1}{2}$$

We conclude that there are three solutions: $x = -3$, $x = 2$, and $x = \dfrac{1}{2}$. But $\dfrac{1}{2}$ is not an integer so the answer is **C**.

All integers are (real) numbers, but not all numbers are integers. In fact a common mistake is to overlook answers that are not integers.

EXAMPLE 2

How many numbers x satisfy $x^2 \leq 1$?

(A) 0
(B) 1
(C) 2
(D) 3
(E) None of the above

Solution: It is easy to see that $(-1)^2 \leq 1$, $(0)^2 \leq 1$, and $(1)^2 \leq 1$ so there are at least three solutions. Some people might choose D at this point, but they would be incorrect. Consider a number between 0 and 1, like $\frac{1}{2}$. Then $\left(\frac{1}{2}\right)^2$ so $= \frac{1}{4} \leq 1$ so $\frac{1}{2}$ is also a solution. Clearly there are more than three solutions so **E** is the answer. In fact there are infinitely many solutions since any number between 0 and 1 would make the inequality true.

You can add, subtract, or multiply integers, and the result is always an integer. Dividing integers may result in a noninteger fraction ($6 \div 10 = 3/5$), may result in an integer ($6 \div 3 = 2$), or may be impossible ($6 \div 0$ is undefined).

The *positive integers* are $\{1, 2, 3, 4, \ldots\}$, and the *negative integers* are $\{\ldots -4, -3, -2, -1\}$. Neither set includes zero. Zero is neither positive nor negative.

EXAMPLE 3

Find all positive integers n so that $n^2 = |n|$.

(A) $n = -1, 1$
(B) $n = -2, -1, 1, 2$
(C) $n = -1, 0, 1$
(D) $n = 1$
(E) None of the above

Solution: We are only looking for positive n so we can substitute n for $|n|$. Thus we need to solve for n in the equation $n^2 = n$.

$$n^2 - n = 0 \text{ [bring everything to one side]}$$
$$n(n - 1) = 0 \text{ [factor]}$$
$$n = 0 \text{ or } n - 1 = 0$$
$$n = 0 \text{ or } n = 1.$$

Zero is not a positive integer but 1 is. The answer is **D**.

Consecutive Integers

A sequence of increasing (or decreasing) integers that increase (or decrease) by one are called consecutive integers. 3, 4, 5, 6, 7 are consecutive integers but 3, 4, 7, 5, 6 are not. Also, $-2, -3, -4, -5$ are consecutive integers but 8, 6, 4, 2 are not.

EXAMPLE 4

The sum of three consecutive integers is 21. What is the smallest of the three integers?

(A) 4
(B) 5
(C) 6
(D) 7
(E) 8

Solution: A conventional way to solve this problem is to use algebra. If the smallest of the three numbers is x, then the three consecutive integers are x, $x + 1$, and $x + 2$. Their sum is 21 so $x + (x + 1) + (x + 2) = 21$, We can solve for x.

$$x + (x + 1) + (x + 2) = 21$$
$$3x + 3 = 21$$
$$3x = 18$$
$$x = 6.$$

> **TIP**
>
> If n is odd, the sum of n consecutive numbers is n times the middle number.

Hence, the smallest of the consecutive integers is 6 so the answer is **C**. Another way to solve this problem is to use the given answers and check which one is correct. Starting with A we would check: is $4 + 5 + 6 = 21$? No. For B we check: is $5 + 6 + 7 = 21$? No. For C we check: is $6 + 7 + 8 = 21$? Yes. The answer is C.

EXAMPLE 5

Column A	Column B
Sum of integers from 1 to 13	Sum of integers from 15 to 19

Solution: Since there are 11 consecutive numbers from 1 to 13 and 7 is the middle number, the sum $1 + 2 + \ldots + 13 = 13 \times 7 = 91$. Similarly, $15 + 16 + 17 + 18 + 19 = 5 \times 17 = 85$. Choose **A**.

Problems

Basic Problems

Column A	Column B

In questions 1–3, x and y are negative integers

1. | $x - y$ | $x + y$ |

2. | xy | $x + y$ |

3. | xy | $x - y$ |

In questions 4–5, a, b, and c, in that order, are consecutive increasing integers.

4. | $a - b$ | $b - c$ |

5. $a - b$	$c - b$

n is an integer so that $n^2 \leq n$

6. n	1

n is an integer so that $n^2 \geq 5$

7. n	2

8. Product of consecutive integers from -5 to 5	Product of consecutive integers from -5 to 10

Sum of 9 consecutive integers is 0

9. Smallest summand	-4

P is the product of 3 consecutive integers

10. Remainder when P is divided by 3	Remainder when P is divided by 2

There are three consecutive integers so that
the product of the first and third is 48

11. The middle number	-7

12. The sum of 5 consecutive integers is 5. What is the smallest summand?

   (A) 5
   (B) 1
   (C) 0
   (D) -1
   (E) -2

13. How many positive integers satisfy $x^2 \leq 9$?

   (A) -3
   (B) 0
   (C) 1
   (D) 2
   (E) None of the above

14. If x and y are integers so that $-3 \leq x \leq 3$ and $-3 \leq y \leq 3$, what is the smallest integer that $x - y$ could be?

   (A) -5
   (B) -3
   (C) -2
   (D) -1
   (E) None of the above

GRE Problems

15. If x and y are integers so that $0 < x \le 4$ and $-3 < y < 6$ what is the smallest that $x - y$ could be?

    (A) 2
    (B) 0
    (C) −1
    (D) −4
    (E) −6

16. For how many integers, x, is $x^2 + x + 1 \le 2$?

    (A) −1
    (B) 0
    (C) 1
    (D) 2
    (E) 3

17. For how many negative integers, x, is $x^3 \ge x^2$?

    (A) 0
    (B) 1
    (C) 2
    (D) 3
    (E) None of the above

18. The product of three consecutive integers is negative. What is the largest value one of those integers could have?

    (A) 1
    (B) 0
    (C) −1
    (D) −2
    (E) −3

19. The average of n consecutive integers is one of those integers. Which of the following could be n?

    (A) 2
    (B) 3
    (C) 4
    (D) 8
    (E) 16

20. Let S be the sum of five consecutive integers. Which of the following *must* be true?

    I. S is a multiple of 5.
    II. S is greater than or equal to 15.
    III. S is odd.

(A) I only
(B) II only
(C) III only
(D) I and III only
(E) II and III

21. Let S be the sum of five consecutive positive integers. Which of the following *cannot* be true?

   I. S is divisible by 5.
  II. S is less than 10.
 III. S is even.

(A) I only
(B) II only
(C) III only
(D) I and III only
(E) II and III

22. The sum of four consecutive integers is 46. What is the sum of the previous four consecutive integers?

(A) 24
(B) 28
(C) 30
(D) 40
(E) 42

23. Take three consecutive integers. Multiply the first by the third then add 1. The result is always

(A) perfect square.
(B) even number.
(C) power of 2.
(D) prime.
(E) the second number.

Column A	Column B

In questions 24–25, a, b are consecutive decreasing integers.

	Column A	Column B
24.	$a^2 - ab$	a
25.	a^2	$a + ab$
26.	Sum of consecutive integers from -5 to 5	Sum of consecutive integers from -10 to 10

NUMBER THEORY

If you divide one integer by another and there is no remainder, then we can write an equation like $24 \div 8 = 3$ or the equivalent relationship $24 = 8 \times 3$. This relationship will illustrate at least four definitions.

8 is a *divisor* of 24 since $24 \div 8 = 3$ with no remainder (3 is also a divisor of 24).

24 is *divisible* by 8 since $24 \div 8 = 3$ with no remainder (24 is also divisible by 3).

24 is a *multiple* of 8 since $24 = 8 \times 3$ (24 is also a multiple of 3).

8 is a *factor* of 24 since $24 = 8 \times 3$ (3 is also a factor of 24).

Note that 0 is divisible by any nonzero number *n*, since *n* divides evenly into zero, zero times. For instance, $0 \div 7 = 0$ so 0 is divisible by 7.

EXAMPLE 1

Which of the following is a multiple of 2 and a factor of 36?

(A) 8
(B) 9
(C) 10
(D) 12
(E) 16

Solution: Multiples of 2 include 2, 4, 6, 8, 10, 12, 14, and 16 so B is not the answer. The factors of 36 are 1, 36, 2, 18, 3, 12, 4, 9, and 6. So the solution is 12—D.

EXAMPLE 2

Which of the following has exactly three positive factors?

(A) 8
(B) 18
(C) 25
(D) 36
(E) 64

Solution: We know that only perfect squares have an odd number of positive factors. As 8 and 18 are not perfect squares, we will check 25, 36, and 64. The positive factors of 25 are 1, 25, and 5. So the answer is **C**. Just to double check we find the positive factors of 36 (1, 2, 3, 4, 6, 8, 12, 18, and 36) and see there are nine of them. Also 64 has seven positive factors (1, 2, 4, 8, 16, 32, and 64).

TIP

- 1 and the number itself are always factors.

- Factors usually come in pairs ($24 = 8 \times 3$ and $24 = 2 \times 12$) but the number of factors is not always even.

- Only perfect squares have an odd number of positive factors. For instance, 36 has nine factors (1, 2, 3, 4, 6, 8, 12, 18, and 36) and 16 has five factors (1, 2, 4, 8, and 16).

Divisibility Rules

There are many rules for checking if an integer is divisible by a specific number. For instance, most people know that a number that ends in 0 is a multiple of ten. We present rules for divisibility by 2, 3, 4, 5, 6, 8, and 9.

- A number is divisible by 2 when the ones digits is 0, 2, 4, 6, or 8.

- A number is divisible by 3 when the sum of its digits is divisible by 3.

- A number is divisible by 4 when the last two digits are divisible by 4.

- A number is divisible by 5 when the ones digits is 0 or 5.

- A number is divisible by 6 when it is divisible by 2 and 3.

- A number is divisible by 8 when the last three digits are divisible by 8.

- A number is divisible by 9 when the sum of its digits is divisible by 9.

> **TIP**
>
> While not applicable for all numbers, a number is divisible by 7 if it can be separated into groups of adjacent digits that are multiples of 7. For instance, 14,287 is divisible by 7 since 14, 28, and 7 are all multiples of 7. This idea works for any divisor, not just 7. You can see that 2,255 is divisible by 11 since 22 and 55 are multiples of 11.

We did not give a rule for divisibility by 7 or other numbers. Rules exist, but in most cases it is just best to divide by 7 and see if the remainder is zero.

EXAMPLE 3

Which of the following is divisible by 3 but not 4?

(A) 144
(B) 84
(C) 48
(D) 40
(E) 30

Solution: $144 = 12 \times 12$ and $12 = 3 \times 4$ so 144 is a multiple of 4 and A is not the answer. In fact any number divisible by 12 will be divisible by 3 and 4. As $84 = 7 \times 12$ and $48 = 4 \times 12$, neither is the answer. Since 40 is divisible by 4 ($40 \div 4 = 10$), it cannot be the answer. That leaves 30 which is divisible by 3, $30 = 3 \times 10$, and not divisible by 4, $30 \div 4 = 7$ R2. The answer is **E**.

EXAMPLE 4

If d represents a single digit from 0 to 9 and $3023783d93$ is divisible by 9, what is d?

(A) 0
(B) 2
(C) 5
(D) 7
(E) None of the above

Solution: To be divisible by 9 the sum of the digits must be divisible by 9. In this case the sum of the digits is $3 + 0 + 2 + 3 + 7 + 8 + 3 + d + 9 + 3 = 38 + d$. The next multiple of 9 after 38 is 45. So $38 + d = 45$ or $d = 7$. The answer is **D**.

EXAMPLE 5

Which of the following is not divisible by 7?

(A) 2,828
(B) 7,357
(C) 7,735
(D) 9,449
(E) 9,114

Solution: 28 is a multiple of 7 so 2,828 is divisible by 7. As 7, 35, and 7 are multiples of 7, 7,357 is also divisible by 7. Similarly 7,735 (77 and 35) and 9,114 (91 = 7 × 13 and 14) are divisible by 7. That leaves 9,449 which is not divisible by 7. In fact long division shows that 9,449 ÷ 7 = 1349 R6. The answer is **D**.

Odds and Evens

An integer that is divisible by 2 is called *even*. If an integer is not even it is called *odd*. There are many equivalent ways to determine if a number is even or odd.

n is even	n is odd
$\Leftrightarrow$ n is a multiple of two	$\Leftrightarrow$ n is one more than a multiple of two
$\Leftrightarrow$ $n \div 2$ has remainder 0	$\Leftrightarrow$ $n \div 2$ has remainder 1
$\Leftrightarrow$ n has ones digit 0, 2, 4, 6 or 8	$\Leftrightarrow$ n has ones digit 1, 3, 5, 7, or 9

Odd and even numbers have many nice properties. Some are illustrated in the table below.

Property	Example
Sum of evens is even	4 + 8 = 12
Sum of two odds is even	7 + 11 = 18
Odd plus even is odd	5 + 6 = 11
Product of odds is odd	5 × 7 = 35
Product of an even integer and any integer is even	6 × 4 = 24 and 6 × 5 = 30

EXAMPLE 6

If E is even and O is odd, which of the following is even?

(A) $E + O$
(B) $5 \times 7 \times 9 \times E$
(C) $5 + 7 + 9 + E$
(D) $O \times (E + 1)$
(E) $O \times (E - 1)$

Solution: An even plus an odd is odd—A is not the answer. Anything (5 × 7 × 9) times an even is even. The answer is **B**. Let's check the other answers, too. In C, 5 + 7 is even since it's odd plus odd. 9 + E is odd since it's odd plus even. So even (5 + 7) plus odd (9 + E) is odd. C is not the answer. Since E is even, $E + 1$ is odd. An odd , O, times an odd, $E + 1$, is odd. D is not the answer. Since E is even, $E - 1$ is odd. An odd, O, times an odd, $E - 1$, is odd. E is not the answer.

Prime Numbers

A positive integer is called *prime* if it has exactly two distinct positive factors.

Number	Positive Factors	Primality
1	1	Not prime
2	1, 2	Prime
3	1, 3	Prime
4	1, 2, 4	Not prime
5	1, 5	Prime
6	1, 2, 3, 6	Not prime
7	1, 7	Prime
8	1, 2, 4, 8	Not prime

Notes:

- 1 is not a prime. It has only one positive factor—itself.

- A prime number can only be the product of two positive integers if they are one and itself. If it can be factored any other way as the product of positive integers then it is not a prime number. For instance, $24 = 4 \times 6$ so 24 is not a prime.

- 2 is the only even prime number.

- There are an infinite number of primes.

- You should recognize small primes like 2, 3, 5, 7, 11, 13, 17, 19, 23, 29, etc. Memorize them if you don't know them.

TIP

To check if a number is prime, you need only see if it is divisible by any primes from 2 up to the square root of the number. Consider 79. $\sqrt{79} \approx 8.9$ so we check if 79 is divisible by primes from 2 to 8.9, that would be 2, 3, 5, and 7. Now $79 \div 2 = 39$ R1, $79 \div 3 = 26$ R1, $79 \div 5 = 15$ R4 and $79 \div 7 = 11$ R2. In all four cases there is a remainder, so 79 is not divisible by any of the primes 2, 3, 5, and 7. Thus 79 is prime.

EXAMPLE 7

Which of the following is prime?

(A) 25
(B) $7^2 - 5^2$
(C) 51
(D) 73
(E) $2 \times 3 \times 5 + 3$

Solution: $25 = 5 \times 5$ so **A** is not prime. Using difference of squares we see that $7^2 - 5^2 = (7 - 5) \times (7 + 5) = 5 \times 12$ so **B** is not prime. Using the commutative and distributive laws $2 \times 3 \times 5 + 3 = 3 \times (2 \times 5 + 1) = 3 \times 11$ so **E** is not prime. To check if 51 is prime we need only check for divisibility by primes up to $\sqrt{51}$, which is a little more than 7 (recall $7^2 = 49$). So we check primes 2, 3, 5, and 7. 51 is odd so it is not divisible by 2. $5 + 1 = 6$ which is divisible by 3, so 51 is divisible by 3 (in fact $51 = 3 \times 17$). So **C** is not prime. That leaves only 73 to be a prime. The answer is **D**.

EXAMPLE 8

If p and q are odd primes, which of the following could be a prime?

(A) pq
(B) $p^2 + p$
(C) $p + q$
(D) $p + q + 1$
(E) $2p + 4q$

Solution: For A we see that pq is not a prime since $pq = p \times q$ (and neither p nor q is 1). For B we factor $p^2 + p = p(p + 1)$ so it is not a prime. For C, p and q are both odd so $p + q$ is even. And $p + q$ cannot be equal to 2, $p + q$ is at least $3 + 5$, so it is not prime. D is one more than C so it is odd, maybe it could be a prime. For E we factor $2p + 4q = 2(p + 2q)$ and see that it is not prime. So **D** is the only possible answer. And if $p = 3$ and $q = 7$ then $p + q + 1 = 11$, which is prime.

Every positive integer can be written uniquely as a product of primes. For example, $30 = 2 \times 3 \times 5$, $45 = 3^2 \times 5$, and $100 = 2^2 \times 5^2$. To find the *prime factorization* of a number first find two factors, then find the factors of the factors. Repeat until all your factors are prime. This is commonly done with a *factor tree*, as seen below.

$$60 = 2 \times 2 \times 3 \times 5 = 2^2 \times 3 \times 5$$

$$210 = 7 \times 2 \times 3 \times 5$$

The prime factorization is often easier to find than a list of all positive factors. Its structure can also identify a lot of information about the number quickly—for instance, the prime factors or the number of positive factors.

EXAMPLE 9

Which of the following has exactly three distinct *prime* factors?

(A) 20
(B) 30
(C) 49
(D) 91
(E) 320

Solution: We used factor trees (not shown) to find the prime factorization of each number.

$$20 = 2^2 \times 5$$
$$30 = 2 \times 3 \times 5$$
$$49 = 7^2$$
$$320 = 2^6 \times 5$$
$$420 = 2^2 \times 3 \times 5 \times 7$$

You can see that 20 has three prime factors (2, 2, and 5), but they are not all distinct. Also 49 has three positive factors (1, 7, and 49), but they are not all prime. Clearly, 30 is the only given number with exactly three prime factors. The answer is **B**.

Greatest Common Factor and Lowest Common Multiple

The GCF(a,b) is the *greatest common factor* of two integers, a and b—the largest number that is a factor of both a and b. It is also the largest integer that is a divisor of both a and b. For example, 15 has positive factors 1, 2, 3, 5, and 15, while 24 has positive factors 1, 2, 3, 4, 6, 8, 12, and 24 so the GCF(15, 24) = 3.

The LCM(a,b) is the *lowest common multiple* of a and b—the smallest positive number that is a multiple of a and is a multiple of b. 15 has multiples 15, 30, 45, 60, 75, 90, 105, 120, 135, etc., while 24 has multiples 24, 48, 72, 96, 120, 144, etc. so LCM(15, 24) = 120.

> **TIP**
>
> - GCF(n,m) $\leq n \leq m \leq$ LCM(n,m).
> - $n \times m \div$ GCF(n,m) = LCM(n,m). This relationship can be very useful for determining one from the other.
> - Another way to determine GCF is to write out the numbers' prime factorizations fully (no exponents) and take what they have in common.
> - Another way to determine LCM is to write out the numbers' prime factorizations fully (no exponents) and for each prime take how may a has or how many b has, whichever is larger.

EXAMPLE 10

Find the GCF(36, 60).

(A) 1
(B) 4
(C) 6
(D) 12
(E) 60

Solution: The positive factors of 36 are 1, 2, 3, 4, 6, 9, 12, 18, and 36. The positive factors of 60 are 1, 2, 3, 4, 5, 6, 10, 12, 15, 20, 30, and 60. Clearly the largest factor they have in common is 12 so the GCF(36, 60) = 12. The answer is **D**.

EXAMPLE 11

If $a = 2^3 \times 3^2 \times 5$ and $b = 3^3 \times 5 \times 7$, find GCF($a,b$) + LCM($a,b$).

(A) 45
(B) 360
(C) $2^3 \times 3^5 \times 5^2 \times 7$
(D) 7,560
(E) 7,605

Solution: There is no nice formula for the sum of the GCF and LCM, this question is simply making you compute both of them. Since the prime factorization is already given to use, we'll use the techniques given in the tips above. First we'll find the GCF.

$$a = 2 \times 2 \times 2 \times \underline{3 \times 3 \times 5}$$

$$b = 3 \times \underline{3 \times 3 \times 5} \times 7$$

The common factors are 3, 3 and 5 so the GCF(a,b) = $3^2 \times 5 = 45$. Now we find the LCM.

$$a = \underline{2 \times 2 \times 2} \times 3 \times 3 \times \underline{5}$$

$$b = \underline{3 \times 3 \times 3} \times 5 \times \underline{7}$$

Hence, LCM(a,b) = $2 \times 2 \times 2 \times 3 \times 3 \times 3 \times 5 \times 7 = 2^3 \times 3^3 \times 5 \times 7 = 7,560$. Here we take three factors of 2 because a has three and b has none, we take three factors of 3 because b has three and a only two, we take one factor of 5 as both have one, and we take one factor of 7 as b has one and a has none.

Another way to compute the LCM, after finding the GCF, would be to take ($a \times b$) ÷ 45, as in the the first tip above. The sum GCF(a,b) + LCM(a,b) is 45 + 7,560 = 7,605. The answer is **E**.

Problems

Basic Problems

Column A	Column B
1. Smallest positive factor of 24	Largest factor of 8
2. Smallest prime factor of 91	Largest prime factor of 63
3. Number of even one-digit positive integers	Number of odd one-digit positive integers

In questions 4 and 5, a and b are positive integers.

Column A	Column B
4. $ab \div$ GCF(a,b)	LCM(a,b)
5. LCM(a,b) × GCF(a,b)	$a \times b$
6. An even prime number	3
7. An odd prime	3

N is prime

Column A	Column B
8. Product of positive factors of N	N

9. The prime factorization of 72 is

(A) 2×7
(B) 2×6^2
(C) $2^3 \times 9$
(D) 8×9
(E) $2^3 \times 3^2$

10. D is a single digit so that $937D24$ is divisible by 2, 3, 4, 8, and 9. What is D?

(A) 0
(B) 1
(C) 2
(D) 3
(E) Greater than 3

11. If x is even and y is odd, which of the following must be odd?

(A) xy
(B) $8x$
(C) $x/2$
(D) $x - y$
(E) $(y + 1) / 2$

GRE Problems

<u>Column A</u>   <u>Column B</u>

In questions 12 and 13, x is a positive integer.

12.	Twice the number of positive divisors of x	Number of positive divisors of $2x$
13.	Number of distinct prime factors of x	Number of distinct prime factors of $2x$
14.	Number of even two digit positive integers	Number of odd two digit positive integers

a and b are positive integers

15.	GCF(a,ab)	GCF(b,ba)
16.	Smallest positive multiple of 7 and 3 that is even	Smallest positive multiple of 7 and 3 that is odd
17.	Smallest positive number divisible by both 5 and 7	70

18.	Largest number that is a factor of both 30 and 90	15

N is greater than 4 and not prime

19.	Product of positive factors of *N*	2*N*

N is positive and divisible by 2, 3, 4, and 8

20.	*N*	192

N is greater than 1,000 and divisible by 8

21.	*N*	1004

22. If the sum of the positive factors of *N* is *N* + 1, then *N* must be

    (A) odd
    (B) even
    (C) a perfect square
    (D) prime
    (E) not prime

23. Which of the following has precisely three positive factors?

    (A) 8
    (B) 12
    (C) 15
    (D) 25
    (E) 39

24. *D* is a single digit so that 728*D*49 is divisible by 3 and 7. What is *D*?

    (A) 0
    (B) 1
    (C) 2
    (D) 3
    (E) Greater than 3

25. If *p* is an odd prime, which of the following could be a prime?

    (A) p^2
    (B) $p + 2$
    (C) $p + 3$
    (D) 17×23
    (E) $71 \times 72 \times 73 + 3$

FRACTIONS

By forming ratios (fractions) of integers, but never dividing by zero, we obtain the rational numbers.

$$\text{Rational numbers} = \left\{ \frac{a}{b} : a,b \text{ are integers}, b \neq 0 \right\}.$$

> **NOTE**
> - Any number that can be expressed as a fraction of integers is called a rational number. $-2, 0, 3/4$, and 5 are all examples of rational numbers as $-2 = -2/1$, $0 = 0/6$, $3/4 = 6/8$ and $5 = 10/2$.
> - All integers are rational numbers, for instance $-5 = -5/1$ but not all rational numbers are integers ($1/2$ is a rational but is not an integer).

Fractions occur naturally in everyday life and thus occur in many GRE questions. If you have 3 chocolate bars and you want to share with 5 of your friends, how will you do it? One way is to divide each bar into 6 pieces and each person gets one piece from each bar. So each person gets 3 pieces of size $\frac{1}{6}$ each. That is $\frac{3}{6}$.

Another way is to divide each bar in half. Now you have 6 equal size portions (each $\frac{1}{2}$ a bar) so each person takes one. In either case each person gets the same amount of chocolate. We see that $\frac{3}{6} = \frac{1}{2}$.

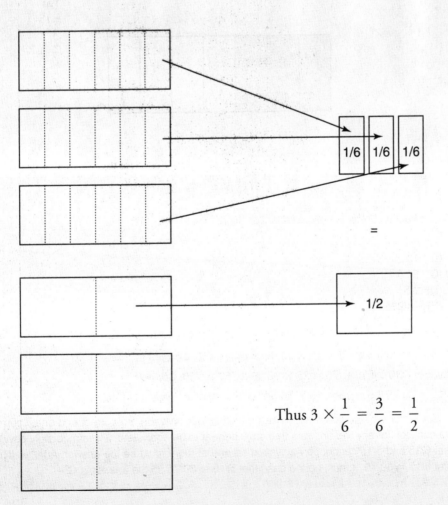

$$\text{Thus } 3 \times \frac{1}{6} = \frac{3}{6} = \frac{1}{2}$$

Equivalent Fractions

Any given fraction can be expressed an infinite number of ways, for example $\frac{1}{2} =$

$\frac{2}{4} = \frac{3}{6} = \frac{4}{8} = \cdots$ These are called *equivalent fractions* since they appear different

but express the same value. One way to check if fractions are equivalent is to cross multiply.

$\frac{a}{b}$ is equivalent (equal) to $\frac{c}{d}$ if $a \times d = b \times c$. For example, $\frac{6}{14}$ is equivalent to $\frac{3}{7}$

since $6 \times 7 = 14 \times 3$.

<table>
<tr><td>

NOTE

Any time you multiply both numerator and denominator of a fraction by the same value, you get an equivalent fraction. For example, multiply $\frac{3}{7}$ by

5 to get

$\frac{3 \times 5}{7 \times 5} = \frac{15}{35}$.

Thus $\frac{3}{7}$ and $\frac{15}{35}$

are equivalent fractions.

</td></tr>
</table>

$\frac{6}{14} = \frac{3}{7}$

EXAMPLE 1

Which fraction below is not equivalent to 30/75?

(A) 6/15
(B) 10/25
(C) 5/15
(D) 2/5
(E) 90/225

Solution: We could check each one using cross multiplication.

6/15 = 30/75 if 6 × 75 = 15 × 30, and 450 = 450. Correct!

10/25 = 30/75 if 10 × 75 = 25 × 30, and 750 = 750. Correct!

5/15 = 30/75 if 5 × 75 = 15 × 30 and 375 ≠ 450 so this is incorrect.

An easier way would be to realize that since four answers are correct and one incorrect we can look for any two answers that don't appear to be equivalent. It is immediately obvious that 6/15 and 5/15 cannot be equivalent so one of them must be the answer. After verifying that 6/15 = 30/75, it must be the case that 5/15 ≠ 30/75 so the answer is **C**.

For a given fractional value, there are many equivalent fractions. So which one should you use for an answer? The preferred answer is always the one *in lowest terms*. That is, the GCF of the numerator and denominator is 1. For example 12/15 is not in lowest terms since the GCF(12,15) is not 1. But 12/15 is equivalent to 4/5 (check $12 \times 5 = 15 \times 4$) and GCF(4,5) is 1. So 4/5 is in lowest terms.

The usual way to find lowest terms is to find common factors for the numerator and denominator and then use the Cancellation Law. *The Cancellation Law* says that if b and c are nonzero numbers, then $\dfrac{a \times b}{c \times b} = \dfrac{a}{c}$. We think of canceling the b's, $\dfrac{a \times \cancel{b}}{c \times \cancel{b}}$

to be left with $\dfrac{a}{c}$. Using this law and sometimes several steps, we can reduce any fraction to lowest terms. For example, $\dfrac{75}{240} = \dfrac{\cancel{5} \times 15}{\cancel{5} \times 48} = \dfrac{15}{48} = \dfrac{\cancel{3} \times 5}{\cancel{3} \times 16} = \dfrac{5}{16}$. Since GCF(5,16) = 1 this fraction is now in lowest terms.

EXAMPLE 2

Which fraction is not in lowest terms?

(A) 2/3
(B) 4/9
(C) 13/39
(D) 10/43
(E) 30/49

Solution: For each fraction we look at the GCF (numerator, denominator). If it is 1, then the fraction is in lowest terms. It's easiest to check each individually.

GCF(2,3) = 1, not A.

GCF(4,9) = GCF(2 × 2, 3 × 3) = 1 so not B.

GCF(13,39) = GCF(13, 3 × 13) = 13. So $\dfrac{13}{39} = \dfrac{13}{3 \times 13} = \dfrac{1}{3}$. So 13/39 is not in lowest terms. The answer is **C**.

Mixed Fractions

A mixed fraction (or mixed number) is an integer and a fraction added together but expressed without the plus sign. For example $3\frac{1}{3}$ (three and one-third), $5\frac{1}{2}$ (five and one-half), and $-3\frac{1}{4}$ (negative three and one-quarter) are all mixed fractions. Be careful, $3\frac{1}{4}$ means $3 + \frac{1}{4}$, not $3 \times \frac{1}{4}$.

A fraction, a/b, can be expressed as a mixed fraction if $a > b$. For instance $\frac{3}{2} = \frac{1}{2} + \frac{1}{2} + \frac{1}{2} = 1 + \frac{1}{2} = 1\frac{1}{2}$. To convert from a fraction to a mixed fraction is easy—just divide b into a. For example, as $7 \div 3 = 2$ R1, we know that $\frac{7}{3} = 2\frac{1}{3}$.

$$7 \div 3 = 2 \text{ R1}$$

$$\frac{7}{3} = 2\frac{1}{3}$$

A mixed fraction, $n\frac{p}{q}$, has an integer part n and a fractional part p/q. To convert to a fraction, first multiply n by q and add p. The result is the numerator, while q is still the denominator. For example $2\frac{1}{3} = (3 \times 2 + 1)/3 = 7/3$.

$$\frac{(2 \times 3) + 1}{3} = \frac{7}{3}$$

EXAMPLE 3

Which of the following mixed fractions are equivalent to 12/5?

(A) $1\frac{2}{5}$

(B) $2\frac{1}{5}$

(C) $2\frac{2}{5}$

(D) $5\frac{1}{2}$

(E) $12\frac{1}{5}$

Solution: Let's convert each answer to a fraction.

$1\frac{2}{5} = \frac{(5 \times 1) + 2}{5} = \frac{7}{5}$, which is clearly not correct.

$2\frac{1}{5} = \frac{(5 \times 2) + 1}{5} = \frac{11}{5}$, which is not correct.

$2\frac{2}{5} = \frac{(5 \times 2) + 2}{5} = \frac{12}{5}$, which is correct!

Alternatively, we could have converted 12/5 to a mixed fraction. $12 \div 5 = 2$ R2 so $\frac{12}{5} = 2\frac{2}{5}$. Either way, the answer is **C**.

Operations on Fractions

It is easy *to add fractions* if they have the same denominator. For instance, two-fifths plus one-fifth equals three-fifths $\left(\dfrac{2}{5} + \dfrac{1}{5} = \dfrac{3}{5}\right)$ in the same way that two apples plus one apple equals three apples. More simply, when they have equal denominators, you add fractions by keeping the denominator and adding the numerators. $\dfrac{a}{b} + \dfrac{c}{b} = \dfrac{a+c}{b}$.

$$\frac{2}{5} + \frac{1}{5} = \frac{3}{5}$$

If they do not have equal denominators, you can use equivalent fractions to find a common denominator. Usually we use the lowest common multiple of the original denominators. For example, the LCM(2,5) = 10 so in the following problem we convert our original fractions to equivalent fractions with denominator 10.

$$\frac{1}{2} + \frac{3}{5} = \frac{?}{10} + \frac{?}{10} = \frac{5}{10} + \frac{6}{10} = \frac{5+6}{10} = \frac{11}{10}$$

$$\frac{1}{2} + \frac{3}{5} = \frac{11}{10}$$

Diagram: Adding fractions

Subtraction is very similar to addition. For example,

$$\frac{3}{5} - \frac{1}{2} = \frac{?}{10} - \frac{?}{10} = \frac{6}{10} - \frac{5}{10} = \frac{6-5}{10} = \frac{1}{10}.$$

To multiply fractions, simply multiply numerator by numerator and denominator by denominator to get the product. For example,

$$\frac{4}{7} \times \frac{2}{3} = \frac{4 \times 2}{7 \times 3} = \frac{8}{21}.$$

You can also see how this works pictorially. The product is the double shaded area in the diagram below.

$$\frac{4}{7} \times \frac{2}{3} = \frac{8}{21}$$

To divide fractions recall that for any numbers x and y, $x \div y = x \times 1/y$. When x and y are fractions, to divide we simply "invert and multiply." For example,

$$\frac{4}{3} \div \frac{2}{3} = \frac{4}{3} \times \frac{3}{2} = \frac{\cancel{4}^2 \times \cancel{3}}{\cancel{3} \times \cancel{2}} = \frac{2}{1} = 2$$

This should seem appropriate since four apples (thirds) divided by two apples (thirds) equals two.

How can we *compare fractions?* Well clearly $\frac{3}{5} < \frac{4}{5}$ (in the same way that three apples (fifths) is less than four apples (fifths)). How can we tell if $\frac{1}{2} > \frac{2}{5}$? The easiest way is to find a common denominator and then compare numerators. In this case LCM(2,5) = 10 so the denominator is 10. So $\frac{1}{2} = \frac{5}{10}$ and $\frac{2}{5} = \frac{4}{10}$. As $\frac{5}{10} > 4/10$, we conclude that $\frac{1}{2} > \frac{2}{5}$.

EXAMPLE 4

Column A	Column B
$\dfrac{3}{10} \times \dfrac{5}{6} + \dfrac{1}{5}$	$\dfrac{3}{10} \div \dfrac{5}{6} - \dfrac{1}{5}$

Solution: First we multiply $\frac{3}{10} \times \frac{5}{6} = \frac{\cancel{3} \times \cancel{5}}{2 \times \cancel{5} \times 2 \times \cancel{3}} = \frac{1}{4}$. Now we add $\frac{1}{4} + \frac{1}{5}$. The LCM(4,5) = 20 so $\frac{1}{4} + \frac{1}{5} = \frac{5}{20} + \frac{4}{20} = \frac{9}{20}$.

Now to divide $\frac{3}{10} \div \frac{5}{6}$, we invert and multiply to get $\frac{3}{10} \times \frac{6}{5} = \frac{3 \times \cancel{2} \times 3}{\cancel{2} \times 5 \times 5} = \frac{9}{25}$. Now to compare 9/20 and 9/25 we could find a common denominator. The LCM(20,25) = 100 and 9/20 = 45/100 and 9/25 = 36/100. We see that 45/100 > 36/100 and thus 9/20 > 9/25.

Alternatively we might note that 9 divided into only 20 parts must be larger than 9 divided into a greater number (25) of parts. Even without subtracting 1/5, which would make B even smaller, we already see that A is larger than B. The answer is **A**.

> **TIP**
>
> - If the numerators are equal, the one with the smaller denominator is larger, for example 9/20 > 9/25.
>
> - Most often people compare fractions by converting them to decimals and then comparing the decimals.
>
> - Another way to compare fractions is to draw an accurate diagram of each fraction and eyeball which is larger.
>
> - A mixed fraction is not necessarily larger than a nonmixed fraction. For instance, $2\frac{3}{5} < \frac{16}{5}$ since $2\frac{3}{5} = \frac{13}{5}$, which is less than $\frac{16}{5}$.

EXAMPLE 5

Which fraction is the largest?

- (A) 11/20
- (B) 5/6
- (C) 5/8
- (D) 3/7
- (E) 2/3

Solution: We'll use equivalent fractions and the first tip above to answer this question. First, we note that $\frac{5}{6} > \frac{5}{8}$ as the numerators are equal and $6 < 8$. So C is not the answer. Then we note that $\frac{2}{3} = \frac{4}{6}$ and $\frac{4}{6} < \frac{5}{6}$ so E is not the answer. By the first tip $\frac{3}{7} < \frac{3}{6}$ and $\frac{3}{6} < \frac{5}{6}$ so D is not the answer. That only leaves A and B. We note that, $\frac{11}{20}$ is close to $\frac{10}{20}$, which equals $\frac{1}{2}$ and we know $\frac{5}{6} > \frac{3}{6} = \frac{1}{2}$. So we think B is the answer. Just to be absolutely certain, we can find a common denominator. As LCM(6,20) = 60 we find equivalent fractions $\frac{11}{20} = \frac{33}{60}$ and $\frac{5}{6} = \frac{50}{60}$. Clearly $\frac{50}{60} > \frac{33}{60}$ so $\frac{5}{6} > \frac{11}{20}$. The answer is **B**.

Simplifying Complex Fractions

Sometime you have to deal with *complex fractions*—fractions where the numerator and denominator are not just numbers but expressions or even other fractions. What is the best way to simplify these expressions? Consider for example, the fraction $\dfrac{\frac{1}{2} + \frac{4}{5}}{\frac{3}{10} - \frac{1}{4}}$.

First, we simplify it using PEMDAS—the numerator and denominator are treated like parentheses.

$$\frac{1}{2} + \frac{4}{5} = \frac{5}{10} + \frac{8}{10} = \frac{13}{10} \text{ and } \frac{3}{10} - \frac{1}{4} = \frac{6}{20} - \frac{5}{20} = \frac{1}{20}$$

$$\text{hence } \frac{\dfrac{1}{2} + \dfrac{4}{5}}{\dfrac{3}{10} - \dfrac{1}{4}} = \frac{\dfrac{13}{10}}{\dfrac{1}{20}} = \frac{13}{10} \times \frac{20}{1} = \frac{13 \times 2 \times 10}{10} = \frac{26}{1} = 26$$

Second, we try an alternate technique called *clearing the denominators.* Multiplying both numerator and denominator does not change the value of the fraction it simply makes an equivalent fraction. So we carefully choose a multiplier as the LCM of all denominators in the expression. LCM(2,5,4,10) is 20. This technique makes numbers larger but reduces the amount of work with fractions. First, we have $\dfrac{20}{20} \times$

$$\frac{\dfrac{1}{2} + \dfrac{4}{5}}{\dfrac{3}{10} - \dfrac{1}{4}} = \frac{20 \times \dfrac{1}{2} + 20 \times \dfrac{4}{5}}{20 \times \dfrac{3}{10} - 20 \times \dfrac{1}{4}}. \text{ Then we use cancellation to obtain } \frac{10 - 16}{6 - 5}$$

which equals $-6/-1$ or 6.

EXAMPLE 6

Column A	Column B
$\dfrac{\dfrac{3}{10} \times \dfrac{3}{10} \times \dfrac{3}{10}}{\dfrac{4}{5} + \dfrac{4}{5}}$	$\dfrac{\dfrac{3}{10} + \dfrac{3}{10} + \dfrac{3}{10}}{\dfrac{4}{5} \div \dfrac{4}{5}}$

Solution: To simplify column A, we'll multiply numerator and denominator by 1,000 (10 × 10 × 10).

$$\frac{\dfrac{3}{10} \times \dfrac{3}{10} \times \dfrac{3}{10}}{\dfrac{4}{5} + \dfrac{4}{5}} \times \frac{1,000}{1,000} = \frac{3 \times 3 \times 3}{200 \times 4 + 200 \times 4} = \frac{27}{1,600}$$

To simplify Column B we multiply numerator and denominator by 10

$$\frac{\dfrac{3}{10} + \dfrac{3}{10} + \dfrac{3}{10}}{\dfrac{4}{5} \div \dfrac{4}{5}} \times \frac{10}{10} = \frac{3 + 3 + 3}{\dfrac{\cancel{4}}{\cancel{5}} \times \dfrac{\cancel{5}}{\cancel{4}} \times 10} = \frac{9}{10}$$

Clearly B is much larger than A.

Solving Fraction Problems with Diagrams

A very valuable technique for solving fractions that is often overlooked is using a diagram. The diagram helps you keep track of the information in the problem and can help avoid difficult calculations—especially in multistep problems. Just be careful to remember what in your diagram represents 1 (the whole). It can change at each step.

EXAMPLE 7

At the first stop on Leroy Street, half the people get off the bus. At the second stop on Leroy Street, two-thirds as many people on the bus, get onto the bus. At the third stop on Leroy

Street, three-fifths leave the bus. At the fourth stop, half get off, and there are 4 left. How many people were on the bus before arriving at Leroy Street?

(A) 0
(B) 1—the driver
(C) 4
(D) 20
(E) 24

Solution: We'll use a chart to see what happens at each stage.

Four are left. This tells us that each small rectangle represents four people. Looking back at step one, we see that the bus can be divided into six small rectangles. Thus there were 6 × 4 = 24 people on the bus at the start. The answer is **E**.

To solve this problem using algebra we could let the number of people on the bus initially be B. Then after stop 1 we have $B/2$ people on the bus. At stop 2 we add 2/3 of $(B/2)$ so we have $B/2 + (2/3 \times B/2)$. At stop 4 we lose three-fifths (and thus retain 2/5). So we have $2/5(B/2 + (2/3 \times B/2))$. Finally at the last stop we lose half and the result is 4. $\frac{1}{2} \times (2/5(B/2 + (2/3 \times B/2))) = 4$. Then we solve for B.

A third approach would be to work backwards. Start with 4. Double it to get 8. Subtracting $\frac{3}{5}$ of a value is the same as taking $\frac{2}{5}$ of the value. So multiply by $\frac{5}{2}$ (the inverse of $\frac{2}{5}$) to get 20. Subtract $\frac{2}{5}$ of 20 to get 12. Double it to get 24. In some ways, this is the simplest approach, though it is very challenging to understand and determine the right fractions to use without a diagram.

Problems

Basic Problems

Column A	Column B
1. $\dfrac{1}{1+\frac{1}{2}}$	$\dfrac{2}{2+\frac{2}{1}}$
2. Reciprocal of $2\frac{2}{3}$	3/7

3.

$$\frac{3}{5} \div \frac{5}{7} \div \frac{7}{9}$$

$$\frac{3}{5} \times \frac{5}{7} \times \frac{7}{9}$$

4.

$$\frac{2}{10} + \frac{3}{7} + \frac{8}{6}$$

$$\frac{6}{14} + \frac{1}{5} + \frac{4}{3}$$

5.

$$\frac{1}{2} - \frac{1}{3} + \frac{1}{4}$$

$$\frac{1}{3} - \frac{1}{4} + \frac{1}{5}$$

6.

The fraction the white part is of the whole

The fraction the shaded part is of the whole

7. What fraction is smallest?

(A) $\frac{11}{20}$

(B) $\frac{5}{6}$

(C) $\frac{3}{8}$

(D) $\frac{2}{7}$

(E) $\frac{1}{3}$

8. Math class has 22 girls and 18 boys. What fraction of the class are girls?

(A) $\frac{22}{18}$

(B) $\frac{11}{9}$

(C) $\frac{11}{20}$

(D) $\frac{9}{20}$

(E) $\frac{9}{11}$

9. If $\dfrac{3}{8}$ of x equals 6, what is $\dfrac{3}{4}$ of x?

(A) 12
(B) 16
(C) 24
(D) 32
(E) 54

GRE Problems

	Column A	Column B

10.

Column A:
$$\dfrac{\dfrac{4}{7}+\dfrac{3}{14}}{1+\dfrac{45}{49}}$$

Column B:
$$\dfrac{\dfrac{4}{7}\times\dfrac{3}{14}}{1\div\dfrac{45}{49}}$$

$$x \neq 0$$

11.

Column A:

Column B:
x

12. 3/7 of 21/6 equals 5/9 of what number?

(A) 7/10
(B) 23/7
(C) 27/9
(D) 27/10
(E) 10/27

13. Two-thirds of the people in Lawrence County are eligible to vote. Only $\dfrac{4}{5}$ of the eligible people register to vote. Only $\dfrac{3}{4}$ of the registered voters actually vote on Election Day. What fraction of the county's population did not vote?

(A) $\dfrac{2}{5}$

(B) $\dfrac{3}{5}$

(C) $\dfrac{4}{5}$

(D) $\dfrac{5}{2}$

(E) $\dfrac{1}{3}$

14. $2\frac{1}{2}$ pounds of steak cost the same as $1\frac{1}{4}$ pounds of lamb. If 4 pounds of lamb cost $18 what would 5 pounds of steak cost?

(A) $5.75
(B) $8
(C) $11.25
(D) $21
(E) $27.25

15. If *S* is the set of all fractions *a/b*, where *a* and *b* are integers so that $1 \le a \le 5$ and $2 \le b < 4$, then

(A) *S* contains 10 distinct numbers
(B) *S* contains no integers
(C) *S* contains 3 fractions that are not integers
(D) *S* contains 3 fractions less than 1
(E) *S* contains 0

16. Northern Lights College has only three majors—music, education, and math (and each student has precisely one major). Half of the students are education majors. One-third of the students are math majors. Three-quarters of the music majors are female. If there are 120 male music majors how many students attend the college?

(A) 160
(B) 240
(C) 960
(D) 1,240
(E) 2,880

17. If $\left(\frac{2}{x}\right)^3 = \left(\frac{x}{-2}\right)^2$, then what is *x*?

(A) -1
(B) 0
(C) 1
(D) $\sqrt{2}$
(E) 2

18. A new scout troop started up in 2006 with 24 boys. In 2007, 8 new boys joined and then $\frac{1}{8}$ quit. In 2008, $\frac{1}{7}$ quit and then three boys joined. What fraction of the troop would have to leave to get back to the original start-up size?

(A) $\frac{1}{9}$

(B) $\frac{1}{8}$

(C) $\dfrac{1}{6}$

(D) $\dfrac{1}{4}$

(E) $\dfrac{1}{3}$

19. A terrible flu has hit the students from Professor Murty's lecture. He can see that $\dfrac{5}{7}$ of them are absent and $\dfrac{1}{3}$ of the remaining students are looking pale. If the pale students leave early, he'll have only 12 students left. How many students are normally in Professor Murty's lecture?

   (A) 48
   (B) 52
   (C) 63
   (D) 67
   (E) 72

20. The chief of police for Smalltown USA notices that, not including himself, $\dfrac{2}{3}$ of his police force carries firearms. If he includes himself, $\dfrac{5}{8}$ of his force carries firearms. How many people on his force do not carry firearms?

   (A) 5
   (B) 7
   (C) 11
   (D) 16
   (E) 24

DECIMALS

Any number can be expressed as combination of powers of 10 and powers of (1/10). For instance $777/5 = 155\dfrac{2}{5}$ or $155\dfrac{4}{10}$, which can be expressed as $1 \times 10^2 + 5 \times 10^1 + 5 \times 10^0 + 4 \times \left(\dfrac{1}{10}\right)^1$. We typically write this as 155.4 where the period is called a decimal point and separates the powers of 10 (left of the decimal point) from the powers of 1/10 (right of the decimal point). This is called the *decimal expansion*. Sometimes the expansion is infinite ($\sqrt{2} = 1.414\dots$), sometimes it's finite ($7/25 = 0.28$), sometimes it has repeating patterns ($23/99 = 0.23232323\dots$), and sometimes it has no patterns ($\pi = 3.141591\dots$). Our system of decimal numbers relies on place value.

<table>
<tr><td>

TIP

- If the denominator has only 2 and 5 as prime factors then the fraction will have a finite (terminating) decimal.

- Otherwise all fractions become infinite repeating decimals.

- Irrational numbers like $\sqrt{2}$ or e have infinite nonrepeating decimals.

- A finite decimal can be written with additional zeros at the end and not change the value of the decimal. For example 2.5 equals 2.50 or even 2.5000.

</td></tr>
</table>

Converting Between Fractions and Decimals

To *convert fractions to decimals* we use long division, placing a decimal point above the decimal point in the dividend.

$$
\begin{array}{r}
0.232 \\
99\overline{)23.000} \\
\underline{198} \\
320 \\
\underline{297} \\
230 \\
\cdots
\end{array}
\qquad
\begin{array}{r}
0.28 \\
25\overline{)7.00} \\
\underline{50} \\
200 \\
\underline{200} \\
0-R
\end{array}
$$

EXAMPLE 1

Which of the following is equal to 0.021021021....?

(A) 7/333
(B) 9/25
(C) 33/40
(D) 21/99
(E) $\sqrt{3}$

Solution: 25 = 5 × 5 and 40 = 2 × 2 × 2 × 5 so by the tip 9/25 and 33/40 have finite decimals. Also $\sqrt{3}$ is irrational so it has an infinite nonrepeating decimal. Thus B, C, and E are not correct. Using long division we see that 21/99 = 0.2121... and 7/333 = 0.021021.... So the answer is **A**.

$$
\begin{array}{r}
0.212\ldots \\
99\overline{)21.000\ldots} \\
\underline{198} \\
120 \\
\underline{99} \\
210 \\
\underline{198} \\
\cdots
\end{array}
\qquad
\begin{array}{r}
0.02102\ldots \\
333\overline{)7.00000\ldots} \\
\underline{666} \\
340 \\
\underline{333} \\
70 \\
\underline{0} \\
700 \\
\underline{666} \\
\cdots
\end{array}
$$

There is no easy way to convert irrational numbers to decimals without a calculator. I recommend you memorize commonly used numbers and their decimal expansion. See the Appendix.

Comparing Decimal Numbers

How do we compare decimal numbers? If one number has more digits to the left of the decimal than the other, it is larger.

EXAMPLE 2

Compare 322.95 and 99.1. We start by writing one above the other aligned at the decimal point: 322.95
99.1 . Notice that 322.95 has three digits to the left of the decimal and 99.1 has two digits to the left of the decimal so 322.95 > 99.1.

If both numbers have the same number of digits to the left of the decimal we compare digits in the same place starting from the left. The first place we find where the digits are not the same, the number with the larger digit is the larger number.

EXAMPLE 3

Compare 341.738 and 341.739.

```
3  4  1 .  7  3  8
↕  ↕  ↕     ↕  ↑
3  4  1 .  7  2  9
```

Notice that 3 = 3, 4 = 4, 1 = 1, 7 = 7, 3 > 2 so 341.738 > 341.729. Note, the fact that 8 < 9 in the final digit is irrelevant.

Operations on Decimals

To add (or subtract) decimals, line them up at the decimal point and add (or subtract) as you would integers. The answer will have a decimal point in the place directly below the other decimal points.

EXAMPLE 4

123.45
+67.891 becomes 123.450
+67.891
191.341

and 123.45
−54.321 becomes 12 3.450
−54.321
69.129

To multiply you do not need to line up the decimals. Treat the numbers as if they are integers and multiply. Then count the number of total number of spaces after the decimals in the factors. There should be that many places after the decimal point in the product.

EXAMPLE 5

```
  7.6
×2.13
  228
  76
152
16188
```

Then since there are a total of three places after the decimal in the factors, we put three places after the decimal in the product. So the product is 16.188.

For division, if the divisor is an integer, we proceed as we saw above. If the divisor is a decimal point we change the problem slightly but so that the result will still be correct. For example, to divide 23.5 by 2.2, we instead divide 235 by 22. Why? Think of equivalent fractions. Multiplying numerator and denominator by 10 shows that 23.5/2.2 = 235/22. In computing $2.2\overline{)23.5}$, move both decimal places one to the right to become

$$
\begin{array}{r}
10.68 \\
22.\overline{)235.00} \\
\underline{22} \\
150 \\
\underline{132} \\
180 \\
\underline{176} \\
4
\end{array}
$$

We could continue this division for some time but as you see 23.5 ÷ 2.2 is approximately 10.68.

EXAMPLE 6

Choose the largest value.

(A) 523.45 + 3.005
(B) 532.45 − 7.089
(C) 23.4 × 18.5
(D) 32.4 ÷ 0.04
(E) 600

Solution: The most direct way to solve this problem is to do each calculation.

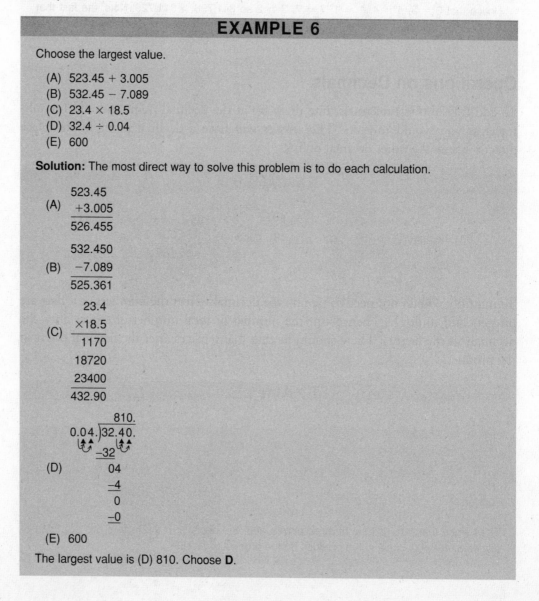

(A)
$$
\begin{array}{r}
523.45 \\
+3.005 \\
\hline
526.455
\end{array}
$$

(B)
$$
\begin{array}{r}
532.450 \\
-7.089 \\
\hline
525.361
\end{array}
$$

(C)
$$
\begin{array}{r}
23.4 \\
\times 18.5 \\
\hline
1170 \\
18720 \\
23400 \\
\hline
432.90
\end{array}
$$

(D)
$$
\begin{array}{r}
810. \\
0.04.\overline{)32.40.} \\
\underline{-32} \\
04 \\
\underline{-4} \\
0 \\
\underline{-0}
\end{array}
$$

(E) 600

The largest value is (D) 810. Choose **D**.

An alternate (better) solution would be to estimate. A is approximately 523 + 3 = 526 and B is approximately 532 − 7 = 525. Both are clearly less than 600 (E). C is less than 25 × 20 which is 500, also less than 600 (E). For D we move the decimal places two to the right and divide 3,240 ÷ 4. This is more than 3,200 ÷ 4 = 800, which is clearly greater than 600 (E). So the answer is **D**.

Multiplying or Dividing by Powers of Ten

Since decimal numbers are based on powers of ten it is extremely easy to multiply or divide by 10^n, where n is a positive integer. To multiply a number by 10^n, just move the decimal place n places to the right. For example, $24.345 \times 10^2 = 2,434.5$.

$$24.34\underset{\frown}{5} \times 10^2 \Rightarrow 2434.5$$

To divide a number by 10^n, just move the decimal place n places to the left. For example, $24.345 \div 10^2 = 0.24345$.

$$\underset{\frown}{24}.345 \div 10^2 \Rightarrow 0.24345$$

EXAMPLE 7

Choose the largest value.

  (A) 0.123×10^5
  (B) $1,23,0000 \div 10^3$
  (C) 0.00123×10^6
  (D) $1,230 \div 10^2$
  (E) $123,000,000 \div 10^7$

Solution: In A we move the decimal five places to the right to get 12,300. In B we move the decimal three places to the left to get 1,230. In C we move the decimal six places to the right to get 1,230. In D we move the decimal two places to the left to get 12.3. In E we move the decimal seven places to the left to get 12.3. The largest value is 12,300. The answer is **A**.

How can we divide or multiply by 10^n when n is less than 0? For example, if you want to divide by 10^{-4} you may instead multiply by 10^4, following the rules above. Likewise, if you are asked to multiply by 10^{-3} you may instead divide by 10^3.

Problems

Basic Problems

	Column A	Column B
1.	$8.023 - 7.032$	$0.401 + 0.5023$
2.	$(0.5)^2$	5×0.5
3.	$(0.1)^3$	$1,000 \div 1,000,000$

4.	$0.15 + 0.0032 - 8.2$		$2.5 \div 1.75 \times 3.1$
5.	34.2×10^5		0.0342×10^9
6.	$1.03 \div 10^4$		$1030 \div 10^7$

7. Choose the largest value.

   (A) 45.6×9
   (B) 0.465×10^3
   (C) 2.33×103.5
   (D) $646.003 - 1.254$
   (E) $1,003 \div 1.5$

8. Choose the smallest value.

   (A) $9.65 - 7.23$
   (B) 0.00345×10^3
   (C) $101 \div 50$
   (D) $646.003 - 647.254$
   (E) $1001.4 - 999.8$

GRE Problems

	Column A		Column B
9.	$(0.99)^9$		$(0.99)^{10}$
10.	0.00923×10^8		$92,300,000 \div 10^2$

11. 39×10^3 is how many times larger than 1.3×10^{-4}?

    (A) 10^{-1}
    (B) 10^7
    (C) $3,000$
    (D) $30,000,000$
    (E) $300,000,000$

12. 0.00015 is how many times smaller than 600?

    (A) $4,000$
    (B) 4×10^6
    (C) 10^7
    (D) $30,000$
    (E) $400,000$

13. Solve for x if $16.44 \times 0.47223 \times x = 4,722.3 \times 1.644$.

    (A) 0.001
    (B) 0.1
    (C) 10
    (D) $1,000$
    (E) $10,000$

14. Solve for x if $6.15 \times 723 \div x = 615 \times 0.0723$.

    (A) 0.01
    (B) 0.1
    (C) 10
    (D) 100
    (E) 1,000

RADICALS AND EXPONENTS

We say that 3 is the square root of 9 and write $\sqrt{9} = 3$ because $3^2 = 9$. Similarly $\sqrt{25} = 5$ because $5^2 = 25$ and $\sqrt{100} = 10$ because $10^2 = 100$. More generally, we define $\sqrt[n]{a}$, the "nth root of a," to be b when $b^n = a$. For example, the cube root of 8, $\sqrt[3]{8}$, is equal to 2 since $2^3 = 8$ and the fifth root of 243, $\sqrt[5]{243}$, is equal to 3 since $3^5 = 243$. Any expression of the form $\sqrt[n]{a}$ can be called a radical.

> **TIP**
>
> - On the GRE you are likely to only encounter square roots, though knowing cube roots or other roots may help with some problems.
> - Although $(-3)^2 = 9$, $\sqrt{9} \neq 3$. Square root is defined as the "principal radical" and only returns positive values or zero.
> - The square root (and more generally nth root for n even) is only defined for positive numbers. The square root of negative four, $\sqrt{-4}$, does not make sense[3] since there is no number whose square is -4.
> - The cube root (and more generally nth root for n odd) is defined for all numbers. For example $\sqrt[3]{-8} = -2$ since $(-2)^3 = -8$.
> - Although $\left(\sqrt{a}\right)^2 = a$, it is not always true that $\sqrt{a^2} = a$. For example $\sqrt{(-3)^2} = \sqrt{9} = 3$ not -3. It is always true that $\sqrt{a^2} = |a|$.

EXAMPLE 1

Which of the following is a positive integer?

(A) $\sqrt{240}$

(B) $\sqrt[5]{64}$

(C) $\sqrt[3]{-64}$

(D) $\sqrt[4]{80}$

(E) $\sqrt{196}$

Solution: For A, we factor 240 and then simplify: $\sqrt{240} = \sqrt{2^4 \times 15} = \sqrt{16} \times \sqrt{15} = 4\sqrt{15}$, which is not an integer. For B, $\sqrt[5]{64} = \sqrt[5]{2^6} = \sqrt[5]{2^5} \times \sqrt[5]{2} = 2\sqrt[5]{2}$, which is not an integer. For C, $\sqrt[3]{-64} = -4$ since $(-4) \times (-4) \times (-4) = -64$. But -4 is not a positive integer. For D, $\sqrt[4]{80} = \sqrt[4]{2^4 \times 5} = \sqrt[4]{2^4} \times \sqrt[4]{5} = 2\sqrt[4]{5}$, which is not an integer. So **E** must be the answer and indeed $\sqrt{196} = \sqrt{2^2 7^2} = \sqrt{2^2} \sqrt{7^2} = 2 \times 7 = 14$. Of course, it helps to solve such problems if you memorize some of the early perfect squares (knowing $14^2 = 196$ should allow you to solve this problem in a few seconds). See the Appendix for a list of suggested things to memorize.

---

[3] *Complex numbers would allow you to solve this problem, but the GRE only concerns itself with real numbers.*

Simplifying Radicals

Expressions involving radicals can be challenging to simplify. You can add or subtract *like* radicals. For instance, $2\sqrt{6} + 3\sqrt{6} = 5\sqrt{6}$ (think two apples plus three apples equals five apples).

When $a \geq 0$ and $b > 0$, we can simplify radicals using the rules $\sqrt{ab} = \sqrt{a}\sqrt{b}$ and $\sqrt{\dfrac{a}{b}} = \dfrac{\sqrt{a}}{\sqrt{b}}$. For instance, $\sqrt{12} = \sqrt{4 \times 3} = \sqrt{4} \times \sqrt{3} = 2\sqrt{3}$ and

$$\sqrt{2.25} = \sqrt{\frac{9}{4}} = \frac{\sqrt{9}}{\sqrt{4}} = 3/2 = 1.5.$$

Using the last rule, radicals are usually simplified to remove any squares under the radical sign. So, you will see $2\sqrt{3}$ and not $\sqrt{12}$, or $3\sqrt{2}$ and not $\sqrt{18}$ (note $\sqrt{18} = \sqrt{9 \times 2} = \sqrt{9} \times \sqrt{2} = 3\sqrt{2}$).

Before calculators were in common use, many answers involved radicals, and it was usually considered bad form to give an answer, like $\dfrac{2}{\sqrt{3}}$, with a radical in the denominator. To *rationalize a denominator*, simply multiply numerator and denominator by the same radical to get an equivalent fraction, without a radical in the denominator.

For example, $\dfrac{2}{\sqrt{3}} \times \dfrac{\sqrt{3}}{\sqrt{3}} = \dfrac{2\sqrt{3}}{3}$ or even $\dfrac{2}{3}\sqrt{3}$.

TIP

- You may not add or subtract different radicals. For example, $\sqrt{9} - \sqrt{4} \neq \sqrt{9-4}$ as $\sqrt{9} - \sqrt{4} = 3 - 2 = 1$, which is not $\sqrt{5}$. An expression like $\sqrt{6} + \sqrt{5}$ cannot be simplified at all.

- Of course, the reverse of the first tip is also invalid. Note that $\sqrt{9-4} \neq \sqrt{9} - \sqrt{4}$ and $\sqrt{6+5} \neq \sqrt{6} + \sqrt{5}$. Still a very common mistake would be to calculate $\sqrt{9+4} = \sqrt{9} + \sqrt{4} = 3 + 2 = 5$. Clearly $\sqrt{13} \neq 5$. Beware—it's an easy trap to fall into!

EXAMPLE 2

If the area of a square is 60, what is the length of each side?

(A) 3,600
(B) 15
(C) $4\sqrt{15}$
(D) $2\sqrt{5}$
(E) $2\sqrt{15}$

Solution: The formula for the area of a square is $A = s^2$, where s is the length of each side. So $60 = s^2$, and we have to solve for s. Taking the square root of each side, we get $s = \sqrt{60}$ (in this case we know $\sqrt{s^2} = s$ since s is positive). We must simplify $\sqrt{60}$. We use a factor tree to factor 60 and discover that $\sqrt{60} = \sqrt{2^2 \times 3 \times 5} = \sqrt{2^2} \times \sqrt{3 \times 5} = 2\sqrt{15}$. The answer is **E**.

EXAMPLE 3

Simplify $\dfrac{5}{2}\sqrt{\dfrac{6}{15}}$.

(A) $\sqrt{\dfrac{3}{2}}$

(B) $2\sqrt{3}$

(C) $\frac{1}{2}\sqrt{10}$

(D) $\sqrt{\dfrac{2}{5}}$

(E) $\sqrt{2} + \sqrt{5}$

Solution: First, we'll factor the numbers under the square root sign and cancel the common factor, $\dfrac{5}{2}\sqrt{\dfrac{6}{15}} = \dfrac{5}{2}\sqrt{\dfrac{3 \times 2}{3 \times 5}} = \dfrac{5}{2}\sqrt{\dfrac{2}{5}}$. Second, we use the rule $\sqrt{\dfrac{a}{b}} = \dfrac{\sqrt{a}}{\sqrt{b}}$ to find that $\dfrac{5}{2}\sqrt{\dfrac{2}{5}} = \dfrac{5}{2}\dfrac{\sqrt{2}}{\sqrt{5}}$. Finally we rationalize the denominator (cancelling as needed) $\dfrac{5\sqrt{2}}{2\sqrt{5}} \times \dfrac{\sqrt{5}}{\sqrt{5}} = \dfrac{5\sqrt{2}\sqrt{5}}{10} = \dfrac{\sqrt{2}\sqrt{5}}{2}$. Finally we combine the radicals using the rule $\sqrt{ab} = \sqrt{a}\sqrt{b}$ and bring the fraction in front to get $\dfrac{\sqrt{2}\sqrt{5}}{2} = \dfrac{\sqrt{10}}{2} = \dfrac{1}{2}\sqrt{10}$. The answer is **C**.

An alternate (challenging, but maybe quick) approach would be to estimate the value of the expression given as a decimal and compare it to each of the given answers.

Defining Powers

An expression like a^n is called a *power*. The *base* of the power is a and the *exponent* is n. When n is an integer, powers are a special notation for repeated multiplication. Pay careful attention to how powers are defined when n is some other kind of number.

If n is a positive integer then we define $a^n = \underbrace{a \times a \times a \times a \ldots \times a}_{n \text{ times}}$. For instance, $2^5 = 2 \times 2 \times 2 \times 2 \times 2 = 32$. When $n = 2$, we call the power a *perfect square*; for example, $9 = 3^2$, and if $n = 3$, we call the power a *perfect cube*, for example $8 = 2^3$.

If n is a negative integer and a is not zero, then we define $a^n = \dfrac{1}{a^{|n|}} = \underbrace{\dfrac{1}{a} \times \dfrac{1}{a} \times \dfrac{1}{a} \times \ldots \times \dfrac{1}{a}}_{n \text{ times}}$. For instance $3^{-2} = \dfrac{1}{3^2} = \dfrac{1}{3} \times \dfrac{1}{3} = \dfrac{1}{9}$. You may not see a negative exponent on the GRE, but they still can be helpful in solving GRE problems.

If n is zero and $a \neq 0$, then define $a^n = 1$. Yes, $4^0 = 1$ and $\pi^0 = 1$.

If a is zero and $n \neq 0$, then $a^n = 0^n = 0$. Yet, 0^0 is undefined.

EXAMPLE 4

Which of the following numbers are less than 1?

I. 5^{-3}

II. $\left(\dfrac{1}{5}\right)^{-3}$

III. 5^0

(A) I only
(B) II only
(C) III only
(D) II and III
(E) I and II

Solution: For I we see that $5^{-3} = \dfrac{1}{5} \times \dfrac{1}{5} \times \dfrac{1}{5} = 1/125$. Recall that $1/(1/5) = 5$ then $\left(\dfrac{1}{5}\right)^{-3} = 5 \times 5 \times 5 = 125$. Finally $5^0 = 1$. So the only answer less than 1 is I. Choose **A**.

When n is a fraction, $n = p/q$ with q positive and p positive or negative, then we define $a^n = a^{\frac{p}{q}} = \left(\sqrt[q]{a}\right)^p$. For instance, $81^{\frac{1}{4}} = \left(\sqrt[4]{81}\right)^1 = \sqrt[4]{81} = 3$ or $8^{\frac{2}{3}} = \left(\sqrt[3]{8}\right)^2 = 2^2 = 4$. As mentioned earlier, only square roots appear frequently on the GRE. So it would be reasonable to expect you to know that $4^{2.5} = 4^{\frac{5}{2}} = \left(\sqrt{4}\right)^5 = 2^5 = 32$, but it may be unreasonable to ask for $2{,}187^{\frac{3}{7}}$.

Rules for Working with Powers

These rules help you simplify expression with powers. $a^{m+n} = a^m a^n$. For example, $2^{2+3} = 2^2 \times 2^3$ as $32 = 4 \times 8$. This rule is used more often to combine powers into one power: "keep the base and add the exponents." For example, $5^4 \times 5^4 = 5^{4+4} = 5^8$.

$a^{m-n} = \dfrac{a^m}{a^n}$. This is just a variation of the previous rule combined with the definition of negative exponents. An example is $4^{5-3} = 4^5 / 4^3$, which makes sense as

$4^{5-3} = 4^2 = 16$ and $4^5 / 4^3 = 4^2/1 = 16$ (using cancellation). More often this rule is used for examples like $5^4 \div 5^5 = 5^{4-5} = 5^{-1} = 1/5$.

$(ab)^n = a^n b^n$. For example, $(2 \times 5)^3 = (2 \times 5) \times (2 \times 5) \times (2 \times 5) = 2 \times 2 \times 2 \times 5 \times 5 \times 5 = 2^3 \times 5^3$.

EXAMPLE 5

Simplify $\dfrac{(10^3)^2 \div 10^5 \times 10^7}{2^3 2^2 5^7}$.

(A) 20
(B) 40
(C) 100
(D) 2/5
(E) 25/2

Solution: First $(10^3)^2 = 10^6$, so the numerator is $10^6 \div 10^5 \times 10^7$, which equals $10^{6-5+7} = 10^8$. Second, combining the powers of 2 in the denominator we get $2^{(3+2)}5^7$. So we are trying to simplify $\dfrac{10^8}{2^5 5^7}$. If we express 10 as 2×5 then we have $\dfrac{(2 \times 5)^8}{2^5 5^7}$, which equals $\dfrac{2^8 5^8}{2^5 5^7}$. Now using our rules for dividing powers we have $2^{8-5}5^{8-7} = 2^3 \times 5 = 40$. Choose **B**.

TIPS

- A common mistake would be "keep the exponent and add the bases." For instance, $2^4 \times 3^4$ is not equal to 5^4, as $2^4 \times 3^4 = 16 \times 81 = 1{,}296$ but $5^4 = 625$. However, $2^4 \times 3^4 = (2 \times 3)^4 = 6^4$.

- Another common mistake would be to try to simplify when powers are added. For instance, $2^3 + 2^5$ is not equal to 2^8, as $2^3 + 2^5 = 8 + 32 = 40$ and $2^8 = 256$.

- There is one special time when you can simplify added powers. When you have two identical powers of two, three identical powers of three, or, generally, n identical powers of n. For instance, $2^3 + 2^3 = 2 \times 2^3 = 2^4$ and $3^2 + 3^2 + 3^2 = 3 \times 3^2 = 3^3$.

Problems

Basic Problems

Column A	Column B
1. $(5^2)^3$	5^5
2. $((1/2)^3)^2$	2^{-6}

3. 10^5	$2^6 5^4$
4. $8/2^5$	$(2^{-2})^{-2}$
5. $\sqrt{\dfrac{8}{9}}$	$2/3$
6. $\sqrt{4+9}$	$\sqrt{4}+\sqrt{9}$
7. $\sqrt{9-4}$	$\sqrt{9}-\sqrt{4}$
8. $(2+3)^2$	2^2+3^2
9. $-\sqrt[3]{8}$	$\sqrt[3]{-8}$
10. $\sqrt{(-4)^2}$	-4

11. If $2^a \times 16^2 = 4^5$ then what is a?

    (A) -3
    (B) -1
    (C) 0
    (D) 1
    (E) 2

12. If $\dfrac{3^x}{9} = \sqrt{81}$, then $x = $?

    (A) 0
    (B) 2
    (C) 4
    (D) 6
    (E) 8

13. Choose the largest value.

    (A) 2^3
    (B) 3^2
    (C) $2^3 \times 3^2$
    (D) $2^3 \times 2^{-3}$
    (E) $(2^3)^2$

GRE Problems

14. Solve for a if $2^{a+6}4^a = 8^3$.

    (A) 0
    (B) 1
    (C) 2
    (D) 3
    (E) 4

15. If $\sqrt{6^n} = \dfrac{2^n}{\sqrt{2}} \times \dfrac{3^n}{\sqrt{3}}$, then what is n?

    (A) -1
    (B) 0
    (C) 1
    (D) 2
    (E) 3

16. Simplify $\sqrt{\dfrac{x^{10}y^8z^5}{x^6y^7z^6}}$.

    (A) $x\sqrt{yz}$

    (B) $\dfrac{x^2\sqrt{xz}}{z}$

    (C) $\dfrac{\sqrt{xyz}}{z}$

    (D) $\dfrac{\sqrt{x^2yz}}{z}$

    (E) $\dfrac{x^2\sqrt{yz}}{z}$

Column A	Column B
17. $\dfrac{\sqrt{40}}{2}$	$\dfrac{20}{\sqrt{10}}$

You are given a square and a circle that have the same area

18. Diameter of the circle	Diagonal of the square

19. $3^4 + 3^4 + 3^4$	3^5

82 *GRE Math Workbook*

20. $2^4 + 2^4 + 2^4$	2^6
21. Average of 2^0, 2^1, 2^2, and 2^3	Average of 3^0, 3^1, and 3^2
22. Average of 3^1, 3^2, and 3^3	Sum of 3^0, 3^1, and 3^2

SOLUTIONS

Numbers

1. (**B**) The dividend is the number you divide into, and the quotient is the result. So this question is asking you to fill in the blank $44 \div \_\_\_ = 11$. Since $4 \times 11 = 44$, the answer is 4. Choose **B**.

2. (**D**) The reciprocal is $1 \div (2/5)$ which equals $1 \times (5/2) = 5/2 = 2.5$. So answers II and III are correct. Answer I is $1 \div (5/2) = 1 \times (2/5) = 2/5 = 0.4$ and is not the correct answer. Choose **D** (II and III only).

3. (**D**) The opposite of a is $-a$. Without knowing the value of a, we can't tell which is larger. If $a < 0$, then $-a > 0$, and $-a$ is larger. If $a > 0$ then $-a < 0$, and a is larger. If $a = 0$ then $-a = 0$, and they are equal. Choose **D**.

4. (**D**) As $abc = 0$, then one of the three values a, b, or c must equal zero. Since $b > 1$, b is not equal to zero. Hence $a = 0$ or $c = 0$. If $a = 0$, c could be anything including zero. That means a and c could be equal ($a = 0 = c$) or one could be larger than the other ($a = 0$ and $c = -3$). Choose **D**.

5. (**A**) The expression in Column A looks complicated and is tedious to compute. Luckily we don't have to compute it. Since it is in absolute value signs, the result must be greater than or equal to zero. But -1, in Column B, is less than zero. Choose **A**.

6. (**A**) This tests your knowledge of order of operations. In Column A, there are no parentheses or exponents so we do multiplication and division in left to right order. In this case that means division, then multiplication. We finish with addition. $2 + 8 \div 4 \times 3 = 2 + 2 \times 3 = 2 + 6 = 8$. In Column B we do whatever is inside parentheses first proceeding from innermost to outermost. Hence we do addition, then division, and finally multiplication. $((2 + 8) \div 4) \times 3 = (10 \div 4) \times 3 = 2.5 \times 3 = 7.5$. Clearly $8 > 7.5$, so choose **A**.

7. (**B**) Here a, b, and c are positive different single digit integers, and $c \div b = a$. As a single-digit integer, the largest c could potentially be is 9. But 9 is only divisible by 1, 3, and 9. Then our division equation would have to be $9 \div 1 = 9$, $9 \div 3 = 3$, or $9 \div 9 = 1$. All of those do not have three different numbers. Hence c cannot be 9 and must be less than 9. Choose **B**.

8. (**D**) If $a = 4$, then the division equation could be $8 \div 2 = 4$. But that is not the only possible equation. We could also have $8 \div 4 = 2$ or $6 \div 3 = 2$ or

$6 \div 2 = 3$. Hence, a could be equal to 4, but it could also be less than 4. Choose **D**.

9. **(B)** What pairs of numbers add to 11? $1 + 10, 2 + 9, 3 + 8, 4 + 7$, and $5 + 6$. The only product that equals 30 is 5×6. So the numbers are $a = 5$ and $b = 6$. Then $a - b = 5 - 6 = -1$ and $a/b = 5/6$. Since $-1 < 5/6$, B is larger. But wait, couldn't $a = 6$ and $b = 5$? Then $a - b = 1$ and $a/b = 6/5$. $1 < 6/5$ so again B is larger. In both cases B is larger so choose **B**.

10. **(B)** The opposite of a is $-a$, and the reciprocal of a is $1/a$. Their quotient is $\dfrac{-a}{\frac{1}{a}} = -a \times \dfrac{a}{1} = -a^2$. The quotient of a and the reciprocal of a is

   $\dfrac{a}{\frac{1}{a}} = a \times \dfrac{a}{1} = a^2$. Even if we took the quotient in the opposite order, the

   result in column A is always negative and the result in column B is always positive. Choose **B**.

11. **(B)** Since a is an integer and $|a| \leq 2$, a must be one of $-2, -1, 0, 1$, or 2. That means that one of the terms in the product $(a + 2)(a + 1)(a)(a - 1)(a - 2)$ must be zero and hence the product is zero. As $4 > 0$, choose **B**.

12. **(A)** As with every absolute value problem, there are three cases: $b - a > 0$, $b - a = 0$ or $b - a < 0$. If $b - a > 0$, then $|b - a| = b - a$ and hence $b - a = a - b$. Add a to both sides and then add b to both sides to see that $2b = 2a$, or $b = a$. But that is impossible as we are told a is not equal to b. If $b - a = 0$, then $b = a$ which is also impossible. Hence the remaining case, $b - a < 0$, must be true. If $b - a < 0$ then $b < a$. Choose **A**.

Integers

1. **(A)** The easiest way to solve this problem is to subtract x from both columns to get $-y$ and y. Which is larger? $-y$ is larger than y, since y is a negative number. Choose **A**.

2. **(A)** Since both x and y and negative, their product is positive and their sum is negative. Choose **A**.

3. **(A)** The product of two negative numbers is positive. But the difference of two negative numbers can also be positive, for example $-6 - (-8) = 2$. It's not hard to see the difference will be largest when $x = -1$ and then $x - y = |y| - 1$. When $x = -1$, $xy = |y|$. But $|y|$ is always greater than $|y| - 1$. Choose **A**.

4. **(C)** Since they are consecutive and increasing, for example $a = 3$, $b = 4$, and $c = 5$, then $a - b = -1$ and $b - c = -1$. Choose **C**.

5. **(B)** In this case, $a - b = -1$ and $c - b = 1$. Choose **B**.

6. **(D)** Which integers, n, have the property that $n^2 \le n$? $1^2 \le 1$. Also $0^2 \le 1$, so n could be 1 or 0 (or possibly other values). Choose **D**.

7. **(D)** Which integers, n, have the property that $n^2 \ge 5$? Clearly $n = 3$ would do as $3^2 = 9 \ge 5$. But -3 is also an integer and $(-3)^2 = 9 \ge 5$. So n could be greater or less than 2. Choose **D**.

8. **(C)** At first glance you might decide to choose B since more numbers are being multiplied. That would be wrong. The consecutive integers from -5 to 5 include zero. Anything times 0 is 0. Hence the product of consecutive integers from -5 to 5 is zero. Likewise the product of consecutive integers from -5 to 10 is zero. Choose **C**.

9. **(C)** For nine consecutive integers to add to 0, they cannot all be positive or all negative. There must be positive and negative integers which mean one of them must be zero and in fact there has to be an equal number on each side of zero. Then the numbers must be $-4, -3, -2, -1, 0, 1, 2, 3$, and 4. So the smallest summand is -4. Choose **C**.

10. **(C)** Every third number is a multiple of three so for any three consecutive integers one of them has to be a multiple of three. Hence their product is also a multiple of three. For example using 4, 5, 6 we see 6 is a multiple of three ($6 = 2 \times 3$). So their product $P = 4 \times 5 \times 6 = 4 \times 5 \times (2 \times 3) = (4 \times 5 \times 2) \times 3$, which is clearly a multiple of three. Hence, the remainder when divided by 3 will be zero. Similarly, every second number is even so the three consecutive numbers include at least one even number (possibly two). Hence P is an even number, and when you divide P by 2 the remainder is 0. Choose **C**.

11. **(D)** If the middle number is -7 then the other numbers are -6 and -8, which do multiply to give 48. Another possibility is 6, 7, and 8. Then $6 \times 8 = 48$ and the middle number is 7. Choose **D**.

12. **(D)** This is a good problem to test the answers given. If the smallest of five summands is C 0 then the sum is $0 + 1 + 2 + 3 + 4 + 5 = 15$, which is way too large. Try D-1 whence the sum is $-1 + 0 + 1 + 2 + 3 = 5$. Choose **D**.

13. **(E)** Test the positive integers (1, 2, 3, ...) to see which satisfy the inequality. If $x = 1$, then $x^2 = 1 \le 9$. If $x = 2$, then $x^2 = 4 \le 9$. If $x = 3$, then $x^2 = 9 \le 9$. If $x = 4$, then $x^2 = 16 \not\le 9$. There are three valid answers. Choose **E**.

14. **(E)** The expression $x - y$ will be smallest when x is smallest (the largest in absolute value negative number it can be) and y is the largest positive number it can be. Take $x = -3$ and $y = 3$. Then $x - y = -6$. Choose **E**.

15. **(D)** Follow the same principle as in problem 14; $x - y$ is smallest when x is smallest and y is largest. Take $x = 1$ (it has to be an integer greater than 0) and $y = 5$ (it has to be an integer less than 6). Then $x - y = 1 - 5 = -4$. Choose **D**.

16. **(D)** Let's test small values of x. If $x = 0$, $x^2 + x + 1 = 0 + 0 + 1 = 1 \le 2$. If $x = 1$, $x^2 + x + 1 = 1 + 1 + 1 = 3 \not\le 2$. Clearly for $x > 1$, it will also be false. If $x = -1$, $x^2 + x + 1 = 1 - 1 + 1 = 1 \le 2$. If $x = -2$, $x^2 + x + 1 = 4 - 2 + 1 = 3 \not\le 2$. Clearly for $x < -2$ it will also be false. So the inequality is only true when $x = 0$ or -1. Choose **D**.

    Alternate solution: Subtract 1 from both sides of the inequality to get $x^2 + x \le 1$. Then factor the left side to get $x(x + 1) \le 1$. So this question is really asking when a product of two consecutive numbers is less than or equal to one. A quick inspection tells us this is impossible unless one of the factors is zero (i.e., $x = 0$ or $x + 1 = 0$). Hence $x = 0$ or $x = -1$ are the only solutions. Choose **D**.

17. **(A)** The cube of a negative integer is always negative. For example $(-2)(-2)(-2) = -8$. The square of a negative integer is always positive. A negative is never greater than or equal to a positive. Choose **A**.

18. **(C)** The product of three numbers being negative means that either one is negative and two are positive or all three are negative. The first case is not possible with consecutive integers. To have both positive and negative in a set of consecutive integers you have to have zero where the product would be zero, not a negative. So all three numbers must be negative. The largest any one of them could be is -1, if we had the numbers -3, -2, and -1. Choose **C**.

19. **(B)** The average of any two consecutive integers is not an integer. For example, $\dfrac{2 + 3}{2} = 2.5$. So A is not the answer. The average of three consecutive integers is always an integer. In fact, it is always the middle number! If the numbers are n, $n + 1$, and $n + 2$, then their average is $\dfrac{n + (n + 1) + (n + 2)}{3} = \dfrac{3n + 3}{3} = n + 1$. For example, the average of 2, 3, and 4 is 3. Choose **B**. For more information on why the other answers cannot be correct see the section in Chapter 5 on averages.

20. **(A)** Five consecutive integers could be three odd and two even, where their sum is odd, or two odd and three even, where their sum is even. So III is not true. Consecutive integers can be negative (e.g., -5, -4, -3, -2, -1) so their sum can be less than 15. So II is not true. Thus I must be true. Choose **A**.

    Alternative solution: If the middle number is x, then the sum of the five consecutive numbers is $5x$. Hence the sum is always a multiple of 5 and I is true. If x is even the sum, $5x$, is also even, but if x is odd, the sum is also odd. So III is not always true. And clearly if $x < 3$, then the sum, $5x$, is less than 15. So II is not always true either. Choose **A**.

21. **(B)** We know from problem 20 that I is always true and III is true when the middle number is even. Thus the answer must be that II cannot be true.

Choose **B**. Note the smallest sum from five consecutive *positive* integers is $1 + 2 + 3 + 4 + 5 = 15$.

22. **(C)** If the first number is x, then $x + (x + 1) + (x + 2) + (x + 3) = 46$. Simplify the left side to get $4x + 6 = 46$, then subtract 6 from each side to get $4x = 40$, and finally divide by 4 to find $x = 10$. The previous four numbers will be 6, 7, 8, and 9. Their sum is 30. Choose **C**.

    Alternative solution: Each summand in the new sum is four less than the corresponding number in the original sum. So the new sum will be $46 - (4 \times 4) = 30$.

23. **(A)** If the first number is x, then the three numbers are x, $x + 1$, and $x + 2$. Multiply the first by the third and add 1: $x(x + 2) + 1 = x^2 + 2x + 1$. You should notice that this factors to $(x + 1)^2$. So the answer is always a perfect square! Choose **A**.

    Note: If we let x be the middle number the answer is even easier. The three numbers are $x - 1$, x, and $x + 1$. Multiply the first by the third and add 1: $(x - 1)(x + 1) + 1 = x^2 - 1 + 1 = x^2$.

24. **(C)** Notice $a^2 - ab = a(a - b)$ and since a,b are consecutive and decreasing $a - b = 1$. Hence $a^2 - ab = a(a - b) = a \times 1 = a$. Choose **C**.

25. **(C)** Notice that $a + ab = a(1 + b)$ and since a,b are consecutive and decreasing $b + 1 = a$. Hence, $a + ab = a(1 + b) = a(a) = a^2$. Choose **C**.

26. **(C)** At first glance, it seems B would be larger since there are more addends, but that is incorrect. Consider carefully that $(-5) + (-4) + (-3) + (-2) + (-1) + 0 + 1 + 2 + 3 + 4 + 5$, and by reordering $5 + (-5) + 4 + (-4) + 3 + (-3) + 2 + (-2) + 1 + (-1) + 0$ it is easy to see the sum is zero. Likewise, for the sum from -10 to 10. Choose **C**.

    Alternate solution: The sum of consecutive integers from -5 to 5 is the sum of 11 consecutive integers so it is 11 times the middle number which is $11 \times 0 = 0$. Likewise, the sum of consecutive integers from -10 to 10 will be $21 \times 0 = 0$. Choose **C**.

Number Theory

1. **(B)** The smallest positive factor of any number is 1. The largest factor of any positive number is the number itself—in this case 8. Choose **B**.

2. **(C)** By testing all primes less than $\sqrt{91} \approx 9.5$, I found that 91 is divisible by 7, and $91 = 7 \times 13$. The smallest prime divisor of 91 is 7. It is easy to start factoring 63 as it is a multiple of 3: $63 = 3 \times 21 = 3 \times 3 \times 7$. The largest prime factor of 63 is 7. Choose **C**.

3. **(B)** Many people will just assume there are an even number of odd and evens. Not so in this case. Positive single digit even numbers are 2, 4, 6, and 8.

Positive single digit odd numbers are 1, 3, 5, 7 and 9. Choose **B**. If we had included 0 there would have been an equal number of odds and evens.

4. **(C)** We know (see tips) that $\dfrac{ab}{GCF(a,b)} = LCM(a,b)$. Choose **C**.

5. **(C)** As $\dfrac{ab}{GCF(a,b)} = LCM(a,b)$, if we multiply both sides of the equation by $GCF(a,b)$, we get $ab = LCM(a,b) \times GCF(a,b)$. Choose **C**.

6. **(B)** The only even prime number is 2 and $2 < 3$. Choose **B**.

7. **(D)** All primes besides 2 are odd. An odd prime could be 3 or it could be larger, say 7. Choose **D**.

8. **(C)** As N is prime, it has only two factors, 1 and itself. So the product of its factors is $1 \times N$, which equals N. Choose **C**.

9. **(E)** We factor 72 as follows: $72 = 2 \times 36 = 2 \times 2 \times 18 = 2 \times 2 \times 2 \times 9 = 2 \times 2 \times 2 \times 3 \times 3$. Using exponents this can be expressed as $2^3 \times 3^2$. Choose **E**. Notice A does not equal 72, while B, C, and D all equal 72 but are not made up of primes.

10. **(C)** To be divisible by 9 the sum of the digits must be a multiple of 9. In this case the sum of the digits is $9 + 3 + 7 + D + 2 + 4 = 25 + D$. As D is a digit from 0 to 9, the only multiple of 9 that $25 + D$ could equal is 27, when $D = 2$. Hence 937,224 is divisible by 9 and thus also divisible by 3. To be divisible by 8 the last three digits must be divisible by 8 and $224 = 28 \times 8$. As 937,224 is divisible by 8, it is also divisible by 4 and 2. Choose **C**.

11. **(D)** The product of an even with any other number is even, so A, xy, is even and B, $8x$, is even. Any even number is divisible by 2, so C, $x/2$, is an integer, but it could be an odd or an even integer. For example $14/2 = 7$ is odd, but $16/2 = 8$ is even. The difference between an even and an odd is always odd. Why? If $x - y = z$, then $y + z = x$. If z was even then we would have odd (y) plus even (z) equal to even (x), which is not true. Choose **D**. Note E is not necessarily odd for reasons similar to B.

12. **(D)** These are equal if x does not have 2 as a factor. For instance, if $x = 25$ then it has three factors (1, 5, 25) and Column A would be $2 \times 3 = 6$. Meanwhile $2x = 50$ has six factors (1, 2, 5, 10, 25, 50). They are not equal if x already has a factor of 2. For instance if $x = 10$, then it has four factors (1, 2, 5, 10), and Column A would be $2 \times 4 = 8$. But $2x = 20$, which has only six factors (1, 2, 4, 5, 10, 20). Choose **D**.

13. **(D)** Note that $2x$ has the same prime factorization as x except it has an extra factor of 2. If x already has 2 as a prime factor, then $2x$ has no new prime factors. For example if $x = 6 = 2 \times 3$, then $2x = 2 \times 6 = 2 \times 2 \times 3$. Both x and $2x$ have two prime factors (2 and 3). If x does not have 2 as a factor

then $2x$ has one more distinct prime factor than x. For example, if $x = 21 = 3 \times 7$, then $2x = 2 \times 21 = 2 \times 3 \times 7$. In this case $2x$ has three distinct prime factors, while x has only two. Choose **D**.

14. **(C)** The even two digit positive integers are 10, 12, . . . , 98, while the odd two digit numbers are 11, 13, . . . , 99. Each even number corresponds to an odd number one more than it, namely $10 \leftrightarrow 11$, $12 \leftrightarrow 13$, . . . , $98 \leftrightarrow 99$. Thus, there is an equal number of each. Choose **C**.

15. **(D)** The GCF(a,ab) is a. The GCF(b,ba) is b. We do not know which is larger, a or b. Choose **D**.

16. **(A)** The LCM(7,3) is 21 since LCM(7,3) = $3 \times 7 \div$ GCF(7,3) = $3 \times 7 \div 1 = 21$. As the lowest common positive multiple of 7 and 3 is odd, any other positive multiple of 7 and 3 will be larger. Choose **A**. In fact, the smallest even multiple is 42.

17. **(B)** The smallest number divisible by both 5 and 7 is the LCM(5,7). Now LCM(5,7) = $5 \times 7 \div$ GCF(5,7) = $5 \times 7 \div 1 = 35$. Since $35 < 70$, choose **B**.

18. **(A)** The largest number that is a factor of both 30 and 90 is the GCF(30,90). Since 30 is a factor of 90, GCF(30,90) = 30. As $30 > 15$, choose **A**.

19. **(A)** Try $N = 6$. Then the product of its factors is $1 \times 2 \times 3 \times 6 = 36$, while $2N = 2 \times 6 = 12$. Try $N = 8$. Then the product of its factors is $1 \times 2 \times 4 \times 8 = 64$, while $2N = 16$. It appears the B will be larger, but can we be certain? Since N is not prime, it has one factor besides 1 and N. That factor must be at least 2. So the product of factors of N is at least $1 \times 2 \times N = 2N$. Could the product ever be equal to $2N$? Only if the only factor of N besides 1 and itself was 2. This only happens when $N = 4$. But $N > 4$. So the product of factors of N is always larger than $2N$. Choose **A**.

20. **(D)** Since 2 divides 8 and 4 divides 8, the smallest number divisible by 2, 3, 4, and 8 is the LCM(3,8), which is 24. But any multiple of 24, like 240, will also be divisible by 2, 3, 4, and 8. Choose **D**.

21. **(A)** To be divisible by 8, the last three digits must be divisible by 8. 1,001 is not divisible by 8 since 1 is not divisible by 8. 1,002 is not divisible by 8 since 2 is not divisible by 8. Continue to see that 1,008 is the first number greater than 1,000 that is divisible by 8. Choose **A**.

22. **(D)** N always has 1 and N as factors. If the sum of its positive factors is $N + 1$, then it has no other positive factors except N and 1. Thus N is a prime number. Choose **D**.

23. **(D)** It's tedious but not difficult to find the factors of each number given until we find the answer. You may also recall that the only positive numbers with exactly three factors are a prime squared, p^2. The positive factors of p^2 are 1, p,

and p^2. Since 25 is the square of a prime, $25 = 5^2$, it has only three positive factors 1, 5, and 25. Choose **D**.

24. **(A)** To be divisible by 3, the sum of the digit must be divisible by 3. Hence $7 + 2 + 8 + D + 4 + 9 = 30 + D$. As 30 is a multiple of 3, D must be a multiple of three. So D could be 0, 3, 6, or 9. Which of those will make the number divisible by 7? We can check each individually by dividing. But we notice that if $D = 0$, then 728049 is the sum of multiples of 7, $700,000 + 28,000 + 49$; hence it is divisible by 7. Choose **A**.

25. **(B)** We investigate each possible answer. A, p^2, is not prime because it has p as a factor. C, $p + 3$, could not be prime because, as the sum of two odds, it is even and divisible by 2. D, 17×23, could not be prime as it has 17 or 23 as factors. Since $72 = 3 \times 24$, $71 \times 72 \times 73$ is a multiple of three and the sum of multiples of three is a multiple of three and thus not prime. That just leaves B. Could $p + 2$ be prime? If $p = 3$, an odd prime, then $p + 2 = 5$, which is also prime. Choose **B**.

Fractions

1. **(A)** We calculate $\dfrac{1}{1 + \frac{1}{2}} = \dfrac{1}{\frac{2}{2} + \frac{1}{2}} = \dfrac{1}{\frac{3}{2}} = 1 \times \dfrac{2}{3} = \dfrac{2}{3}$, while $\dfrac{2}{2 + \frac{2}{1}} = \dfrac{2}{2 + 2} = \dfrac{2}{4} = \dfrac{1}{2}$. As 2/3 is greater than ½, choose **A**.

   Alternative approach: $\dfrac{1}{1 + \frac{1}{2}} = \dfrac{1}{1 + \frac{1}{2}} \times \dfrac{2}{2} = \dfrac{2}{2 + 2 \times \frac{1}{2}} = \dfrac{2}{2 + 1} = \dfrac{2}{3}$

2. **(B)** First we convert the mixed fraction to a regular fraction: $2\frac{2}{3} = \dfrac{3 \times 2 + 2}{3} = \dfrac{8}{3}$. Put another way $2\frac{2}{3} = 2 + \frac{2}{3} = 1 + 1 + \frac{2}{3} = \frac{3}{3} + \frac{3}{3} + \frac{2}{3} = \dfrac{8}{3}$. Now the reciprocal of 8/3 is 3/8 and $3/8 < 3/7$. So choose **B**.

3. **(A)** We note that $\dfrac{3}{5} \div \dfrac{5}{7} \div \dfrac{7}{9} = \dfrac{3}{5} \times \dfrac{7}{5} \times \dfrac{9}{7}$ which is certainly larger than $\dfrac{3}{5}$ as $\dfrac{7}{5}$ and $\dfrac{9}{7}$ are larger than 1. Meanwhile $\dfrac{3}{5} \div \dfrac{5}{7} \div \dfrac{7}{9}$ is less than $\dfrac{3}{5}$ since $\dfrac{5}{7}$ and $\dfrac{7}{9}$ are less than 1. Choose **A**.

4. **(C)** Upon inspection we note that $\dfrac{2}{10} = \dfrac{1}{5}$, $\dfrac{3}{7} = \dfrac{6}{14}$, and $\dfrac{8}{6} = \dfrac{4}{3}$. So both columns are adding the same numbers, just in different orders. Choose **C**.

5. **(A)** It is possible to compute each and compare, but we will work on both columns at once:

Add $\dfrac{1}{4}$ to both columns:

$$\dfrac{1}{2} - \dfrac{1}{3} + \dfrac{1}{4} + \dfrac{1}{4} \qquad \dfrac{1}{3} - \dfrac{1}{4} + \dfrac{1}{5} + \dfrac{1}{4}$$

$$1 - \dfrac{1}{3} \qquad\qquad \dfrac{1}{3} + \dfrac{1}{5}$$

Subtract $\dfrac{1}{3}$ from both columns:

$$1 - \dfrac{1}{3} - \dfrac{1}{3} \qquad \dfrac{1}{3} + \dfrac{1}{5} - \dfrac{1}{3}$$

$$\dfrac{1}{3} \qquad\qquad \dfrac{1}{5}$$

Clearly 1/3 > 1/5 so choose **A**.

6. **(C)** In Column A, white is 4 of 6 equal parts, or $\dfrac{2}{3}$. In Column B, shaded is 6 of 9 equal parts or $\dfrac{2}{3}$. Choose **C**.

7. **(D)** You could convert them all to decimals or use common denominators to compare fractions but we demonstrate how to use some estimation. A, $\dfrac{11}{20}$, is greater than $\dfrac{10}{20} = \dfrac{1}{2}$. B, $\dfrac{5}{6}$, is close to $\dfrac{6}{6} = 1$. C, $\dfrac{3}{8}$, is less than $\dfrac{4}{8} = \dfrac{1}{2}$ but more than $\dfrac{2}{8} = \dfrac{1}{4}$. D, $\dfrac{2}{7}$, is close to $\dfrac{2}{8} = \dfrac{1}{4}$. E, $\dfrac{1}{3}$, is less than $\dfrac{1}{2}$ but more than $\dfrac{1}{4}$. Clearly A and B are too large. Now, as $\dfrac{1}{7} < \dfrac{1}{6}$, we know $\dfrac{2}{7} < \dfrac{2}{6} = \dfrac{1}{3}$. So E is not the smallest. Also $\dfrac{1}{8} > \dfrac{1}{9}$, so $\dfrac{3}{8} > \dfrac{3}{9} = \dfrac{1}{3}$. So C is greater than E. That leaves D as the smallest. Choose **D**.

8. **(C)** There are 22 + 18 = 40 kids in the class. As 22 out of 40 are girls, the fraction of the class that is girls is 22/40 = 11/20. Choose **C**.

9. (**A**) We know that $\frac{3}{8}x = 6$. If we multiply both sides of the equation by 2 and cancel appropriately, $\cancel{2} \times \frac{3}{\cancel{8}_4}x = 2 \times 6$, we find that $\frac{3}{4}x = 12$. Choose **A**.

 Alternatively we could have found x: $\frac{3}{8}x = 6 \Rightarrow \frac{8}{3} \times \frac{3}{8}x = \frac{8}{\cancel{3}} \times \cancel{6}^2 \Rightarrow$

 $x = 16$. Then $\frac{3}{4}x = \frac{3}{\cancel{4}} \times \cancel{16}^4 = 12$.

10. (**A**) First, we simplify Column A and take a rough estimate of its value.

 $\dfrac{\frac{4}{7}+\frac{5}{14}}{1+\frac{45}{49}} = \dfrac{\frac{8}{14}+\frac{5}{14}}{\frac{49}{49}+\frac{45}{49}} = \dfrac{\frac{13}{14}}{\frac{94}{49}} \approx \frac{1}{2}$. Then we see that $\dfrac{\frac{\cancel{4}^2}{7} \times \frac{3}{\cancel{14}^7}}{1 \div \frac{45}{49}} = \dfrac{\frac{6}{49}}{\frac{49}{45}} \approx \dfrac{\frac{6}{48}}{1} = \frac{1}{8}$. Although these are rough approximations, it is clear that A will be larger. Choose **A**.

11. (**D**) First simplify $\dfrac{1}{\left(\dfrac{1}{\frac{1}{x}}\right)} = \dfrac{1}{\left(1 \div \frac{1}{x}\right)} = \dfrac{1}{\left(1 \times \frac{x}{1}\right)} = \dfrac{1}{x}$. Now which is larger, x or $1/x$? That depends on x. If $x = 2$, then $1/x = \frac{1}{2} < 2 = x$. If $x = \frac{1}{2}$, then $1/x = 1/(\frac{1}{2}) = 2 > \frac{1}{2} = x$. Choose **D**.

12. (**D**) As an equation, $\frac{3}{7} \times \frac{21}{6} = \frac{5}{9} \times x$. To solve for x, multiply both sides by $\frac{9}{5}$: $\frac{9}{5} \times \frac{3}{\cancel{7}} \times \frac{\cancel{21}}{\cancel{6}^2} = \frac{\cancel{9}}{5} \times \frac{\cancel{5}}{\cancel{9}} \times x$. Then $\frac{27}{10} = x$. Choose **D**.

13. (**B**) $\frac{3}{4}$ of the registered voters voted, registered voters are $\frac{4}{5}$ of those eligible to vote, and those eligible are $\frac{2}{3}$ of the population. Hence those who voted are $\frac{3}{4} \times \frac{4}{5} \times \frac{2}{3} = \frac{2}{5}$ of the population. Hence $\frac{3}{5}$ of the population did not vote. Choose **B**.

14. **(C)** This is really a conversion problem: $(5 \text{ lb steak}) \times \dfrac{1.25 \text{ lb lamb}}{2.5 \text{ lb steak}} \times$

$\dfrac{\$18}{4 \text{ lb lamb}}$, which equals $\cancel{5} \times \dfrac{1.25}{\cancel{2.5}} \times \dfrac{\cancel{18}^{9}}{\cancel{4}} = 1.25 \times 9 = 11.25$ dollars.

Choose **C**.

Alternatively, if we say 4 lb of lamb is approximately 3 times $1\frac{1}{4}$ lb of lamb

then $1\frac{1}{4}$ lb of lamb cost about $\$18/3 = \$6$. Then 5 lb of steak is twice 2.5 lb

of steak or twice the price of $1\frac{1}{4}$ lb of lamb. That is $2 \times \$6 = \$12$. As C is the

only answer near \$12, choose **C**.

15. **(D)** First note that a can be 1, 2, 3, 4, or 5 and b can be 2 or 3. Then

$S = \left\{ \dfrac{1}{2}, \dfrac{1}{3}, \dfrac{2}{2}, \dfrac{2}{3}, \dfrac{3}{2}, \dfrac{3}{3}, \dfrac{4}{2}, \dfrac{4}{3}, \dfrac{5}{2}, \dfrac{5}{3} \right\}$. If we reduce these fractions to

lowest terms we have $S = \left\{ \dfrac{1}{2}, \dfrac{1}{3}, 1, \dfrac{2}{3}, \dfrac{3}{2}, 1, 2, \dfrac{4}{3}, \dfrac{5}{2}, \dfrac{5}{3} \right\}$, which is only

nine distinct numbers. We see that A, B, C, and E are not true. So the answer
must be **D**.

16. **(E)** Since $\dfrac{1}{2}$ of the students major in education and $\dfrac{1}{3}$ major in math, the rest

must study music. That is $1 - \dfrac{1}{3} - \dfrac{1}{2} = \dfrac{1}{6}$ study music. As $\dfrac{3}{4}$ of the music

students are female, only $\dfrac{1}{4}$ are male. That is $\dfrac{1}{4}$ of $\dfrac{1}{6}$, or $\dfrac{1}{24}$, of all students

are male music majors. That group is 120 students. So the college has $24 \times$
$120 = 2{,}880$ students. Choose **E**. This is a good problem to use a diagram.

Education

Math

Music

Female Music

Male Music 120

17. (**E**) First we expand: $\left(\dfrac{2}{x}\right)^3 = \left(\dfrac{x}{-2}\right)^2 \Rightarrow \dfrac{8}{x^3} = \dfrac{x^2}{4}$. Then multiply both

    sides by $4x^3$ to clear the denominators: $\dfrac{8}{x^3} = \dfrac{x^2}{4} \Rightarrow 4x^3 \times \dfrac{8}{x^3} = 4x^3 \times$

    $\dfrac{x^2}{4} \Rightarrow 32 = x^5$. This implies that $x = 2$. Choose **E**.

18. (**A**) After the 8 joined in 2007, there were 32 boys in the troop. As $\dfrac{1}{8}$ of

    $32 = 4$, after 4 quit there were 28 left. In 2008, $\dfrac{1}{7}$ of 28, or 4, left. There

    remained 24 until 3 joined, so that 27 remained. To get back to the original

    size, 3 out of 27 would have to quit. As $\dfrac{3}{27} = \dfrac{1}{9}$, choose **A**.

19. (**C**) Let x be the class size. As $\dfrac{5}{7}$ of his students are absent, only $\dfrac{2}{7}$ are attend-

    ing. $\dfrac{1}{3}$ of those attending are getting sick, so $\dfrac{2}{3}$ of those attending are not get-

    ting sick and will remain. Hence $\dfrac{2}{3}$ of $\dfrac{2}{7}$ of $x = 12$. Solve for x: $\dfrac{2}{3} \times \dfrac{2}{7} \times$

    $x = 12 \Rightarrow \dfrac{4}{21}x = 12 \Rightarrow x = 12 \times \dfrac{21}{4} = 63$. Normally Professor Murty

    has 63 students in his class. Choose **C**.

20. (**B**) Assume that the chief has $n + m$ officers, n carry firearms and m do not.
    Then $\dfrac{n}{n + m} = \dfrac{3}{5}$ and $\dfrac{n + 1}{n + m + 1} = \dfrac{5}{8}$. If we cross multiply, we get the
    two equations $5n = 3n + 3m$ and $8n + 8 = 5n + 5m + 5$. The first
    equation simplifies to $n = 1.5m$, which we substitute into the second equation
    to get $8(1.5m) + 8 = 5(1.5m) + 5m + 5$. This simplifies to $m = 6$.
    Plug $m = 6$ and thus $n = 1.5 \times 6 = 9$. Check: $9/(6 + 9) = 9/15 = 2/3$
    and $(9 + 1)/(9 + 6 + 1) = 10/16 = 5/8$. There are 6 officers on his force
    who do not carry firearms. Choose **B**. Another way to look at this problem
    is that you want a fraction equivalent to 3/5 (like 6/10, 9/15, . . .) so that if
    you add 1 to both numerator and denominator you get a fraction equivalent
    to 5/8 (like 10/16, 15/24, . . .). Then some guesswork could lead you to
    the answer.

Decimals

1. **(A)** Estimating, $8.02 - 7.03$ is 0.99, while $0.40 + 0.50 = 0.90$. Choose **A**.

2. **(B)** Straight calculation shows that $(0.5)^2 = (0.5)(0.5) = 0.25$, while $5 \times 0.5 = 2.5$. Alternatively, if we divide both columns by 0.5, we are left with 0.5 in Column A and 5 in Column B. Either way, choose **B**.

3. **(C)** $(0.1)^3 = (0.1)(0.1)(0.1) = 0.001$ since the product is 1 with three places to the right of the decimal point. Also to find $1,000 \div 1,000,000$, we move the decimal point in $1,000.0$ six places to the left and get 0.001. Choose **C**.

4. **(B)** Since -8.2 is so large compared to the other two values, the answer in Column A will be negative, while the answer in Column B will be positive. Choose **B**.

5. **(B)** In Column A we move the decimal five places to the right to get $342,000$. In Column B we move the decimal 9 places to the right to get $34,200,000$. Choose **B**.

6. **(C)** Multiply both columns by 10^4 and now we have 1.03 in A and $1,030 \div 10^3$ in B. To find $1,030 \div 10^3$, move the decimal three places to the left and get 1.03. Choose **C**.

7. **(E)** We use estimation. A is less than $50 \times 10 = 500$, B is 465, C is approximately $2.33 \times 100 = 233$, D is approximately 645, and E is approximately $1,000 \div (3/2) = 1,003 \times 2/3 \approx 667$. Because the last two approximations are very good, we can confidently say the answer is **E**.

8. **(D)** We use estimation. A is approximately 2, B is 3.45, C is approximately $100 \div 50 = 2$, D is approximately -1, and E is approximately 1.5. Only D is less than zero so choose **D**.

9. **(A)** Divide both sides by $(0.99)^9$. Then Column A is 1 and Column B is 0.99. Choose **A**.

10. **(C)** In Column A move the decimal eight places to the right to find $923,000$. In Column B move the decimal two places to the left to find $923,000$. Choose **C**.

11. **(E)** Another way to ask this question is, what do I have to multiply 1.3×10^{-4} by to get 39×10^3? First , $1.3 \times 3 = 3.9$, so $1.3 \times 30 = 39$. Second $10^{-4} \times 10^7 = 10^3$. So the answer is 30×10^7 or $300,000,000$. Choose **E**.

12. **(B)** Another way to ask this question is what do we multiply 0.00015 by to get 600? We note that $0.00015 \times 10^5 = 15$, that $15 \times 4 = 60$, and $60 \times 10 = 600$. In total we multiplied by $10^5 \times 4 \times 10 = 4 \times 10^6 = 4,000,000$. Choose **B**.

13. **(D)** To solve $16.44 \times 0.47223 \times x = 4,722.3 \times 1.644$, we divide. Then $x = 4,722.3 \times 1.644 \div 16.44 \div 0.47223 = (4,722.3 \div 0.47223) \times$

(1.644 ÷ 16.44). In the first set of parentheses the decimal moved four places so the answer is 10^4. In the second set of parentheses the decimal moved one place so the answer is 10^{-1}. Hence $x = 10^4 \times 10^{-1} = 10^3 = 1{,}000$. Choose **D**.

14. (**D**) We'll approach this problem differently. First solve $6.15 \div \underline{\quad} = 615$. Since the decimal moves two place to the right, the answer is 10^{-2}. Second solve $723 \div \underline{\quad} = 0.0723$. Since the decimal moves four places to the left the answer is 10^4. Then $x = 10^{-2} \times 10^4 = 10^2 = 100$. Choose **D**. You may find it easier to multiply both sides of the equation by x and then approach this as a multiplication problem instead of a division problem.

Radicals and Exponents

1. (**A**) Many people incorrectly add the exponents and decide the answer is C. The rule is to multiply the exponents so $(5^2)^3 = 5^6$. Choose **A**.

2. (**C**) Much like problem 1, Column A is $((1/2)^2)^3 = (1/2)^6 = 1/(2^6)$. Column B is $2^{-6} = 1/(2^6)$. Choose **C**.

3. (**A**) Since $10 = 2 \times 5$, then $10^5 = (2 \times 5)^5 = 2^5 5^5$. Divide both columns by what they have in common, $2^5 5^4$, and you'll have Column A is 5 and Column B is 2. Choose **A**.

4. (**B**) As $8 = 2^3$, $\dfrac{8}{2^5} = 2^3 \div 2^5 = 2^{-2} = \dfrac{1}{2^2} = \dfrac{1}{4}$. Meanwhile $(2^{-2})^{-2} = 2^4 = 16$. Choose **B**.

5. (**A**) The easiest way to solve this problem is to square both columns. Then A is 8/9 and B is $\left(\dfrac{2}{3^2}\right) = \dfrac{2^2}{3^2} = \dfrac{4}{9}$. Choose **A**.

6. (**B**) This is commonly mistaken to be a rule and thus equal when it is not. Note that $\sqrt{4+9} = \sqrt{13}$, which is between 3 and 4, since $3^2 < 13 < 4^2$. Meanwhile $\sqrt{4} + \sqrt{9} = 2 + 3 = 5$. Choose **B**.

7. (**A**) This is also not a rule. Note that $\sqrt{9-4} = \sqrt{5}$, which is between 2 and 3 since $2^2 < 5 < 3^2$. Also $\sqrt{9} - \sqrt{4} = 3 - 2 = 1$. Choose **A**.

8. (**A**) Here is another nonrule. We see $(2+3)^2 = 5^2 = 25$, while $2^2 + 3^2 = 4 + 9 = 13$. Choose **A**.

9. (**C**) Note that $\sqrt[3]{8} = 2$ since $2^3 = 8$. Hence $-\sqrt[3]{8} = -2$. Also $\sqrt[3]{-8} = -2$ since $(-2)^3 = -8$. Choose **C**.

10. **(A)** Be careful! These are not equal, as $\sqrt{(-4)^2} = \sqrt{16} = 4$. Choose **A**.

11. **(E)** To solve for a in $2^a \times 16^2 = 4^5$, it is best to change all powers to have a base of 2. Then $2^a \times 16^2 = 4^5 \Rightarrow 2^a \times (2^4)^2 = (2^2)^5 \Rightarrow 2^a \times 2^8 = 2^{10} \Rightarrow 2^{a+8} = 2^{10}$. Now that the bases are equal we can equate the exponents. As $a + 8 = 10$, then $a = 2$. Choose **E**.

12. **(C)** We simplify and change all powers to have a base of 3: $\dfrac{3^x}{9} = \sqrt{81} \Rightarrow$

    $\dfrac{3^x}{3^2} = 9 \Rightarrow 3^{x-2} = 3^2$. Now we can equate exponents $x - 2 = 2$, and see that

    $x = 4$. Choose **C**.

13. **(C)** As C is the product of A and B, C is larger than either of them. Also as $3^2 = 9$ is larger than $2^{-3} = 1/8$, C is larger than D. Now E is $(2^3)^2 = 2^6 = 64$, while C is $2^3 3^2 = 8 \times 9 = 72$. Choose **C**.

14. **(B)** Change all powers to a base of two: $2^{a+6} 4^a = 8^3 \Rightarrow 2^{a+6} (2^2)^a = (2^3)^3 \Rightarrow 2^{a+6} 2^{2a} \Rightarrow 2^9 \Rightarrow 2^{(a+6)+2a} 2^9 \Rightarrow 2^{3a + 6} = 2^9$. Now we can equate exponents and solve for a: $3a + 6 = 9 \Rightarrow 3a = 3 \Rightarrow a = 1$. Choose **B**.

15. **(C)** We write 6 as 2×3, change our radicals to exponents and simplify.

    $$\sqrt{6^n} = \frac{2^n}{\sqrt{2}} \times \frac{3^n}{\sqrt{3}} \Rightarrow \left((2 \times 3)^n\right)^{\frac{1}{2}} = \frac{2^n}{2^{\frac{1}{2}}} \times \frac{3^n}{3^{\frac{1}{2}}} \Rightarrow (2 \times 3)^{\frac{n}{2}} = 2^{n-\frac{1}{2}} 3^{n-\frac{1}{2}}$$

    $$\Rightarrow 2^{\frac{n}{2}} 3^{\frac{n}{2}} = 2^{n-\frac{1}{2}} 3^{n-\frac{1}{2}}.$$ Now we can see that we need to solve $n/2 = n - (1/2)$.

    Multiply both sides by 2 to clear the fractions, and we get $n = 2n - 1 \Rightarrow -n = -1 \Rightarrow n = 1$. Choose **C**.

16. **(E)** First we simplify under the radical: $\sqrt{\dfrac{x^{10} y^8 z^5}{x^6 y^7 z^6}} = \sqrt{x^{10-6} y^{8-7} z^{5-6}} =$

    $\sqrt{x^4 y z^{-1}}$. Since none of the answers have negative exponents, we move z back

    into the denominator, $\sqrt{\dfrac{x^4 y}{z}}$, and apply the radical to all parts:

    $\dfrac{\sqrt{x^4} \sqrt{y}}{\sqrt{z}} = \dfrac{x^2 \sqrt{y}}{\sqrt{z}}$. Finally we rationalize the denominator: $\dfrac{x^2 \sqrt{y}}{\sqrt{z}} \times$

    $\dfrac{\sqrt{z}}{\sqrt{z}} = \dfrac{x^2 \sqrt{yz}}{z}$. Choose **E**.

17. **(B)** First we rationalize the denominator in B: $\dfrac{20}{\sqrt{10}} \times \dfrac{\sqrt{10}}{\sqrt{10}} = \dfrac{20\sqrt{10}}{10} =$

    $2\sqrt{10}$. Then we simplify the radical in A: $\dfrac{\sqrt{40}}{2} = \dfrac{\sqrt{4}\sqrt{10}}{2} = \dfrac{\cancel{2}\sqrt{10}}{\cancel{2}} =$

    $\sqrt{10}$. Clearly $2\sqrt{10}$ is greater than $\sqrt{10}$. Choose **B**.

18. **(B)** Let r be the radius of the circle, d, its diameter, and s, the side length of the square. The area of the circle is πr^2. Since $r = \dfrac{d}{2}$, the area of the circle is

    also $\pi\left(\dfrac{d}{2}\right)^2 = \dfrac{\pi d^2}{4}$. The area of the square is s^2.

    Then $s^2 = \dfrac{\pi d^2}{4}$ and thus $s = \sqrt{\dfrac{\pi d^2}{4}} = \sqrt{\dfrac{\pi}{4}}d$.

    But we want the diagonal of the square, which is $\sqrt{2}s$ (see Appendix A). So

    $\sqrt{2}s = \sqrt{2}\sqrt{\dfrac{\pi}{4}}d = \sqrt{\dfrac{2\pi}{4}}d$. As $2\pi > 4$, $\sqrt{\dfrac{2\pi}{4}} > 1$, and thus $\sqrt{2}s > d$.

    Choose **B**.

    Alternative solution: Draw a diagram so that the diameter of the circle and the diagonal of the square are equal. Then the square would fit inside the circle and hence not have equal area. To have equal area, the diagonal of the square would have to be increased. That is why the diameter is smaller.

19. **(C)** $3^4 + 3^4 + 3^4 = 3 \times (3^4) = 3^5$. Choose **C**.

20. **(B)** In Column A, $2^4 + 2^4 + 2^4 = 3 \times 2^4$. In Column B, $2^6 = 2^2 2^4 = 4 \times 2^4$. Since $4 > 3$, choose **B**.

21. **(B)** In Column A the average is

    $\dfrac{2^0 + 2^1 + 2^2 + 2^3}{4} = \dfrac{2^0 + 2^1 + 2^2 + 2^3}{2^2} = 2^{-2} + 2^{-1} + 2^0 + 2^1 =$

    $\dfrac{1}{4} + \dfrac{1}{2} + 1 + 2 = 3\dfrac{3}{4}$. In Column B the average is $\dfrac{3^0 + 3^1 + 3^2}{3} = 3^{-1}$

    $+ 3^0 + 3^1 = \dfrac{1}{3} + 1 + 3 = 4\dfrac{1}{3}$. Choose **B**.

22. **(C)** In Column A the average is $\dfrac{3^1 + 3^2 + 3^3}{3} = 3^0 + 3^1 + 3^2$. So they are equal. Choose **C**.

Algebra

Algebra can be very helpful in solving some problems, but most problems on the GRE quantitative exam can be solved without any complicated algebra. The algebra that is required is much less than what is typically taught in your high school math classes. Use this chapter to brush up on your algebra skills and practice GRE-style questions that could involve algebra.

What is algebra? The essential concept is representing an unknown number with a symbol (usually a letter) that we call a *variable*. For example, in the expression $2x + 3$, x is a variable representing an unknown number that we would like to double and add 3 to. It is called a variable because we can think of x taking on different values (varying). If $x = 3$, then $2x + 3 = 9$. If $x = 5$, then $2x + 3 = 13$. If $x = 37$, then $2x + 3 = 77$.

POLYNOMIALS AND FACTORING

A *monomial* is the product of a number with zero or more variables. A *binomial* is the sum (or difference) of two monomials; a *trinomial* is the sum (or difference) of three monomials, and so on. A *polynomial* is a sum (or difference) of one or more monomials.

Name	Examples
Monomial	$3x^2$, $-6st$, $1/2u^3v^5$, $8y$, 13
Binomial	$3x + 5$, $4y^3 - y$, $x^2 + y^2$, $4 + w$
Trinomial	$x^2 + x + 1$, $3x + 2y + z$, $9 + x^2 - y^2$
Polynomial	23, $4x + 5$, $3y^2 + y + 11$, $4x^5 + 3x^2 - x + 2$, $x^7 - x^6 + x^5 - x^4 + x^3 - x^2 - x + 1$

The number multiplied by the variables in a monomial is called the *coefficient*. The monomials in a polynomial are called the *terms* of the polynomial. In the polynomial $4x^5 + 3x^2 - x + 2$, the terms are $4x^5$, $3x^2$, $-x$, and 2. The coefficient of x^5 is 4 and the coefficient of x is -1.

Although the GRE quantitative exam may never refer explicitly to polynomials by name, they do appear in a few questions. We'll first learn how to do basic operations with polynomials.

To *add polynomials* we collect like terms and add coefficients. That is we put terms with the same variables together and add their coefficients. You can only add like terms—3 apples plus 2 apples equals 5 apples but you can't add 3 apples to 2 oranges.

EXAMPLE 1

Addition

$$(3x^2 - x + 5) + (2x^2 + 4x - 9) = (3x^2 + 2x^2) + (-x + 4x) + (5 - 9) = 5x^2 + 3x - 4$$

$$(4x^4 - x - 7) + (2x^3 + x^2 - 3x + 11) = (4x^4) + (2x^3) + (x^2) + (-x - 3x) + (-7 + 11)$$
$$= 4x^4 + 2x^3 + x^2 - 4x + 4$$

To *subtract polynomials* we simply distribute the negative and then add the results. When distributing, be sure every term in the second polynomial is multiplied by negative one.

EXAMPLE 2

Subtraction

$$(2x^2 - 2x + 5) - (2x^2 + 4x + 3) = 2x^2 - 2x + 5 - 2x^2 - 4x - 3 = (2x^2 - 2x^2) +$$
$$(-2x - 4x) + (5 - 3) = -6x + 2$$

$$(x - 7) - (2x^3 - 11) = x - 7 - 2x^3 + 11 = (-2x^3) + (x) + (-7 + 11) = -2x^3$$

To *multiply polynomials* we use the distributive property (sometimes multiple times).

EXAMPLE 3

A monomial times a binomial:

$$(3x)(2x^2 + 5) = (3x \times 2x^2) + (3x \times 5) = 6x^3 + 15x$$

EXAMPLE 4

A binomial times a binomial:

$$(2y + x)(3y^2 - 2x) = (2y + x)(3y^2) + (2y + x)(-2x)$$

$$= (2y \times 3y^2) + (x \times 3y^2) + (2y \times (-2x)) + (x \times (-2x))$$

$$= 6y^3 + 3xy^2 - 4xy - 2x^2$$

Notice, we distributed the first binomial to each term, then we distributed again. Some people prefer to think of this as multiplying each term in the first polynomial times each term in the second polynomial.

EXAMPLE 5

A binomial times a binomial:

$$(2y + x)(3y^2 - 2x) = (2y \times 3y^2) + (x \times 3y) + (2y \times (-2x)) + (x \times (-2x))$$
$$= 6y^3 + 3xy - 4xy - 2x^2 = 6y^3 - xy - 2x^2$$

EXAMPLE 6

Simplify $(5x - 2)(x + 3) - (2x + 3)(x - 5)$

(A) $3x^2 + 5x - 21$
(B) $3x^2 + 20x + 9$
(C) $7x^2 + 5x - 21$
(D) $5x - 21$
(E) 0

Solution: First we compute $(5x - 2)(x + 3) = (5x)(x) + (-2)(x) + (5x)(3) + (-2)(3) = 5x^2 - 2x + 15x - 6 = 5x^2 + 13x - 6$. Then we compute $(2x + 3)(x - 5) = (2x)(x) + (2x)(-5) + (3)(x) + (3)(-5) = 2x^2 - 10x + 3x - 15 = 2x^2 - 7x - 15$. So the difference is $(5x - 2)(x + 3) - (2x + 3)(x - 5) = (5x^2 + 13x - 6) - (2x^2 - 7x - 15) = 5x^2 + 13x - 6 - 2x^2 + 7x + 15 = (5x^2 - 2x^2) + (13x + 7x) + (-6 + 15) = 3x^2 + 20x + 9$. Choose **B**. A common mistake would be to not distribute the negative to all parts of the second polynomial and result in the incorrect answer A.

Three products appear frequently when dealing with polynomials. In fact, they may be the only products that appear on the GRE. These are well worth memorizing.

The first is called the rule for squaring a binomial. We explain using multiplication.

$$(A + B)^2 = (A + B)(A + B) = (A + B)(A) + (A + B)(B) = (A \times A) + (B \times A) + (A \times B) + (B \times B) = A^2 + BA + AB + B^2 = A^2 + 2AB + B^2$$

TIP

$(A + B)^2 = A^2 + 2AB + B^2$

$(A - B)^2 = A^2 - 2AB + B^2$

$(A - B)(A + B) = A^2 - B^2$

Orally you might remember this as "To square a binomial, square the first term, multiply the first term by the second term and double it, square the last term."

The second is just the square of a difference. You really don't have to memorize it if you think of it as a variation on the first.

$$(A - B)^2 = (A + (-B))^2 = A^2 + 2(A)(-B) + (-B)^2 = A^2 - 2AB + B^2$$

The third is called the difference of squares since the product is a difference of perfect squares.

$$(A - B)(A + B) = (A - B)(A) + (A - B)(B) = (A \times A) + (-B \times A) + (A \times B) + (-B \times B) = A^2 - BA + AB - B^2 = A^2 - B^2$$

EXAMPLE 7

Expand each of the following: (i) $(2x + 4)^2$, (ii) $(3 - x)^2$, (iii) $(5x - 6y)(5x + 6y)$

Solution:

(i) $(2x + 4)^2 = (2x)^2 + 2(2x)(4) + (4)^2 = 4x^2 + 16x + 16$
(ii) $(3 - x)^2 = 3^2 - 2(3)(x) + x^2 = 9 - 6x + x^2$
(iii) $(5x - 6y)(5x + 6y) = (5x)^2 - (6y)^2 = 25x^2 - 36y^2$.

EXAMPLE 8

Simplify $(3x + 7)^2 - (3x - 7)^2$

(A) 98
(B) $18x^2$
(C) $9x^2 + 42x + 49$
(D) $84x$
(E) $-18x^2$

Solution: Using our special multiplication rules $(3x + 7)^2 = (3x)^2 + 2(3x)(7) + 7^2 = 9x^2 + 42x + 49$, while $(3x - 7)^2 = (3x)^2 - 2(3x)(7) + 7^2 = 9x^2 - 42x + 49$. So $(3x + 7)^2 - (3x - 7)^2 = (9x^2 + 42x + 49) - (9x^2 - 42x + 49) = 9x^2 - 42x + 49 - 9x^2 + 42x - 49 = 84x$. Choose **D**.

The opposite of multiplying polynomials together is called factoring. In general this can be a difficult challenge, but for the GRE there are only a few types of problems you will encounter.

In *common factoring* you simply identify what the terms have in common and divide it out of each term. For example in the polynomial $4rst + 6r^2t - 2s^2t$, you can see that each term is divisible by 2 and by t. So we look try to fill in the blanks $4rst + 6r^2t - 2s^2t = (2t)$ (___ + ___ + ___) to make the equation valid. By thinking about multiplication, we can see that $(2t)(2rs) = 4rst$, $(2t)(3r^2) = 6r^2t$, and $(2t)(-s^2) = -2s^2t$. Hence $4rst + 6r^2t - 2s^2t = (2t)(2rs + 3r^2 - s^2)$.

EXAMPLE 9

Use common factoring to factor $3x^2y + 6x - 2xy$.

Solution: Note that $3x^2y + 6x - 2xy = 3xxy + (2)(3)x - 2xy$. In this form it should be clear that 3 is common to the first two terms, and 2 is common to the last two terms, but there is no constant common to all three terms. Also the second term has no y, so y cannot be a common factor. But all three terms have one x. So the largest common factor is just x. Then $3x^2y + 6x - 2xy = x(3xy + 6 - 2y)$. Each term of the trinomial $3xy + 6 - 2y$ was chosen so that when multiplied by x would result in the original expression $3x^2y + 6x - 2xy$.

The most common type of factoring on the GRE comes from *special factoring rules*— really the special multiplication rule used in reverse.

$$A^2 + 2AB + B^2 = (A + B)^2$$
$$A^2 - 2AB + B^2 = (A - B)^2$$
$$A^2 - B^2 = (A - B)(A + B)$$

EXAMPLE 10

Factor each of the following: (i) $x^2 + 2xy + y^2$, (ii) $x^2 - 6x + 9$, (iii) $4x^2 - 36$.

Solution: (i) $x^2 + 2xy + y^2 = (x + y)^2$ a straightforward application of the first special factoring rule. (ii) Because of the negative and the fact that $9 = 3^2$, we suspect it is the second special factoring rule. And indeed $-2(x)(3)$ does give the middle term $-6x$. Hence, $x^2 - 6x + 9 = (x - 3)^2$. (iii) Because we have a difference of squares, we see it is the third special factoring rule. $4x^2 - 36 = (2x)^2 - (6)^2 = (2x - 6)(2x + 6)$. We should recognize this factors further using common factoring. $(2x - 6)(2x + 6) = 2(x - 3)2(x + 3) = 4(x - 3)(x + 3)$.

Alternatively, you might also have common factored first to see that $4x^2 - 36 = 4(x^2 - 9) = 4(x^2 - 3^2) = 4(x - 3)(x + 3)$.

Using difference of squares, we can provide an alternate answer to Example 8:

Notice that $(3x + 7)^2 - (3x - 7)^2 = [(3x + 7)-(3x - 7)][(3x + 7) + (3x - 7)] = (3x + 7 - 3x + 7)(3x + 7 + 3x - 7) = 14(6x) = 84x$.

A common type of problem you may encounter on the GRE uses the special factoring rules to avoid ugly calculations.

EXAMPLE 11

Find $(1.62)^2 - (1.38)^2$.

(A) 0.682342
(B) 0.72
(C) 0.72044
(D) 1.7202
(E) 2.4

Solution: The tedious way to do this problem is to calculate each square and subtract. It doesn't take too long, but it would be easy to make a mistake: $(1.62)^2 - (1.38)^2 = 2.6244 - 1.9044 = 0.72$. Another way to solve this problem is to use the difference of squares factoring rule: $(1.62)^2 - (1.38)^2 = (1.62 + 1.38)(1.62 - 1.38) = 3(0.24) = 0.72$. The computations are so much easier, you may even be able to do the second technique in your head. Choose **B**.

Problems

Basic Problems

1. Add: $(2 - 3x + 5x^3) + (7 + 4x - x^5)$.

(A) $9 - 7x + 4x^3$
(B) $9 + x + 4x^3$
(C) $9 + x + 5x^3$
(D) $9 + x + 5x^3 - x^5$
(E) $14 - 12x^2 - 5x^8$

2. Simplify: $(1 + 2x) - (3x + 4x^2) + (5x^2 + 6x^3) - (7x^3 + 8x^4)$.

   (A) $1 - 3x + 4x^2 + 6x^3 - 8x^4$
   (B) $1 - x + 9x^2 + 13x^3 + 8x^4$
   (C) $1 + 5x + 9x^2 + 13x^3 - 8x^4$
   (D) $1 - x + x^2 - x^3 - x^4$
   (E) $1 - x + x^2 - x^3 - 8x^4$

3. Multiply: $(2 + x)(3 - 2x)$.

   (A) $6 - x + 2x^2$
   (B) $6 - x - 2x^2$
   (C) $6 + 3x - 2x^2$
   (D) $6 + 3x + 2x^2$
   (E) $6 + x - 2x^2$

4. Which of the following is a correct use of the distributive property?

   (A) $(x^{100} - 1)(2 + x^{10}) = x^{10}(x^{100} + 2) - 1(x^{100} + 2)$
   (B) $(x^{100} - 1)(2 + x^{10}) = x^{100}(x^{10} + 2) + 1(2 + x^{10})$
   (C) $(x^{100} - 1)(2 + x^{10}) = 2(x^{100}) - x^{10}(x^{100} - 1)$
   (D) $(x^{100} - 1)(2 + x^{10}) = x^{100}(2 + x^{10}) - 1(2 + x^{10})$
   (E) $(x^{100} - 1)(2 + x^{10}) = 2(x^{100} - 1) + x^{100}(x^{10} - 1)$

Column A	Column B
5. $\quad 4 - y^2$	$(2 - y)(2 + y)$
6. $\quad t^2 + 9$	$(t + 3)(t - 3)$
7. $\quad 3ab^2 - 2a^3b + 4ab$	$ab(3b - 2a^2 + 2)$
8. $\quad 99 \times 101$	100^2

GRE Problems

9. Find the value of $\dfrac{x - y}{x^2 - y^2}$ if $x = 0.01$ and $y = 0.99$.

   (A) 0.0099
   (B) 0.99
   (C) 1
   (D) 1.99
   (E) $9,900$

10. Find the value of $\dfrac{b^2 - a^2}{b + a}$ if $a = 43$ and $b = 57$.

    (A) 1/100
    (B) 1.96
    (C) 14
    (D) 1,400
    (E) 1,960

11. I have 77 positive numbers and 44 negative numbers. Their sum is $77^2 - 44^2$. What is their average?

    (A) −33
    (B) 33
    (C) -33^2
    (D) 33^2
    (E) 1/121

Column A	Column B
12. $(x-1)(x)(x+1)$	$(x-2)(x)(x+2)$

$ab = 2$

Column A	Column B
13. $(a+b)^2$	$(a-b)^2$

$s > 0$

Column A	Column B
14. $(s+t)^2$	$(s-t)^2$

$a - b = 24$
$a + b = 25$

Column A	Column B
15. $a^2 - b^2$	ab

$x > 0$ and $y > 0$

Column A	Column B
16. $\dfrac{x-y}{x+y}$	$\dfrac{x^2 - y^2}{(x+y)^2}$

Column A	Column B
17. $(0.63)^2 - (0.37)^2$	1/4

$x \neq 0$

Column A	Column B
18. $\dfrac{1}{x} - \dfrac{1}{x^2}$	$\dfrac{x-1}{x^2}$

Column A	Column B
19. $(x+1/2)^2 - (x-1/2)^2$	$|x|$

$x + y = 3$

Column A	Column B
20. $x^2 + 2xy + y^2$	$6 + x + y$

SOLVING EQUATIONS

Equations show that two quantities are equal. For example, $3x = 4$, $a + b = a - b$, and $x^2 + 2x - 3 = 0$. An equation that involves only one variable can often be solved; this means to determine values of the variable that make the equation true.

The basic rule for solving equations is "whatever you do to one side of the equation, do to the other." If you start with two equal quantities and do the same thing to them, they remain equal.

Rule in Words	Rule in Symbols	Example
Add same number to both sides of the equation	If $a = b$, then $a + c = b + c$.	If $x - 3 = 4$, then $x - 3 + 3 = 4 + 3$, (i.e, $x = 7$).
Subtract same number from both sides of the equation	If $a = b$, then $a - c = b - c$.	If $2x = 4 + x$, then $2x - x = 4 + x - x$ (i.e, $x = 4$).
Multiply both sides of the equation by the same nonzero number	If $a = b$, then $ac = bc$.	If $x/2 = 3$, then $2(x/2) = 2(3)$ (i.e, $x = 6$).
Divide both sides of the equation by the same nonzero number	If $a = b$, then $a/c = b/c$.	If $3x = 15$, then $(3x)/3 = 15/3$ (i.e, $x = 5$).
Square both sides	If $a = b$, then $a^2 = b^2$.	If $\sqrt{x} = 3$, then $\left(\sqrt{x}\right)^2 = 3^2$ (i.e, $x = 9$).

By combining the basic rules you can solve many equations. Generally, you try to bring to one side all terms involving the variable you are solving for, and everything else to the other side.

EXAMPLE 1

Solve for x if $3x - 2 = 5x + 8$.

Solution:

Add 2 to both sides	$3x - 2 + 2 = 5x + 8 + 2$
	$3x = 5x + 10$
Subtract $5x$ from both sides	$3x - 5x = 5x + 10 - 5x$
	$-2x = 10$
Divide both sides by -2	$-2x/(-2) = 10/(-2)$
	$x = -5.$

We have determined that $x = -5$. We can check our answer by substituting $x = -5$ in to the original equation.

Check

$$3x - 2 = 5x + 8$$
$$3(-5) - 2 = 5(-5) + 8$$
$$-15 - 2 = -25 + 8$$
$$-17 = -17$$

It's correct!

EXAMPLE 2

If $(x + 2)5 = 3(x + 7)$, then solve for x.

(A) 5/3
(B) 5
(C) 5.5
(D) 7
(E) 8

Solution:

First we expand to get rid of the parentheses	$(x + 2)5 = 3(x + 7)$
	$5x + 10 = 3x + 21$
Subtract $3x$ from both sides to get all x's on one side.	$2x + 10 = 21$
Subtract 10 from both sides.	$2x = 11$
Divide by 2 to isolate x.	$x = 5.5$

TIP

Squaring both sides of an equation can introduce invalid solutions. If $-\sqrt{x} = 3$, and we square both sides, we get $\left(-\sqrt{x}\right)^2 = 3^2$ or $x = 9$. Check this answer in the original equation, and we see that $-\sqrt{9} \neq 3$, so $x = 9$ is not a valid solution. In fact the original equation has no solutions. You can see that more easily if we multiply both sides of the original equation by -1. $-\left(-\sqrt{x}\right) = -(3)$ is equivalent to $\sqrt{x} = -3$. The result of any square root cannot be negative, so there are no solutions.

There are other rules for working with equations, but these require some special care when used.

Rule in Words	Rule in Symbols	Example
If two nonzero values are equal, their reciprocals are equal.	$a = b$ and $a \neq 0$, then $1/a = 1/b$	$\frac{1}{x} = \frac{1}{2} \Rightarrow \frac{1}{\frac{1}{x}} = \frac{1}{\frac{1}{2}} \Rightarrow x = 2$
If the squares of values are equal, then the values are equal or opposites.	$a^2 = b^2$ implies $a = b$ or $a = -b$.	$x^2 = 25 \Rightarrow x = 5$ or $x = -5$
If the powers are equal and they have same positive base (not equal to 1), then their exponents are equal.	$a^x = a^y$, $a > 0$, and $a \neq 1$ implies that $x = y$.	$2^{x + 3} = 2^{2x - 3} \Rightarrow x + 3 = 2x + 3 \Rightarrow x = 6$
If the product of two values is zero then one of the values has to be zero.	If $xy = 0$, then $x = 0$ or $y = 0$.	$(x + 1)x = 0 \Rightarrow x + 1 = 0$ or $x = 0 \Rightarrow x = -1$ or 0

EXAMPLE 3

Solve for x, if $x^2 + 4 = 2x^2 - 5$.

(A) -3
(B) 3
(C) 1
(D) 3 and -3
(E) 0 or 3

Solution: First subtract x^2 from both sides:

$$x^2 + 4 - x^2 = 2x^2 - 5 - x^2$$
$$4 = x^2 - 5$$

Add 5 to both sides:

$$4 + 5 = x^2 - 5 + 5$$
$$9 = x^2$$

Now using the second rule above, we get $x = 3$ or $x = -3$. Choose **D**.

An alternate answer would be to continue from $4 = x^2 - 5$ by subtracting 4 from both sides to see $0 = x^2 - 9$. Now factor using difference of squares to see $(x - 3)(x + 3) = 0$. Since the product is zero, either $x - 3 = 0$ or $x + 3 = 0$. Hence $x = 3$ or $x = -3$.

EXAMPLE 4

If $5^{b+1} = 25^{2-b}$, then solve for b.

(A) 2
(B) 1
(C) $\dfrac{2}{3}$
(D) 0
(E) -1

Solution: First represent 25 as 5^2; then simplify using laws of exponents: $5^{b+1} = (5^2)^{2-b} \Rightarrow$ $5^{b+1} = 5^{4-2b}$. Now we can equate the exponents and solve: $b + 1 = 4 - 2b \Rightarrow 3b = 3 \Rightarrow$ $b = 1$. Choose **B**.

TIP

- You don't always have to solve for the variable in the problem. Sometimes you can solve directly for what is asked.

- As discussed in Chapter 2, for a multiple-choice question, you can check each of the five answers to find the correct one.

- If there are many variables in a problem and you have to solve for just one of them, treat the other variables as numbers.

- If an equation involves fractions, clear the denominators by multiplying both sides of the equation by the LCM of the denominators.

EXAMPLE 5

Column A	Column B
$x + 5 = 27$	
$2x + 12$	$3x - 10$

Solution: We could solve for *x*, but we will follow the tip above and try to directly find $2x + 12$ and $3x - 10$. Since $x + 5 = 27$, multiply both sides by 2 to get $2x + 10 = 54$. Now add two to both sides, and we have $2x + 12 = 56$. As $x + 5 = 27$, multiply both sides by 3 to get $3x + 15 = 81$. Subtract 25 from both sides and we have $3x - 10 = 56$. Surprisingly, $2x + 12 = 56 = 3x - 10$. Choose **C**.

EXAMPLE 6

If $y < -1 < x$, solve for *x* in terms of *y*: $\dfrac{x}{y + 2} = \dfrac{y}{x + 2}$

(A) $-y$
(B) $-y - 2$
(C) $y + 2$
(D) $y + 1$
(E) y

Solution: To clear fractions, we multiply both sides by $(x + 2)(y + 2)$ (this is the same as cross multiplying).

$$(x + 2)\,\cancel{(y + 2)}\,\frac{x}{\cancel{y + 2}} = \cancel{(x + 2)}\,(y + 2)\frac{y}{\cancel{x + 2}}$$

We are left with $(x + 2)x = (y + 2)y$, which expands to $x^2 + 2x = y^2 + 2y$. It's not clear how to proceed from here, but if we add one to both sides, we now have perfect squares, $x^2 + 2x + 1 = y^2 + 2y + 1$, which can be factored as $(x + 1)^2 = (y + 1)^2$. If we take square roots, we find that $x + 1 = y + 1$ or $x + 1 = -(y + 1)$. Solving both cases $x = y$ or $x = -y - 2$. But we were given that $y < x$ so the first case is not possible. Hence $x = -y - 2$. Choose **B**.

Solving Systems of Linear Equations

Being able to solve a system of two linear equations in two unknowns is a useful basic skill. It appears very frequently in many different types of math problems. While not always *required* to solve a GRE problem, it does give you a skill you can count on at all times. You may know it as the *substitution method*. We explain the technique with an example.

EXAMPLE 7

Find *x* and *y* so that $2x + 3y = 13$ and $x - 2y = 3$.

Solution:

Number your equations. This helps us identify what happens in each step.	$2x + 3y = 13$ ① $x - 2y = 3$ ②
First we choose an equation and isolate one of the variables. Since *x* in equation 2 has no coefficient it is a good target. We add $2y$ to both sides.	Solve for *x* in ② $x = 3 + 2y$
Now substitute that value for *x* back into the other equation. This will eliminate one of the variables.	Substitute $x = 3 + 2y$ into ① $2(3 + 2y) + 3y = 13$

Solve for y.	$6 + 4y + 3y = 13$ $6 + 7y = 13$ $7y = 7$ $y = 1$
Now we use this solution for one variable to find the other. You can substitute into one of the original equations and solve for x. The easiest way to do this is to use the expression we found for x in the second step. (optional) Check your answer by substituting into the original equations.	Substitute $y = 1$ into $x = 3 + 2y$ $x = 3 + 2(1) = 3 + 2 = 5$ $x = 5$, $y = 1$ Substitute $x = 5$, $y = 1$ into ① and ②. $2(5) + 3(1) = 13$ $(5) - 2(1) = 3$

Of course these problems are rarely so explicit. You will often find them as word problems or parts of other problems.

EXAMPLE 8

Three times a number plus a second number equals two. The sum of the numbers is four. What are the numbers?

(A) 1 and 5
(B) 1 and −5
(C) −1 and 5
(D) −1 and −5
(E) 1 and 2

Solution: Let a be the first number and b the second number. Then $3a + b = 2$ and $a + b = 4$.

We use the substitution method.
$$3a + b = 2 \; ①$$
$$a + b = 4 \; ②$$

Solving for b in ②, we find $b = 4 - a$. Substitute $b = 4 - a$ into ① to find $3a + (4 - a) = 2$ $\Rightarrow 2a + 4 = 2 \Rightarrow 2a = -2 \Rightarrow a = -1$. Now substitute $a = -1$ into $b = 4 - a$, and $b = 4 - (-1) = 4 + 1 = 5$. Hence the numbers −1 and 5. Choose **C**.

There is another standard technique for solving linear equations. It involves adding or subtracting multiples of equations, and may be called the *elimination method*. We illustrate with an alternate solution to Example 7.

Number your equations. This helps us identify what happens in each step.	$2x + 3y = 13 \; ①$ $x - 2y = 3 \; ②$
We try to add (or subtract) a multiple of one equation to the other in order get rid of one variable. In this case we multiply ② by 2 and subtract the result from ①.	Multiply ② by 2. $2x - 4y = 6$ Subtract this from ①. $\quad 2x + 3y = 13$ $\underline{-(2x - 4y = 6)}$ $\qquad\qquad 7y = 7$
Now we can solve for y.	$y = 1$

Now we use this solution for one variable to find the other. You can substitute into one of the original equations and solve for x.

Substitute $y = 1$ into ②
$$x - 2(1) = 3$$
$$x - 2 = 3$$
$$x = 5$$

Now you have a solution.

$x = 5$ and $y = 1$

(Optional) Check your answer by substituting into the original equations.

Substitute $x = 5$, $y = 1$ into ① and ②.
$$2(5) + 3(1) = 13$$
$$(5) - 2(1) = 3$$

EXAMPLE 9

Column A	Column B

$$2x + 4y = 5$$
$$2x - y = -5$$

Column A	Column B
x	y

Solution: We follow the elimination method.

$2x + 4y = 5$ ①
$2x - y = -5$ ②

First we subtract ② from ①.

$$
\begin{array}{r}
2x + 4y = 5 \\
-(2x - y = -5) \\
\hline
5y = 10
\end{array}
$$

Hence $y = 2$. Now substitute $y = 2$ into ②, to get $2x - (2) = -5 \Rightarrow 2x = -5 + 2 \Rightarrow 2x = -3 \Rightarrow x = -1.5$.

Thus we have a solution, $x = -1.5$ and $y = 2$. Choose **B**.

EXAMPLE 10

Column A	Column B

$$3x - 4y = 7$$
$$2y - x = 5$$

Column A	Column B
$x - y$	10

Solution: You could solve for x and y using the substitution or elimination method. But let's follow the tip and just add the equations together to get $(3x - 4y) + (2y - x) = 7 + 5$. This simplifies beautifully to $2x - 2y = 12$. Just divide by 2 to see $x - y = 6$. Choose **B**.

TIP

If you are given two or more equations and are unsure of how to proceed, consider adding them or subtracting them. With surprising frequency, this produces a quick solution to the problem.

EXAMPLE 11

$a - b + c = 1$
$b - c + a = 2$
$c - a + b = 3$

What is $a + b + c$?

(A) 1
(B) 2
(C) 3
(D) 6
(E) 9

Solution: Just like our method for solving two linear equations in two unknowns, there is a method for solving three equations in three unknowns. Even if you know this method, you should suspect there is a simpler answer. Try adding all the equations together.

We get $(a - b + c) + (b - c + a) + (c - a + b) = 1 + 2 + 3$ and conveniently many variables cancel out to leave $a + b + c = 6$. Choose **D**.

Problems

Basic Problems

1. If $2x + 3 = 6 - x$, then $x =$
   (A) 1
   (B) 3
   (C) −3
   (D) − 1
   (E) 0

2. Solve for a: $a(a - 3) = (a + 2)(a - 1)$.
   (A) 2
   (B) −2
   (C) $\frac{1}{2}$
   (D) −0.5
   (E) $\frac{1}{4}$

3. Find all solutions for $(t + 2)(3 - t) = (t + 2)$.
   (A) 2
   (B) −2
   (C) −2 and 2
   (D) 0 and 2
   (E) −2, 0, and 2

4. Solve for z in terms of x and y if $2x - y + 3z = 2 + y$.
   (A) $1 + y - x$
   (B) $2(y - x)/3$
   (C) $(2 + 2y - 2x)/3$
   (D) $(1 + y - x)/3$
   (E) $y + x$

5. Solve for b if $2b^2 - 8 = 1 - b^2$.
   (A) −3 and 3
   (B) $\sqrt{3}$ and 3
   (C) $\sqrt{3}$
   (D) $-\sqrt{3}$
   (E) $\sqrt{3}$ and $-\sqrt{3}$

6. Solve for x if $\dfrac{1}{x+1} = \dfrac{2}{x-1}$

(A) -3
(B) -1
(C) 0
(D) 1
(E) $\dfrac{1}{2}$

| Column A | Column B |

$$m + n = 7$$
$$3 - n = 6$$

7. | m | | 9 |

$$x - y = 3$$
$$2x + 3y = 2$$

8. | x | | y |

GRE Problems

9. If $y \neq z$ and $(x + y)z = y(x + z)$, then solve for x in terms of y and z.

(A) 0
(B) $\dfrac{xy}{z}$
(C) $\dfrac{y(x + z)}{yz}$
(D) $y - z$
(E) $y + z$

10. If $2x - 3 = 17$, then $2x + 2 = ?$

(A) 22
(B) 7
(C) 10
(D) 16
(E) 24

11. If RS and TU are straight lines that meet at the center of the circle, find a.

(A) 10
(B) 15
(C) 30
(D) $13\dfrac{1}{3}$
(E) 180

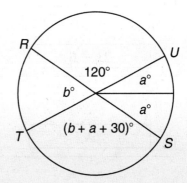

12. If $4^{b+1} = 2^{3b} \div 4$, then solve for b.

   (A) 0
   (B) 2
   (C) 4
   (D) 1.5
   (E) −1

13. If $8^{a/3} = 2^3 8^{1-a}$ then solve for a.

   (A) 0
   (B) 2
   (C) 4
   (D) 1.5
   (E) −1

14. The volume of a sphere is given by $V = 4\pi r^3/3$. What is the radius, r, in terms of V?

   (A) $\dfrac{3V}{4\pi}$

   (B) $\sqrt{\dfrac{3V}{4\pi}}$

   (C) $\sqrt{\dfrac{3\pi}{4V}}$

   (D) $\sqrt{\dfrac{4\pi}{3V}}$

   (E) $\dfrac{4V}{3\pi}$

	Column A		Column B
		$x^2 - 4 = 0$	
15.	x		2
		$x(2(x+3)+3) = 3(4+3x)$	
16.	x		6
		$3x - 6 = 4$	
17.	$2x - 6$		$x - 4$
		$3x - y = 2$ $3x + y = 4$	
18.	x		y

$$3x + 2y + z = -2$$
$$2x + y + z = 10$$

19. | Average of x and y | | z |

---

20. If $r - s = 3$ and $t + s = 11$, what is the average of r and t?

(A) 3
(B) 5
(C) 5.5
(D) 6
(E) 7

21. If $ax^2 - bx + c = 0$ and $-bx^2 + ax - c = 0$, then which of the following is true:

   I. If $a \neq b$, then $x = 0$ or -1
   II. If $x \neq 0$, then $a = b$.
   III. If $x = 2$, then $a = b$.

(A) I only
(B) II only
(C) III only
(D) I and III
(E) II and III

22. Derek has twice as many marbles as Jason. Cornelia has one-third as many marbles as Derek. Together these three have 55 marbles. How many does Derek have?

(A) 60
(B) 40
(C) 30
(D) 15
(E) 10

23. Jillian doubled her favorite number, added 1, divided by 3 and subtracted 2. The result was her favorite number! What is Jillian's favorite number?

(A) 5
(B) 17
(C) 21
(D) −3
(E) −5

INEQUALITIES

EXAMPLE 1

Column A	Column B
$3x - 2$	4

The GRE exam will never ask you to directly solve an inequality problem like: "if $3x - 2 > 4$ solve for x." Yet, all two column questions are implicitly asking you to work with inequalities. The example above is asking you to work with the inequality $3x - 2 > 4$.

Solution: Rather than solve the inequality directly, we will try some values of *x*. When *x* = 0, we have 3(0) − 2 = −2, which is less than 4. When *x* = 5, we have 3(5) − 2 = 13, which is greater than 4. Since there are no restrictions on *x*, A or B could be greater depending on *x*. The answer is **D**.

The classical solution you may have learned in high school might look like:

Since 3*x* − 2 > 4, add 2 to both sides to get 3*x* > 6. Now divide both sides by 3 to get *x* > 2. Thus 3*x* − 2 is greater than 4 when *x* is greater than 2. When *x* > 2, like *x* = 5, A > B and when *x* < 2, like *x* = 0, A < B. Since *x* can be any real number, again the answer is **D**.

We'll discuss the standard rules for inequalities and then see how they are useful in solving two column (and other) questions. They are very important whether you intend to try solving inequalities directly or use any of the other techniques we suggest.

- *Add or subtract the same number from both sides.* If *a* < *b*, then for any number *c*, *a* + *c* < *b* + *c* and *a* − *c* < *b* − *c*. Consider the true inequality −2 < 5. Add 2 to both sides, and we have −2 + 2 < 5 + 2, which is 0 < 7 (true). Subtract two from both sides and we have −2 − 2 < 5 − 2, which is −4 < 3 (also true).

- *Multiply or divide by a positive number.* If *a* < *b* and *c* < 0, then *ca* < *cb* and *a*/*c* < *b*/*c*. Consider the inequality 3 < 6. If we multiply by 2, we get 3 × 2 < 6 × 2, which is 6 < 12 (true). If we divide by 3, we get 3/3 < 6/3, which is 1 < 2 (also true).

- *Multiply or divide by a negative number.* If *a* < *b* and *c* < 0, then *ca* > *cb* and *a*/*c* > *b*/*c*. It is very important to notice that this is the one time that the inequality reverses. Consider the inequality −4 < 2. If we multiply by −1, we get −4 × −1 > 2 × −1, which is 4 > −2, (true). If we divide by −2, we get (−4)/(−2) > 2/(−2) which is 2 > −1 (also true).

EXAMPLE 2

Column A	Column B
Assume *x* < 4	
5 − 2*x*	3*x* + 1

Solution: Let's solve 5 − 2*x* < 3*x* + 1. First add 2*x* to both sides to get 5 < 5*x* + 1. Now subtract 1 from both sides to get 4 < 5*x*. Finally divide both sides by 5 to see that 4/5 < *x* or *x* > 0.8. So A < B when *x* > 0.8, but it was assumed that *x* must be less than 1. So if *x* is between 0.8 and 1 (like 0.9) A < B. But if *x* < 0.8 (like 0), then A > B. So the answer is **D**.

There are other important rules for inequalities that are very useful on the GRE. Some will defy your intuition so study them carefully.

- *Squaring both sides.* If *a* < *b*, then $a^2 < b^2$ when *a* and *b* are nonnegative. For example, if $\sqrt{x} < \sqrt{2}$, then *x* < 2. When at least one of *a* or *b* is negative, other things can happen. For instance −3 < 2 but $(−3)^2 = 9$, which is not less than 2^2. Also, −3 < −2 but $(−3)^2 = 9$, which is greater than $(−2)^2 = 4$.

- *Take the square root of both sides.* If $a < b$, then $\sqrt{a} < \sqrt{b}$, as long as a and b are nonnegative. For example, if $x^2 < 4$, then $\sqrt{x^2} < \sqrt{4}$. Simplifying that means $|x| < 2$ or x is between -2 and 2.

- *Take the reciprocal of both sides.* If $a < b$, then $1/a > 1/b$ as long as a and b have the same sign (they are both positive or both negative). For instance, $2 < 3$ so $\dfrac{1}{2} > \dfrac{1}{3}$.

  Also $-3 < -2$ so $-\dfrac{1}{3} > -\dfrac{1}{2}$. What happens if $a < 0 < b$? Then $1/a < 1/b$.

  Consider $-3 < 2$ and $-\dfrac{1}{3} < \dfrac{1}{2}$.

EXAMPLE 3

Column A	Column B
Assume x is negative	
$4 - x$	$x/2 - 10$

Solution: The easiest solution is by careful observation. As x is negative, $-x$ is positive. Hence $4 - x = 4 + (-x)$ is the sum of positive numbers and is thus positive. So A > 0. As x is negative, so is $x/2$. So a negative minus 10 is also negative. Hence B < 0. Clearly A > B. So the answer is A.

If we choose to solve the inequality directly, we would proceed as follows:
Assume A < B, that is $4 - x < x/2 - 10$.
Multiply both sides by 2 to clear the denominators.
$2(4 - x) < 2(x/2 - 10)$ becomes $8 - 2x < x - 20$.
Add $2x$ to both sides and obtain $8 < 3x - 20$.
Add 20 to both sides: $28 < 3x$.
Divide both sides by 3: $28/3 < x$. $28/3$ is approximately 7.3.
So A < B when $x > 7.3$. But $x < 0$ so A > B. The answer is **A**.

We can treat inequalities as objects and add them together to get true results. Be careful about subtracting, multiplying, or dividing inequalities; the results will usually be false (though occasionally true).

> *Add two inequalities together.* If $a < b$ and $c < d$, then $a + b < c + d$. If $x < 3$ and $y < 5$, then $x + y < 8$.

TIP

Some inequalities that you might think are obviously true are not always true. Try substituting numbers between 0 and 1 or negative numbers to get a counterexample.

- $a < a^2$ is not true for all a. When $a > 1$, then $a < a^2$ but when $0 < a < 1$, then $a > a^2$. For example, if $a = 2$, then $2 < 2^2 = 4$. If $a = \frac{1}{2}$, then $\frac{1}{2} > \frac{1^2}{2} = 1/4$. Of course if $a = 1$, then $a = a^2$ ($1 = 1^2$). If $a < 0$, then $a < a^2$. Any negative number will be less than its square since squares are always positive. For instance $-2 < (-2)^2 = 4$.

- $a > 1/a$ is not true for all a. When $a > 1$, then $a > 1/a$, but when $0 < a < 1$, then $a < 1/a$. For example, if $a = 2$, then $2 > \frac{1}{2}$. If $a = 1/2$, then $\frac{1}{2} < 1/\frac{1}{2} = 2$. Of course, if $a = 1$, then $a = 1/a$ ($1 = 1/1$).

- $a > \sqrt{a}$ is not true for all a. When $a > 1$, then $a > \sqrt{a}$, but when $0 < a < 1$, then $a < \sqrt{a}$. For example, if $a = 4$, then $4 > \sqrt{4} = 2$. If $a = \frac{1}{4}$, then $\frac{1}{4} < \sqrt{\frac{1}{4}} = \frac{1}{2}$. Of course, if $a = 1$, then $a = a^2$ ($1 = 1^2$).

EXAMPLE 4

Given $\frac{1}{2} < a < 1$, choose the smallest value.

- (A) a^2
- (B) a
- (C) $\sqrt{a}$
- (D) $1/a$
- (E) $a - a^2$

Solution: We know from our rules above that when a is between 0 and 1 (and it is in this case) that $a^2 < a$, $a < \sqrt{a}$, $a < 1/a$. So the answer is not B, C, or D. That leaves A and E. Which is smaller a^2 or $a - a^2$? A picture helps, but remember, a could be close to $\frac{1}{2}$ or very close to 1.

We'll solve directly. Assume $a^2 < a - a^2$. Divide by a (a positive number) to get $a < 1 - a$. Add a to both sides: $2a < 1$. Divide by 2: $a < \frac{1}{2}$. So $a^2 < a - a^2$ when $a < \frac{1}{2}$. But $a > \frac{1}{2}$ so $a^2 > a - a^2$. The answer is **E**.

Problems

Basic Problems

Column A	Column B
Assume $a - b > 0$	

1.

$-a$	$-b$

Let $a = 0.7$

2.
| $(a^2)^2$ | $\sqrt{\sqrt{a}}$ |

Assume $x < y$

3.
| $x - y$ | $y - x$ |

Let $x = -1$

4.
| $x^4 - x^3$ | $x^3 - x^4$ |

Assume $x < 2$

5.
| $4x - 3$ | $3x + 4$ |

6.
| $\left(\dfrac{1}{4}\right)^2$ | $\sqrt{\dfrac{1}{4}}$ |

Let $|-y| = 5$

7.
| y | 5 |

8.
| $\sqrt{x^2}$ | x |

9. If $x > 1$ and $y < -1$, which of the following must be true?

   I. $x + y < 0$
   II. $xy < -1$
   III. $x - y > 0$

   (A) II only
   (B) III only
   (C) II and III
   (D) I and II
   (E) I, II, and III

10. Given $a > 2$, choose the smallest value.

    (A) a^2
    (B) a
    (C) $\sqrt{a}$
    (D) $1/a$
    (E) $1/a^2$

GRE Problems

Column A	Column B

11.
| $(1/9)^9$ | $(1/9)^{10}$ |

12.

| 5^6 | 6^5 |

13.

| $2^{10} - \left(\dfrac{1}{2}\right)^{10}$ | $2^9 + \left(\dfrac{1}{2}\right)^9$ |

Let $x > 4$

14.

| $\dfrac{2}{x} - \dfrac{3}{x^2}$ | 1 |

15.

| $x^4 - x^2$ | $x^2 - x^4$ |

Let $a^* = 1/a$

16.

| $\left(7^*\right)^*$ | $\left(\dfrac{1}{7^*}\right)^*$ |

17. If $0 < xy < 1$, which of the following is not possible?

   (A) $x + y = 1$
   (B) $x > 100$
   (C) $x < 0 < y$
   (D) $y < -100$
   (E) $x - y = 1$

18. If $0 < xy < 1$, which of the following is possible?

   (A) $y < 0 < x$
   (B) $x < -2$ and $y > 2$
   (C) x and y are both integers
   (D) $x + y = 10$
   (E) $1/x < 0 < 1/y$

19. Given $a > 1$, choose the largest value.

   (A) a^2
   (B) a
   (C) $\sqrt{a}$
   (D) $1/a$
   (E) $a - a^2$

FUNCTIONS

A function is a rule that assigns to each input exactly one output. A simple example is "multiply the number by 3 and then add 1". Then an input of 5 returns an output of $3 \times 5 + 1$, which equals 16. In grade school you were often given a table of inputs and out-

Input	Output
0	0
1	1
2	4
3	9
−2	4

puts and asked to find the rule. For the table on page 120 you might guess the rule is "square the input," and you would be correct. Notice that although each input can have only one output you can have two inputs that have the same output. For instance, $2^2 = 4$ and $(-2)^2 = 4$.

A good application of this is the square root function. Many people say $\sqrt{9} = \pm 3$, that is $\sqrt{9} = 3$ or $\sqrt{9} = -3$. As square root is a function, it cannot have two outputs for one input; square root is defined strictly as the nonnegative root, so $\sqrt{9} = 3$. (Yes, there are two numbers, 3 and -3, whose squares are equal to 9 but only one of them, 3, is the square root of 9.)

There is standard notation for defining functions. For the "multiply the number by 3 and then add 1" function, we write $f(x) = 3x + 1$. Here x is the input, f is the name of the function, and $3x + 1$ is the output.

EXAMPLE 1

Which function would produce the following table?

(A) $2x^2 + 1$
(B) $2x^2 - 1$
(C) $-6x - 1$
(D) $3x + 1$
(E) $20 + x$

x Input	$f(x)$ Output
-3	17
-2	7
-1	1
0	-1
1	1
2	7

Solution: We could produce a table for each of the given functions but that would be very tedious. We'll just evaluate the functions at a few values and see which match the given table. It is easiest to evaluate a function at zero:

(A) $2x^2 + 1 = 2(0)^2 + 1 = 1$
(B) $2x^2 - 1 = (0)^2 - 1 = -1$
(C) $-6x - 1 = -6(0) - 1 = -1$
(D) $3x + 1 = 3(0) + 1 = 1$
(E) $20 + x = 20 + (0) = 20$

Only B and C agree with the table and produce a value of -1. Now we'll try evaluating at 1: B $2x^2 - 1 = 2(1)^2 - 1 = 1$ while C $-6x - 1 = -6(1) - 1 = -7$. Only B agrees with the table. Choose **B**.

Functions appear implicitly in many mathematical problems and the GRE is no exception to that.

EXAMPLE 2

Orange, Inc., is a world-famous computer manufacturer. It costs them $240{,}000 + 300L$ dollars to produce L laptops at a new facility. These laptops are sold for 600 dollars each. How many do they have to sell in order to break even?

(A) 80
(B) 300
(C) 800
(D) 2,400
(E) 3,000

> **Solution:** The function here is the profit, depending on the number of laptops produced and sold. Profit is revenue ($600L$) minus cost ($240,000 + 300L$). Hence $P(L) = 240,000 + 300L - 600L$ or $P(L) = 240,000 - 300L$. The question is asking for the value of L so that $P(L) = 0$. We can solve $240,000 - 300L = 0$ by adding $300L$ to both sides, $240,000 = 300L$ and dividing by 300, to get $800 = L$. If they sell 800 laptops they will break even. Choose **C**.

Functions are rarely expressed explicitly using the standard notation on the GRE. If a function is defined, it is usually using some nonstandard notation. This can be very confusing for many students, so study the following examples carefully.

EXAMPLE 3

If $r^* = 1/r$, then what is $\left(1 - \left(\frac{1}{2}\right)^*\right)^*$?

(A) $\dfrac{1}{2}$

(B) $-\dfrac{1}{2}$

(C) 0

(D) -1

(E) 2

Solution: First we find $\left(\frac{1}{2}\right)^* = 1/\left(\frac{1}{2}\right) = 2$. So $\left(1 - \left(\frac{1}{2}\right)^*\right)^* = (1 - 2)^* = (-1)^* = 1/(-1) = -1$. Choose **D**.

Functions of two or even more variables also appear on the GRE, though usually in some nonstandard guise. A standard function of two variables might be $f(x,y) = x^2 + y^2$. It takes two numbers as input and returns the sum of their squares. Here's one way this same function could appear on the GRE.

EXAMPLE 4

If $x \wedge y = x^2 + y^2$ then which of the following are valid rules?

 I. $r(x \wedge y) = (rx) \wedge (ry)$

 II. $(-x) \wedge (-y) = x \wedge y$

III. $x \wedge y = y \wedge x$

(A) I only

(B) II only

(C) III only

(D) I and II

(E) II and III

Solution: Note $r(x \wedge y) = r(x^2 + y^2) = rx^2 + ry^2$ while $(rx) \wedge (ry) = (rx^2) \wedge (ry^2) =$ $r^2x^2 + r^2y^2$. Hence I is not valid. Also, $(-x) \wedge (-y) = (-x^2) \wedge (-y^2) = x^2 + y^2$ which equals $x \wedge y$, so II is valid. We see that $x \wedge y = x^2 + y^2 = y^2 + x^2 = y \wedge x$; hence III is also valid.

As II and III are valid, choose **E**.

Problems

Basic Problems

Column A	Column B

In problems 1 and 2, $r^* = 1 - r$.

1.

| $(-2)^*$ | 2^* |

2.

| $3^*2^*1^*$ | $0^*(-1)^*(-2)^*$ |

$$x_\clubsuit = 1/x$$

3.

| $(1/10)_\clubsuit$ | $10_\clubsuit$ |

4. If $x \odot y = \dfrac{x}{y}$, what is $(75 \odot 15)(15 \odot 75)$?

(A) 25
(B) 15
(C) 5
(D) 2.5
(E) 1

5. For the function $F(x) = mx - 9$, what is $F(m)$?

(A) $m - 9$
(B) $(m - 3)(m + 3)$
(C) $m^2 - 9m$
(D) m
(E) $(m + 3)^2$

6. If $G(x,y,z) = x + y - z$, what is $G(2,3,4) + G(3,4,2) + G(4,2,3)$?

(A) 1
(B) 2
(C) 5
(D) 9
(E) 15

GRE Problems

7. If $[\![\,y\,]\!] = \dfrac{2}{y}$, then what is $\left[\!\left[\dfrac{1}{y}\right]\!\right] = [\![\,y\,]\!]$?

    (A) $\dfrac{2y - 2}{y}$

    (B) $\dfrac{2(y - 1)(y - 1)}{y}$

    (C) $2 - \dfrac{2}{y}$

    (D) $\dfrac{1 - y^2}{y}$

    (E) $2 - y$

8. If $r \, \textcircled{\smile} \, t = r^2 - t^2$, then what is $(x - y) \, \textcircled{\smile} \, (x + y)$?

    (A) 0
    (B) $-2y^2$
    (C) $2x^2 - 4xy + 2y^2$
    (D) $-4xy$
    (E) $x^2 - y^2$

9. For the function $f(x) = Mx - 2$, $f(2) = 2$ and $f(3) = 4$. What is $f(5)$?

    (A) 3
    (B) 4
    (C) 6
    (D) 8
    (E) 9

10. Define $\begin{vmatrix} a & b \\ c & d \end{vmatrix} = (a - b)(c - d)$. Which of the following are true?

    I. $\begin{vmatrix} x & 1 \\ 1 & x \end{vmatrix} = (x - 1)^2$

    II. $\begin{vmatrix} 1 & x \\ x & 1 \end{vmatrix} = -(x - 1)^2$

    III. $\begin{vmatrix} x & x \\ 1 & 1 \end{vmatrix} = 0$

    (A) I only
    (B) II only
    (C) III only
    (D) I and II
    (E) II and III

Column A | Column B

In problems 11–13, $\mapsto t = 2 - t$ and $\boxed{s} = \dfrac{1}{s}$.

11. $\mapsto \dfrac{1}{2}$ $\boxed{\dfrac{1}{2}}$

12. $\boxed{\mapsto 3}$ $\mapsto \boxed{3}$

$x \neq 0$

13. $\mapsto (\mapsto x^2)$ $\boxed{x^2}$

SOLUTIONS

Polynomials and Factoring

1. **(D)** We collect like terms and add: $(2 - 3x + 5x^3) + (7 + 4x - x^5) = (2 + 7) + (-3x + 4x) + (5x^3) + (-x^5) = 9 + x + 5x^3 - x^5$. Choose **D**.

2. **(E)** We distribute the negatives, then collect like terms and simplify. $(1 + 2x) - (3x + 4x^2) + (5x^2 + 6x^3) - (7x^3 + 8x^4) = 1 + 2x - 3x - 4x^2 + 5x^2 + 6x^3 - 7x^3 - 8x^4 = 1 + (2x - 3x) + (-4x^2 + 5x^2) + (6x^3 - 7x^3) - 8x^4 = 1 - x + x^2 - x^3 - 8x^4$. Choose **E**.

3. **(B)** We use FOIL. It's best to treat the second factor as $3 + (-2x)$. Then $(2 + x)(3 - 2x) = (2)(3) + (2)(-2x) + (x)(3) + (x)(-2x) = 6 - 4x + 3x - 2x^2 = 6 - x - 2x^2$. Choose **B**.

4. **(D)** Let's distribute the first factor over the second and see if it looks like any of the answers. $(x^{100} - 1)(2 + x^{10}) = (x^{100} - 1)(2) + (x^{100} - 1)(x^{10})$. None of the answers seem to match. We'll be careful to treat $(x^{100} - 1)$ as $x^{100} + (-1)$ and distribute the second factor over the first. $(x^{100} - 1)(2 + x^{10}) = (x^{100})(2 + x^{10}) + (-1)(2 + x^{10})$. Choose **D**.

5. **(C)** Follow the rule for difference of squares to see that $4 - y^2 = 2^2 - y^2 = (2 - y)(2 + y)$. Choose **C**.

6. **(A)** Using the rule for difference of squares $(t + 3)(t - 3) = t^2 - 9$, which is not equal to $t^2 + 9$. Is one always larger than the other? Yes, $(t^2 - 9) + 18 = t^2 + 9$. So $t^2 + 9$ is always 18 larger than $t^2 - 9$. Choose **A**.

7. **(D)** Let's multiply out B: $ab(3b - 2a^2 + 2) = (ab)(3b) + (ab)(-2a^2) + (ab)(2) = 3ab^2 - 2a^3b + 2ab$, which is not the same as A. So which is larger? If $a = 0$, both are zero. If $a = b = 1$, then A is $3 - 2 + 4 = 5$ while B is $3 - 2 + 2 = 3$. So sometimes one is larger and sometimes they are equal. Choose **D**.

8. **(B)** There are many ways to do this problem (including plain multiplication). One way is to use the distributive property: $99 \times 101 = 99 \times (100 + 1) = 99 \times 100 + 99 \times 1 = 9{,}900 + 99 = 9{,}999$, which is less than $100^2 = 10{,}000$. Another way is to use difference of squares: $99 \times 101 = (100 - 1)(100 + 1) = 100^2 - 1$, which is clearly less than 100^2. Either way, choose **B**.

9. **(C)** We factor and simplify before substituting:
$$\frac{x - y}{x^2 - y^2} = \frac{\cancel{x - y}}{\cancel{(x - y)}\,(x + y)} = \frac{1}{x + y}.\ 1/(x + y) = 1/(0.01 + 0.99) =$$
$1/1 = 1$. Choose **C**.

10. **(C)** We factor and simplify before substituting:
$$\frac{b^2 - a^2}{b + a} = \frac{(b - a)\,\cancel{(b + a)}}{\cancel{(b + a)}} = b - a\,.\ \text{Then}\ b - a = 57 - 43 = 14.$$
Choose **C**.

11. **(B)** There are a total of $77 + 44$ numbers so to find the average we divide: $(77^2 - 44^2)/(77 + 44)$. It is easier to factor and cancel before simplifying.
$$\frac{77^2 - 44^2}{77 + 44} = \frac{(77 - 44)\,\cancel{(77 + 44)}}{\cancel{77 + 44}} = 77 - 44 = 33.\ \text{Hence, the average}$$
is 33. Choose **B**.

12. **(D)** It's clear that if $x = 0$ then both columns are zero. If $x = 1$, then A is zero, while B is $(1 - 2)(1)(1 + 2) = -3$. Similarly, if $x = 2$, then B is zero, while A is $(2 - 1)(2)(2 + 1) = 6$. Clearly it depends on the value of x. Choose **D**.

13. **(A)** First we know that $(a + b)^2 = a^2 + 2ab + b^2$ which, as $ab = 2$, equals $a^2 + 2(2) + b^2 = a^2 + b^2 + 4$. Meanwhile $(a - b)^2 = a^2 - 2ab + b^2$, which as $ab = 2$, equals $a^2 - 2(2) + b^2 = a^2 + b^2 - 4$. Since a^2 and b^2 are nonnegative, $a^2 + b^2 + 4 > a^2 + b^2 - 4$. Choose **A**.

14. **(D)**

	A	B
	$(s + t)^2$	$(s - t)^2$
Expand	$s^2 + 2st + t^2$	$s^2 - 2st + t^2$
Subtract $s^2 + t^2$	$-(s^2 + t^2)$	$-(s^2 + t^2)$
	$2st$	$-2st$

Even knowing $s > 0$, since t could be positive or negative, A or B could be larger. Choose **D**.

15. **(A)** We see that $a^2 - b^2 = (a - b)(a + b) = (24)(25) = 600$. We know that $(a + b)^2 = a^2 + 2ab + b^2$ while $(a - b)^2 = a^2 - 2ab + b^2$, so $(a + b)^2 - (a - b)^2 = 2ab - (-2ab) = 4ab$. But $(a + b)^2 - (a - b)^2$ is also equal to $25^2 - 24^2 = (25 - 24)(25 + 24) = 1(49) = 49$. As $4ab = 49$, $ab = 49/4$, clearly much less than 600. Choose **A**.

An alternate solution would be to add the given equations together $(a - b) + (a + b) = 24 + 25 \Rightarrow 2a = 49$. Hence $a = 24.5$. As $a + b = 25$, this means that $b = 0.5$. Now we can evaluate $a^2 - b^2 = (24.5)^2 - (0.5)^2$ and $ab = (24.5)(0.5)$. Even without evaluating, we can see that A > B.

16. **(C)** Start by factoring and simplifying B, $\dfrac{x^2 - y^2}{(x + y)^2} = \dfrac{(x - y)\cancel{(x + y)}}{(x + y)\cancel{(x + y)}} =$

$\dfrac{x - y}{x + y}$. As x and y are positive, we did not cancel zero. Hence A = B. Choose **C**.

17. **(A)** Factor before simplifying: $(0.63)^2 - (0.37)^2 = (0.63 + 0.37)(0.63 - 0.37) = (1)(0.26) = 0.26$. This is greater than $\dfrac{1}{4} = 0.25$. Choose **A**.

18. **(C)** One approach is to factor $\dfrac{1}{x} - \dfrac{1}{x^2} = \dfrac{1}{x}\left(1 - \dfrac{1}{x}\right) = \dfrac{1}{x}\left(\dfrac{x}{x} - \dfrac{1}{x}\right) =$

$\dfrac{1}{x}\dfrac{x - 1}{x} = \dfrac{x - 1}{x^2}$. Choose **C**. Another approach would be to start with B

and split it into two fractions $\dfrac{x - 1}{x^2} = \dfrac{\cancel{x}}{x^{\cancel{2}}} - \dfrac{1}{x^2} = \dfrac{1}{x} - \dfrac{1}{x^2}$.

19. **(D)** One way to simplify A is to factor using difference of squares. $\left(x + \tfrac{1}{2}\right)^2 -$

$\left(x - \tfrac{1}{2}\right)^2 = \left(\left(x + \tfrac{1}{2}\right) - \left(x - \tfrac{1}{2}\right)\right)\left(\left(x + \tfrac{1}{2}\right) + \left(x - \tfrac{1}{2}\right)\right) = (1)(2x) = 2x$.

How does $2x$ compare to $|x|$? When $x = 0$, they are equal. When $x = 1$, they are not. Choose **D**.

20. **(C)** As $x^2 + 2xy + y^2 = (x + y)^2$, A is equal to $3^2 = 9$. Meanwhile B is $6 + (x + y) = 6 + 3 = 9$. Choose **C**.

Solving Equations

1. **(A)** We add x to both sides: $2x + 3 + x = 6 - x + x \Rightarrow 3x + 3 = 6$. Then we subtract 3 from both sides: $3x + 3 - 3 = 6 - 3 \Rightarrow 3x = 3$. Now divide both sides by 3, $3x/3 = 3/3$, and we have $x = 1$. Choose **A**.

2. **(C)** First expand $a(a - 3) = (a + 2)(a - 1) \Rightarrow a^2 - 3a = a^2 + a - 2$. Then subtract a^2 from both sides: $a^2 - 3a - a^2 = a^2 + a - 2 - a^2 \Rightarrow -3a = a - 2$. Now add $3a$ to both sides: $-3a + 3a = a - 2 + 3a \Rightarrow 0 = 4a - 2$. Add 2 to both sides: $0 + 2 = 4a - 2 + 2 \Rightarrow 2 = 4a$. Finally divide both sides: by 4: $2/4 = 4a/4 \Rightarrow 1/2 = a$. Choose **C**.

3. **(C)** Expand $(t + 2)(3 - t) = (t + 2) = 3t + 6 - t^2 - 2t = t + 2 \Rightarrow t + 6 - t^2 = t + 2$. Subtract t from both sides, $t + 6 - t^2 - t = t + 2 - t \Rightarrow 6 - t^2 = 2$. Subtract 6 from both sides $6 - t^2 - 6 = 2 - 6 \Rightarrow -t^2 = -4$, and divide by -1 to get $t^2 = 4$. This implies that $t = 2$ or $t = -2$. Choose **C**.

Alternatively, notice that if $t + 2 = 0$, and hence $t = -2$, then both sides of the equation are zero and thus equal. Otherwise, we can cancel $t + 2$ from both sides to get $3 - t = 1$. Add t to both sides to get $3 = 1 + t$, then subtract 1 from both sides, and we have $t = 2$. So the solutions are 2 and -2.

4. **(C)** To isolate z, we start by subtracting $(2x - y)$ from both sides, $2x - y + 3z - (2x - y) = 2 + y - (2x - y) \Rightarrow 3z = 2 + y - 2x + y = 3z = 2 + 2y - 2x$. Now divide by 3, and we have $z = (2 + 2y - 2x)/3$. Choose **C**.

5. **(E)** First add b^2 to both sides, $2b^2 - 8 + b^2 = 1 - b^2 + b^2 \Rightarrow 3b^2 - 8 = 1$. Now add 8 to both sides $3b^2 - 8 + 8 = 1 + 8 = 3b^2 = 9$. Divide by 3, $3b^2/3 = 9/3 \Rightarrow b^2 = 3$. This implies that $b = \sqrt{3}$ or $b = -\sqrt{3}$. Choose **E**.

6. **(A)** Multiply both sides by $(x + 1)(x - 1)$ to clear the denominators: $\cancel{(x + 1)}(x - 1)\dfrac{1}{\cancel{x + 1}}(x + 1)\cancel{(x - 1)}\dfrac{2}{\cancel{x - 1}}$, which simplifies to $x - 1 = 2(x + 1)$. Expanded this is $x - 1 = 2x + 2$. Subtract x from both sides $x - 1 - x = 2x + 2 - x \Rightarrow -1 = x + 2$. Then subtract 2 from both sides $-1 - 2 = x + 2 - 2 \Rightarrow -3 = x$. Choose **A**.

7. **(A)** If we add the given equations, $(m + n) + (3 - n) = 7 + 6$, it simplifies nicely to $m + 3 = 13$. Subtract 3 from both sides, and we have $m = 10$. Choose **A**.

8. **(A)** Multiply the first equation by 3, to get $3x - 3y = 9$. Add this to the second equation to get $(3x - 3y) + (2x + 3y) = 9 + 2 \Rightarrow 5x = 11 \Rightarrow x = 11/5 = 2.2$. If we substitute $x = 2.2$ back into the first equation, we have $(2.2) - y = 3$, so $y = 2.2 - 3 = -0.8$. As $2.2 > -0.8$, choose **A**.

   Alternate answer: as $x - y = 3$, $x = y + 3$. So x is always 3 more than y, and hence larger than y. Choose **A**.

9. **(A)** First we expand: $(x + y)z \Rightarrow y(x + z) \Rightarrow xz + yz = yx + yz$. We want to get all terms involving x on one side of the equation. Subtract yx from both sides $xz + yz - yx = yx + yz - yx \Rightarrow xz - yx + yz = yz$. Then subtract yz from both sides $xz - yx + yz - yz = yz - yz \Rightarrow xz - yx = 0$. Now factor out an x on the left side $x(z - y) = 0$. Hence $x = 0$ or $z = y$. But we were given that $z \neq y$, so $x = 0$. Choose **A**.

10. **(A)** A quick way to solve this problem is to notice that $2x + 2 = (2x - 3) + 5 = 17 + 5 = 22$. Choose **A**.

11. **(C)** By comparing opposite (vertical) angles at the center of the circle we can get two nice equalities. First $b = 2a$ and second $120 = b + a + 30$. If we substitute the first in the second, we have $120 = 2a + a + 30 \Rightarrow 120 = 3a + 30 \Rightarrow 120 - 30 = 3a \Rightarrow 90 = 3a \Rightarrow a = 30$. Choose **C**.

12. **(C)** First we use 2 as the base for all powers: $4^{b+1} = 2^{3b} \div 4 \Rightarrow (2^2)^{b+1} = 2^{3b} \div 2^2$. Now we use rules of exponents to simplify $2^{2b+2} = 2^{3b-2}$. For the

equality to hold, we must have $2b + 2 = 3b - 2$. Subtract $2b$ from each side, $2b + 2 - 2b = 3b - 2 - 2b$, and we have $2 = b - 2$. Add 2 to each side, and we conclude that $b = 4$. Choose **C**.

13. **(D)** First we change 2^3 to 8, so that we may use 8 as the base for all the powers. Then $8^{a/3} = 2^3 8^{1-a} \Rightarrow 8^{a/3} = (8)8^{1-a}$. Now using rules for exponents we have $8^{a/3} = 8^{1 + (1 - a)} \Rightarrow 8^{a/3} = 8^{2-a}$. Since the bases are equal, we must have $a/3 = 2 - a$. Multiply both sides by 3, $3(a/3) = 3(2 - a) \Rightarrow a = 6 - 3a$. Add $3a$ to both sides $a + 3a = 6 - 3a + 3a \Rightarrow 4a = 6$. Divide by 4 and we have $a = 6/4 = 3/2 = 1.5$. Choose **D**.

14. **(B)** First multiply both sides by 3, to get rid of the fraction: $V \times 3 = (4\pi r^3/3) \times 3 \Rightarrow 3V = 4\pi r^3$. Then we divide both sides by 4π to get $3V/(4\pi) = r^3$.

Finally, take cube roots to get $r = 3\sqrt{\dfrac{3V}{4\pi}}$. Choose **B**.

15. **(D)** As, $x^2 - 4 = 0$, then $x^2 = 4$. Which means that $x = 2$ or $x = -2$. In one case A and B are equal and in the other A $<$ B. Choose **D**.

16. **(A)** Start by expanding $x(2(x + 3) + 3) = 3(4 + 3x) \Rightarrow x(2x + 6 + 3) = 12 + 9x \Rightarrow x(2x + 9) = 12 + 9x \Rightarrow 2x^2 + 9x = 12 + 9x$. We subtract $12 + 9x$ to bring everything to one side: $2x^2 + 9x - (12 + 9x) = 0 \Rightarrow 2x^2 - 12 = 0$. Add 12 to both sides and then divide by 2 to get $x^2 = 6$. This means $x = \sqrt{6}$ or $x = -\sqrt{6}$. In either case it is less than 6. Choose **A**.

17. **(A)** Starting with $3x - 6 = 4$, divide by 3 to get $(3x - 6)/3 = 4/3 \Rightarrow x - 2 = 4/3$. Now multiply by 2 and $2(x - 2) = 2 \times 4/3 \Rightarrow 2x - 4 = 8/3$. Finally subtract 2 to get $2x - 4 - 2 = 8/3 - 2 \Rightarrow 2x - 6 = 2/3$. Going back to $x - 2 = 4/3$, we subtract 2 to get $x - 2 - 2 = 4/3 - 2 \Rightarrow x - 4 = -2/3$. Choose **A**.

18. **(C)** If we add the two given equations then $(3x - y) + (3x + y) = 2 + 4 \Rightarrow 6x = 6 \Rightarrow x = 1$. We can substitute $x = 1$ in the second equation $3(1) + y = 4 \Rightarrow 3 + y = 4$. Subtract 3 from each side, and we have $y = 1$. Since both x and y are 1, choose **C**.

19. **(D)** If we subtract the second equation from the first we get $(3x + 2y + z) - (2x + y + z) = -2 - 10 \Rightarrow x + y = -12$. Now divide both sides by 2 and we have $(x + y)/2 = -6$. Thus the average of x and y is -6. What is z? z can take on almost any value. Note $2x + y + z = 10$ can be rewritten as $x + (x + y) + z = 10$. As $x + y = -12$ this means $x + (-12) + z = 10 \Rightarrow x + z = 22$. When x is very large, say 100, $z = -78$. When x is small, say $x = 0$, then $z = 22$. So z can be larger or smaller than -6. Choose **D**.

20. **(E)** Add the two equations together, to get $(r - s) + (t + s) = 3 + 11 = r + t = 14$. Then divide by 2 to see that $(r + t)/2 = 7$. Hence the average of r and t is 7. Choose **E**.

21. **(D)** Not being certain what else to do, add the two equations together: $(ax^2 - bx + c) + (-bx^2 + ax - c) = 0$. Then collect like terms and simplify $(a - b)x^2 + (a - b)x = 0$. If we factor, then we have $(a - b)(x^2 + x) = 0 \Rightarrow (a - b)(x)(x + 1) = 0$. As the product is zero, $a - b = 0$, $x = 0$ or $x + 1 = 0$. Put another way, $a = b$ or $x = 0$ or $x = -1$. Now we can consider the options. I: if $a \neq b$ then $x = 0$ or -1 is true. II: If $x \neq 0$ then $a = b$ or $x = -1$. So II does not have to be true. III: If $x = 2$, then $(a - b)(x)(x + 1) = 0$ becomes $(a - b)(2)(2 + 1) = 0$ and hence $a - b = 0$, or $a = b$. III is true. Choose **D**.

22. **(C)** Let Derek have d marbles, Jason have j marbles, and Cornelia have c marbles. Then $d = 2j$, $c = (1/3)d$, and $d + c + j = 55$. As $d = 2j$, $j = d/2$. Then substitute $j = d/2$ and $c = (1/3)d$ into $d + c + j = 55$ to get $d + (1/3)d + d/2 = 55$. Multiply both sides by 6 to clear the denominators, $6d + 2d + 3d = 330$. Hence $11d = 330$ or $d = 30$. Choose **C**.

23. **(E)** Let Jillian's favorite number be J. Then Jillian doubled her favorite number, $2J$, added one, $2J + 1$, divided by three, $(2J + 1)/3$, and subtracted two, $(2J + 1)/3 - 2$. This was her favorite number so $(2J + 1)/3 - 2 = J$. To solve we first multiply both sides by 3 to clear the denominators, whence $(2J + 1) - 6 = 3J$. Subtract $2J$ from both sides and $1 - 6 = J$, or $J = -5$. Choose **E**.

Inequalities

1. **(B)** As $a - b > 0$, subtract a from both sides: $(a - b) - a > 0 - a \Rightarrow -b > -a$. Choose **B**.

2. **(B)** First note that $(a^2)^2 = a^4$, while $\sqrt{\sqrt{a}} = \left((a)^{1/2}\right)^{1/2} = a^{\frac{1}{4}}$. For numbers between 0 and 1 (like 0.7) taking the fourth power gives a smaller result, $a^4 < a$, but taking the fourth root gives a larger result, $a^{\frac{1}{4}} > a$. Hence $a^{\frac{1}{4}} > a > a^4$. Choose **B**.

3. **(B)** As $x < y$, subtracting y from both sides gives $x - y < y - y \Rightarrow x - y < 0$. If we multiply this inequality by -1 (reversing the inequality sign) we get $-1(x - y) > -1 \times 0 \Rightarrow y - x > 0$. Hence $x - y < 0 < y - x$. Choose **B**.

4. **(A)** Remember that -1 raised to any even power is 1 and raised to any odd power is -1. If we evaluate A, $x^4 - x^3 = (-1)^4 - (-1)^3 = 1 - (-1) = 2$. Now $x^3 - x^4 = -1(x^4 - x^3) = -1(2) = -2$. Choose **A**.

5. **(B)** One way to solve this problem is to ask when they are equal: $4x - 3 = 3x + 4 \Rightarrow 4x - 3 - 3x = 3x + 4 - 3x \Rightarrow x - 3 = 4 \Rightarrow x - 3 + 3 = 4 + 3 \Rightarrow x = 7$. Since they are equal when $x = 7$, when $x < 7$, (as in this case),

one is always larger than the other. If $x = 1$, $4x - 3 = 4(1) - 3 = 1$ and $3x + 4 = 3(1) + 4 = 7$. So, when $x < 2$, $3x + 4$ is always larger. Choose **B**.

Alternate answer: Notice that $3x + 4 = (4x - 3) + (7 - x)$. As $x < 2$, $7 - x$ is always positive. So $3x - 4$ is always a positive number larger than $4x - 3$. Hence $3x + 4$ is larger.

6. **(B)** For number between 0 and 1 (like $\frac{1}{4}$), squaring gives a smaller result, $\left(\frac{1}{4}\right)^2 < \frac{1}{4}$, but taking the square root gives a larger result $\sqrt{\frac{1}{4}} > \frac{1}{4}$.

Hence $\left(\frac{1}{4}\right)^2 < \frac{1}{4} < \sqrt{\frac{1}{4}}$. Choose **B**. In this case you could have computed

the values and compared, $\left(\frac{1}{4}\right)^2 = \frac{1}{4} \times \frac{1}{4} = \frac{1}{16}$ while $\sqrt{\frac{1}{4}} = \frac{1}{2}$ since $\left(\frac{1}{2}\right)^2 = \frac{1}{4}$.

7. **(D)** As $|-y| = 5$, $-y = 5$, or $-y = -5$. In the first case, $y = -5$ and the second $y = 5$. Since we don't know which value y has, we could have A < B or A = B. Choose **D**.

8. **(D)** Remember that $\sqrt{x^2}$ is not always equal to x. If $x = -3$, then $\sqrt{x^2} = \sqrt{(-3)^2} = \sqrt{9} = 3$. If $x = 3$, then $\sqrt{x^2} = \sqrt{(3)^2} = \sqrt{9} = 3$. Choose **D**.

9. **(C)** As $y < -1$, if we multiply by -1 (and switch the inequality sign), we have $-y > 1$. Now add this to $x > 1$, and we have $x + (-y) > 1 + 1 \Rightarrow x - y > 2$. So III is true. As $x > 1$ and $y < -1$, x is positive and y is negative. The product of a positive and a negative is negative. So $xy < 0$, and II is true. I is not true. If $x = 2$ and $y = -2$, then $x + y = 0$. Choose **C**.

10. **(E)** First, we know that for numbers greater than 1 that $a^2 > a > \sqrt{a}$. So A and B are not the smallest. As $a > 2$, $\sqrt{a} > \sqrt{2} > 1$. We also know that as $a > 2$ that $1/a < 1/2 < 1$. So D is less than C. Finally as $a^2 > a > 0$, then $1/a^2 < 1/a$. Choose **E**.

11. **(A)** The easiest way to solve this problem is to clear the denominators by multiplying both columns by 9^{10}. Then A $= 9^{10} \times (1/9)^9 = 9$ and B $= 9^{10} \times (1/9)^{10} = 1$. As $9 > 1$, choose **A**. Alternatively, remember that $9^9 < 9^{10}$ implies that $1/9^9 > 1/9^{10}$.

12. **(A)** This is challenging as there is no way to avoid doing some calculations. I suggest you divide both columns by 5^5. Then A becomes 5 and B becomes $(6/5)^5 = (1.2)^5$. Since $12^2 = 144$, we know that $(1.2)^5 = (1.2)^2(1.2)^2(1.2) = (1.44)(1.44)(1.2)$. As $14^2 = 196$, $(1.44)^2$ is approximately 2. Thus B is approximately $2 \times 1.2 = 2.4$, nowhere near 5. Choose **A**.

13. **(A)** Multiply both columns by 2^{10} to clear the denominators. Then A becomes

$$\left[2^{10} - \left(\frac{1}{2}\right)^{10}\right]2^{10} = 2^{10}2^{10} - \frac{1}{2^{10}}2^{10} = 2^{20} - 1$$

while B becomes

$$\left[2^9 + \left(\frac{1}{2}\right)^9\right]2^{10} = 2^9 2^{10} + \frac{1}{2^9}2^{10} = 2^{19} + 2$$

Now $2^{20} - 1 = 2 \times 2^{19} - 1 = 2^{19} + 2^{19} - 1$. As $2^{19} - 1 > 2$, A is greater than B. Choose **A**.

14. **(B)** First clear the denominators by multiplying both columns by x^2. As $x > 4$ there is no possibility that this would change the inequality between A and B. Then A is $2x - 3$, while B is x^2. Then $2x - 3 = 2(x - 1.5) < 2x < 4x < x^2$. So B is greater than A. You could also solve $2x - 3 = x^2 \Rightarrow x^2 - 2x + 3 = 0 \Rightarrow (x - 3)(x + 1) = 0 \Rightarrow x - 3 = 0$ or $x + 1 = 0 \Rightarrow x = 3$ or $x = -1$. Then for $x > 3$, either $x^2 > 2x - 3$ or $x^2 < 2x - 3$. But $4^2 > 2(4) - 3$. So $x^2 > 2x - 3$. Either way, choose **B**.

    Alternate answer: $\dfrac{2}{x} - \dfrac{3}{x^2} = \dfrac{2}{x}\left(1 - \dfrac{3}{2x}\right)$. As $x > 4$, $2/x$ is between 0 and 1. As $x > 4$, $2x > 8$, so $3/(2x)$ is also between 0 and 1. The product of numbers between 0 and 1 is between 0 and 1. Choose **B**.

15. **(D)** Note that $-1(x^4 - x^2) = -x^4 + x^2 = x^2 - x^4$. So these numbers are opposites. Except when $x = 0$, both are zero. So sometimes A = B, and sometimes not. Choose **D**.

16. **(A)** $(7^*)^* = (1/7)^* = (1/(1/7)) = 1 \times (7/1) = 7$. Put another way, * takes the reciprocal of a number and the reciprocal of the reciprocal is the original number. Now $\left(\dfrac{1}{7^*}\right)^* \left(\dfrac{1}{\frac{1}{7}}\right)^* = 7^* = \dfrac{1}{7} = 1/7$. Choose **A**.

17. **(C)** A is possible as $(1/2) + (1/2) = 1$ and $0 < (1/2)(1/2) < 1$ since $(1/2)(1/2) = 1/4$. B is possible as we can make y very small so that x can be large and their product still be small. Let $x = 200$ and $y = 1/400$. Then $x > 100$ and $0 < (200)(1/400) < 1$ as $(200)(1/400) = 1/2$. C is not possible. If $x < 0 < y$, then x is negative and y is positive. Then xy would be negative and hence not between 0 and 1. Choose **C**.

    D is possible if $y = -200$ and $x = -1/400$. Then $xy = 1/2$. E is possible if $x = 3/2$ and $y = 1/2$. Then $x - y = 3/2 - 1/2 = 1$ and $(3/2)(1/2) = 3/4$, which is between 0 and 1.

18. **(D)** The product of positive and negative cannot be positive so A, B, and E are not possible. The product of integers is an integer and there are no integers between 0 and 1, so C is not possible. Choose **D**. If $x = 10 - 1/1{,}000$ and $y = 1/1{,}000$, then xy is greater than zero and less than $10(1/1{,}000) = 1/100 < 1$.

19. **(A)** First we know that for numbers greater than 1, that $a^2 > a > $. So B and C are not the largest. Also when $a > 1$, $0 < 1/a < 1 < a$. So D is not the largest. Finally as $a^2 > a$, $a - a^2 < 0 < a$. So E is not the largest. Choose **A**.

Functions

1. **(A)** Since $r^* = 1 - r$, $(-2)^* = 1 - (-2) = 3$. Also $2^* = 1 - 2 = -1$. Choose **A**.

2. **(A)** You can compute this answer directly: $3^* 2^* 1^* = (1 - 3)(1 - 2)(1 - 1) = (-2)(-1)(0) = 0$, while $0^*(-1)^*(-2)^* = (0 - 1)(-1 - 1)(-2 - 1) = (-1)(-2)(-3) = -6$. Choose **A**.

3. **(A)** Notice that this function just takes reciprocals of numbers. The reciprocal of $1/10$ is $10/1 = 10$. The reciprocal of 10 is $1/10$. Choose **A**.

4. **(E)** Because of cancellation you don't have to calculate $(75 \odot 15)$ completely. You just need to notice we are taking the product of reciprocals: $(75 \odot 15)$

$$(15 \odot 75) = \frac{75}{15} \times \frac{15}{75} = 1.$$ Choose **E**.

5. **(B)** To evaluate the function, we simply put m everywhere that x was, so $F(m) = m(m) - 9 = m^2 - 9$. Unfortunately $m^2 - 9$ is not an option. But remembering our difference of squares, $m^2 - 9 = (m - 3)(m + 3)$. So choose **B**.

6. **(D)** $G(2,3,4) + G(3,4,2) + G(4,2,3) = (2 + 3 - 4) + (3 + 4 - 2) + (4 + 2 - 3) = (2 + 2 - 2) + (3 + 3 - 3) + (4 + 4 - 4) = 2 + 3 + 4 = 9$. Choose **D**.

7. **(B)** $\left[\!\left[\frac{1}{y}\right]\!\right] - [\![y]\!] = \frac{2}{\left(\frac{1}{y}\right)} - \frac{2}{y} = 2y - \frac{2}{y}$. This is not an option so we combine the fractions.

$$2y - \frac{2}{y} = 2y\frac{y}{y} - \frac{2}{y} = \frac{2y^2}{y} - \frac{2}{y} = \frac{2y^2 - 2}{y}$$

This is still not an option so we factor the numerator.

$$\frac{2y^2 - 2}{y} = \frac{2(y^2 - 1)}{y} = \frac{2(y - 1)(y + 1)}{y}$$

Choose **B**.

8. **(D)** $(x - y) \, \odot \, (x + y) = (x - y)^2 - (x + y)^2$, which we can factor using difference of squares, into $((x - y) + (x + y))((x - y) - (x + y))$. Simplifying, we have $(2x)(-2y) = -4xy$. Choose **D**.

9. **(D)** Since $f(2) = 2$, we know that $M(2) - 2 = 2$. Since $f(3) = 4$ we know that $M(3) - 2 = 4$. Let's add these two equations together: $(2M - 2) + (3M - 2) = 2 + 4 \Rightarrow 5M - 4 = 6$. Add 2 to both sides, and we have $5M - 2 = 8$. But $f(5) = M(5) - 2$. So $f(5) = 8$. Choose **D**.

10. **(E)** First $\begin{vmatrix} x & 1 \\ 1 & x \end{vmatrix} = (x - 1)(1 - x) = (x - 1)(-1)(x - 1) = -(x - 1)^2$.

    So I is not true. Now $\begin{vmatrix} 1 & x \\ x & 1 \end{vmatrix} = (1 - x)(x - 1) = -(x - 1)(x - 1) =$

    $-(x - 1)^2$. So II is true. Finally $\begin{vmatrix} x & x \\ 1 & 1 \end{vmatrix} = (x - x)(1 - 1) = 0 \times 0 = 0$.

    Thus III is true. Choose **E**.

11. **(B)** We see that $\mapsto \dfrac{1}{2} = 2 - \dfrac{1}{2} = 1.5$. While $\boxed{\dfrac{1}{2}} = 1/(1/2) = 2/1 = 2$.

    Choose **B**.

12. **(B)** First $\mapsto 3 = 2 - 3 = -1$. So $\boxed{\mapsto 3} = \boxed{-1} = \dfrac{1}{-1} = -1$. Then

    $\boxed{3} = \dfrac{1}{3}$ so $\mapsto \boxed{3} = \mapsto \dfrac{1}{3} = 2 - \dfrac{1}{3} = \dfrac{5}{3}$. Choose **B**.

13. **(C)** First we see that $\mapsto x^2 = 2 - x^2$, so $\mapsto (\mapsto x^2) = 2 - (2 - x^2) = x^2$. Also $\boxed{x^2} = \dfrac{1}{x^2}$, so $\boxed{\boxed{x^2}} = \boxed{\dfrac{1}{x^2}} = \dfrac{1}{\dfrac{1}{x^2}} = x^2$. Thus, as long as $x \neq 0$,

    they are equal. Choose **C**.

Data Analysis

PERCENTAGES

Percents are needed to understand any business report, political poll, or medical drug dosage. A percent expresses a number of parts per hundred. For instance, 4 apples is 8% of 50 apples since if we divide 50 apples into 100 parts (each part will be half an apple) then 4 whole apples will be 8 half apples or 8 parts. We could also note that 4 out of 50 apples is the fraction 4/50 which is equivalent to 8/100 so 4 apples is 8% of 50 apples.

Typically we calculate percentages using fractions or decimals.

$$8\% \text{ of } 50 = 8/100 \times 50 = 0.08 \times 50 = 4$$

You'll note that 8% = 0.08 = 8/100.

If asked to compute a fixed percentage of a number we just multiply.

> What is b% of c?
>
> $$\frac{b}{100} \times c = \underline{\hspace{2cm}}$$

EXAMPLE 1

Bob saved 10% of his paycheck for his Friday night date. If his paycheck was $435 how much can he spend on the date?

Solution: 10% of 435 = 10/100 × 435 = 43.5. If you prefer decimals, 10% of 435 = 0.10 × 435 = 43.5. Bob has $43.50 for his date.

> *a is what percentage of c?*
>
> *a =* ____ *% of c*

If asked to find a percentage we can set up a fraction and convert to a decimal.

EXAMPLE 2

Ellen paid $14 of the $35 dinner bill on a date with Bob. What percentage of the bill did she pay? Was the bill split equally?

Solution: You might directly compute 14/35 = 0.4, which is 40/100 or 40%. Why does this work? We need to find what percentage of 35 will equal 14, that is x % of 35 = 14. $\dfrac{x}{100} \times 35 = 14$ so $x = 14 \times \dfrac{100}{35} = \dfrac{14}{35} \times 100 = 40$. Thus Ellen paid only 40% of the bill—not an equal share.

> *a is b% of what?*
>
> *a = b% of* ____

If asked to find a number so that a fixed percentage of it will be a given number, we can divide.

EXAMPLE 3

If Ellen has only $14 and wants to pay 50% of the dinner bill, what should they spend on dinner?

Solution: We set up an equation and solve for x.
50% of x = $14 so 50/100 $\times$ x = $14 or 1/2 $\times$ x = $14, hence x = 2 $\times$ $14 = $28. If you prefer decimals, 0.50 $\times$ x = $14 so x = $14/0.50 = $28. Thus Ellen can afford 50% of the bill if it is $28 (or less).

We often use percentages to describe changes to a value. The percentage involved might compare the change (increase or decrease) to the old value or it might compare the new value to the old value. You must read a question carefully to distinguish between these two situations.

EXAMPLE 4

Ellen's salary was increased by 150% from 2007 to 2008. If she earned $50,000 in 2007, what does she earn in 2008?

   (A) $65,000
   (B) $75,000
   (C) $125,000
   (D) $150,000
   (E) $200,000

Solution: In this case, we compare the *increase* in Ellen's salary to her original (2007) salary. So the increase (new− old) is 150% of $50,000 = 150/100 $\times$ $50,000 = $75,000. Thus Ellen's salary was increased by $75,000. Ellen's new salary is $50,000 + $75,000 = $125,000. Choose **C**.

EXAMPLE 5

Bob's salary for 2008 is 150% of his 2007 salary. If he earned $50,000 in 2007, what does he earn in 2008?

(A) $65,000
(B) $75,000
(C) $125,000
(D) $150,000
(E) $200,000

Solution: In this case we compare Bob's 2008 salary with his 2007 salary. His 2008 salary is 150% of $50,000 = 150/100 × $50,000 = $75,000. Bob's salary in 2008 is $75,000. Choose **B**.

EXAMPLE 6

Column A	Column B

Ellen was given a raise of x %. Her salary increased from $80,000 to $85,000.

x %	6 %

Solution: Let's compare the raise to her salary. She got a raise of $5,000. That is what percentage of $80,000? x % of $80,000 = $5,000 so x/100 × $80,000 = $5,000. Hence x = $5,000/$80,000 × 100 = 6.25. So Ellen received a 6.25% raise. Choose **A**.

Alternatively, 6% of $80,000 = 6/100 × $80,000 = 6 × $800 = $4,800. Her raise was more than $4,800 so x % must be more than 6%.

> **TIP**
>
> a% of b is equal to b% of a.

EXAMPLE 7

Column A	Column B
25% of $40	40% of $25

Solution: First, 25% of $40 = 0.25 × $40 = $\frac{1}{4}$ × $40 = $10. Second, 40% of $25 = 0.40 × $25 = $\frac{4}{10}$ × $25 = $\frac{\$100}{10}$ = $10. In either case, we get the same value, so 25% of $40 = 40% of $25. Choose **C**.

To calculate prices with tax at a % just multiply by $1 + a/100$.

EXAMPLE 8

A shirt costs $20 and sales tax is 7%. What is the total cost including tax?

(A) $27.00
(B) $21.40
(C) $21.07
(D) $21.04
(E) $20.07

Solution: The tax paid is 7% of $20 = 0.07 × $20 = $1.40. The total cost is $20 + $1.40 = $21.40. Choose **B**. Alternatively, the total cost is 1.07 × $20 = $21.40. The techniques are equivalent because of the distributive property: $21.40 = $20 + $1.40 = $20 + ($20 × 0.07) = $20 × (1 + 0.07) = $20 × 1.07.

It does not matter if you add tax before or after a percentage cut in price.

EXAMPLE 9

If there was a 20% discount, what would the total paid for the shirt be?

(A) $16.00
(B) $16.07
(C) $16.13
(D) $17.12
(E) $17.40

Solution: If we calculate tax first, we get $21.40 and then discount it by 20% to get $21.40 less 20% of $21.40 = $21.40−(0.2 × $21.40) = $21.40 − $4.28 = $17.12. If we calculate the discount first, we get $20 less 20% of $20, which is $20 − (0.2 × $20) = $20 − $4 = $16. We then add 7% tax by multiplying $16 × 1.07 = $17.12. It may seem surprising, but either way you get the same result. Why? Because 0.8 × (1.07 × $20) = 1.07 × (0.8 × $20). Choose **D.**

If a number is decreased by a percentage and then increased by the same percentage, the result is LESS than the original number. The larger the percentage the greater the difference will be.

EXAMPLE 10

Column A	Column B

Norma accepted a 10% pay cut rather than lose her job. One year later the company gave her a 10% raise.

Norma's original salary	Norma's final salary

Solution: Assume Norma made $100 (it's a nice easy number to deal with even if it is unrealistic). After the pay cut her salary was $90. Then they increased her salary by 10%. But 10% of $90 is just $9. So now her salary is $99, which is less than her original salary of $100. Generalizing we can see that her salary will be only 99% of its original value. Choose **A.**

Problems

Column A	Column B

35 is x % of 50

	Column A	Column B
1.	x% of 100	$2x$
2.	6% of 60	60% of 6
3.	200% of $35,000	35% of $180,000

4. Mary's salary was $50,000. She now earns $75,000. The percentage increase in her salary was

   (A) 25%
   (B) 50%
   (C) 75%
   (D) 150%
   (E) 200%

5. Mary's old salary was $60,000. Her new salary is 150% of her old salary. What is her new salary?

   (A) $60,000
   (B) $75,000
   (C) $80,000
   (D) $90,000
   (E) $150,000

	Column A	Column B
6.	$10 less 20% plus 8% tax	$8 less 10% plus 20% tax

$$62\% \text{ of } x = 84$$

7.	x	84% of x, plus 10%

8. If Ellen invested $5,000 in a real estate deal and was repaid $5,700, what percentage profit did she earn?

   (A) 5%
   (B) 7%
   (C) 10%
   (D) 14%
   (E) 15%

9. The first 50 questions on the exam were multiple choice and worth 80% of the grade. The last four questions were essay style and worth 20% of the grade. Questions of each type are weighted equally. If Bob scored 73% on the exam and answered only one essay question, how many multiple-choice questions could he have answered correctly?

   (A) 30
   (B) 34
   (C) 40
   (D) 45
   (E) 46

10. A "Wake Me Up" is made up of six ounces of cola (1% caffeine), 3 ounces of coffee (3% caffeine), and 1 ounce of espresso (10% caffeine). What percentage of a "Wake Me Up" is caffeine?

    (A) 1%
    (B) 1.5%
    (C) 2%
    (D) 2.5%
    (E) 3%

AVERAGES

How can you describe a large set of numbers with only one value? There are three common ways to describe the "central tendencies" of a set of values: *mean, median,* and *mode*.

The *mean* is the sum of the values divided by the number of values. This is more commonly called the average of the numbers. To be clear, on the GRE this is always referred to as the "average (arithmetic mean)." For example, 6 is the average (arithmetic mean) of 4, 8, 5, and 7 since $\frac{4 + 8 + 5 + 7}{4} = \frac{24}{4} = 6$.

If you list a set of values in order (from lowest to highest), the value in the middle is the *median*. For instance $200K is the median price among this list of home sale prices: $145K, $190K, $200K, $201K, $205K. If there is an even number of values, there is no middle value so we take the average of the two middle values as the median.

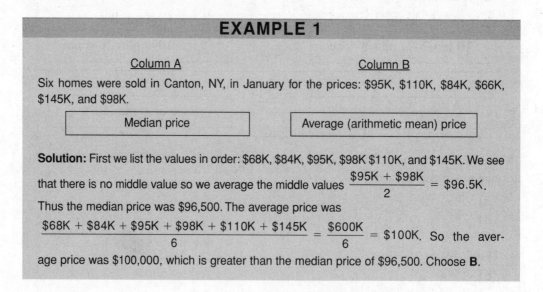

EXAMPLE 1

Column A	Column B

Six homes were sold in Canton, NY, in January for the prices: $95K, $110K, $84K, $66K, $145K, and $98K.

Median price	Average (arithmetic mean) price

Solution: First we list the values in order: $68K, $84K, $95K, $98K $110K, and $145K. We see that there is no middle value so we average the middle values $\frac{\$95K + \$98K}{2} = \$96.5K$.

Thus the median price was $96,500. The average price was

$\frac{\$68K + \$84K + \$95K + \$98K + \$110K + \$145K}{6} = \frac{\$600K}{6} = \$100K$. So the average price was $100,000, which is greater than the median price of $96,500. Choose **B**.

In a list of values the *mode* is the most frequently occurring value. For example 6 is the mode for the set of values: {2, 3, 7, 6, 6, 8, 2, 6} since 6 occurs three times. The value 2 only occurs twice, and all other values occur once. Unlike mean and median, the mode of a set may not be unique. All of the values that occur most frequently can be called the mode. In the worse case, like {1, 2, 3, 4}, every value is the mode.

EXAMPLE 2

Column A	Column B

Consider the set of values $S = \{1, 1, 2, 3, 3, 4, 4, 5, 5\}$

Median of S	Mode of S

Solution: The median is 3, but the mode is not unique. All of 1, 3, 4, and 5 are the mode. The median could be greater than the mode, $3 > 1$, equal to the mode, $3 = 3$, or less than the mode, $3 < 4$. Choose **D**.

The average of 83, 84, and 85 is 84 because

$$\frac{83 + 84 + 85}{3} = \frac{(84 - 1) + 84 + (84 + 1)}{3} = \frac{84 + 84 + 84}{3} = 84$$

If there are an even number of values in the sequence the average is the mean of the two middle values.

> **TIP**
>
> The average of any sequence of consecutive numbers is always the middle value.

EXAMPLE 3

What is the average of the integers from 9 through 16 inclusive?

(A) 12
(B) 12.5
(C) 13
(D) 13.5
(E) 14

Solution: In this case there are eight summands: 9, 10, 11, 12, 13, 14, 15, and 16. The middle terms are 12 and 13 whose mean is $\frac{12 + 13}{2} = 12.5$. So the average of the integers 9 through 16 is 12.5. Choose **B**.

   This property is also true for any arithmetic sequence—one where values are separated by a fixed value.

EXAMPLE 4

What is the average of 81, 85, 89, 93, and 97?

(A) 87
(B) 88
(C) 89
(D) 90
(E) 91

Solution: This is an arithmetic sequence since there is a common difference of 4. Thus the average is the middle term, 89. Choose **C**.

It is easy to understand this property and other properties of averages if you think of averaging as sharing. When you average a set of numbers, you redistribute their values so that they all will have equal values. It is easy to see why this works for an arithmetic sequence but is also valid in general.

EXAMPLE 5

Find the average of 305, 310, and 315.

Solution: Think of sharing—take 5 from 315 and give it to 305.

305	310	315
+5		−5
310	310	310

Now all three values will be the same—310. Thus 310 is the average.

EXAMPLE 6

Mary earned 80, 83, 84, 89, and 89 on five tests. What is her average?

(A) 83
(B) 84
(C) 84.5
(D) 85
(E) 89

Solution: First we take 4 from 89 and give it to 80. Then we take 1 from the other 89 and give it to 83. Now we have 84, 84, 84, 88, and 85. We take three from 88 and share it among the 84's, giving each one. Now we see that Mary's average is 85. Choose **D**.

80	83	84	89	89
+4	+1		−1	−4
84	84	84	88	85
+1	+1	+1	−3	
85	85	85	85	85

TIP

To find the average of unknown values don't try to solve for the values. Try adding the equations together and look for the average.

This technique is not good in all situations. But it can be useful for values that are relatively close in value and values that would be tedious to add.

EXAMPLE 7

Column A	Column B
$2x + y = 8$ and $x + 2y = 10$	
Average (arithmetic mean) of x and y	4

Solution: Adding the two equations together, we find that $3x + 3y = 18$. If we divide by 3 we see that $x + y = 6$. We want to find the average of x and y, that is $\frac{x + y}{2}$. So we divide $x + y = 6$ by 2 to get $\frac{x + y}{2} = 3$. Thus the average of x and y is 3. Choose **B**.

Sometimes you do not need to find the average—rather you are asked to find the total of the values. Knowing that Average = Total/n we see that the Total = Average × n.

EXAMPLE 8

If the average weight of a U.S. penny is 2.5 g, what is the weight of $1,000 in pennies?

(A) 2,500 g
(B) 25 kg
(C) 25,000 g
(D) 250 kg
(E) 1,000 kg

Solution: $1,000 equals 100,000 pennies. The total weight is the average weight times the number of pennies. Then 2.5 g × 100,000 = 250,000 g, which is 250 kg. Choose **D**.

A very common type of problem on the GRE involves completing a data set to get a desired average. Knowing how to get the total from the average is the key skill to solving this kind of problem.

EXAMPLE 9

Harold has caught three bass at the fishing tournament. They weight 4 lb, 6 lb, and 4.5 lb. If he needs four fish with an average weight of 5 lb each to win the tournament, how big a fish does he need to catch?

(A) 3.5 lb
(B) 5 lb
(C) 5.5 lb
(D) 6 lb
(E) 6.5 lb

Solution: If he had four fish with an average of 5 lb, their total weight is the average times the number of fish, that is $4 \times 5 = 20$ lb. His current three fish weight a total of $4 + 6 + 4.5 = 14.5$ lb. He needs $20 - 14.5 = 5.5$ lb more. Choose **C**.

 Alternate Solution: If you prefer algebra, let F be the weight of Harold's fourth fish. We need $(F + 4 + 4.5 + 6)/4 = 5$. Multiply both sides by 4 to get $F + 4 + 4.5 + 6 = 20$. Subtract and we have $F = 5.5$. It's really the same computations—we just think about it differently.

Problems

Column A	Column B
Average (arithmetic mean) of 4, 7, 9	Average (arithmetic mean) of 4, 7, 10

1.

$$A = \{1, 1, 1, 2, 2, 3, 3, 3, 3, 5, 7, 9\}$$

Mode of A	Median of A

2.

Average (arithmetic mean) of A	3

3.

4. Mary received 82, 84, 90, and 88 on her first four tests. What score on test five would give her exactly an 85 average?

(A) 70
(B) 81
(C) 82
(D) 85
(E) 90

5. Seven houses were sold last month in Potsdam, NY. The sale prices in thousands of dollars were $85K, $57K, $104K, $90K, x, y, and $99K. If the mode was $57K and the median price was $90K, then which of the following could be x and y?

   (A) x = $57K and y = $75K
   (B) x = $88K and y = $75K
   (C) x = $57K and y = $95K
   (D) x = $88K and y = $75K
   (E) x = $98K and y = $107K

6. If the average (arithmetic mean) of 7 consecutive odd integers is 21, what is the smallest of the 7 odd integers?

   (A) 1
   (B) 11
   (C) 15
   (D) 18
   (E) 27

7. If the average (arithmetic mean) of six consecutive integers is 9.5, then what is the largest of the six integers?

   (A) 8
   (B) 9
   (C) 10
   (D) 12
   (E) 14

8. Mary needs an average of 85 in her math class to keep her scholarship. She received 82, 84, 90, and 88 on her first four tests. She expects to fail test five but do well on test six—the final test. What is the lowest grade she could get on test five and still possibly keep her scholarship?

   (A) 66
   (B) 68
   (C) 70
   (D) 86
   (E) 90

9. Mary received the same grade on her first four tests and 10 points better on her fifth test. If her average is 82 what score did she receive on her fifth test?

   (A) 80
   (B) 84
   (C) 90
   (D) 92
   (E) 100

10. The average score on the surprise quiz was 7/10. Three students earned a 0, two earned only 1, and one earned a 2. No student earned a perfect score. What is the least number of students there could have been in the class?

(A) 5
(B) 11
(C) 23
(D) 25
(E) 100

11. The average score on the surprise quiz was 8.5/10. If no one earned a perfect score and there are 10 students in the class, what is the lowest score a student could have earned?

(A) 0
(B) 1
(C) 2
(D) 3
(E) 4

12. Let a and b be integers so that $0 < a < 10$ and $20 < b < 30$. If A is the average of a and b, then which of the following MUST be true?

(A) $A < 15$
(B) $A > 15$
(C) $11 < A$
(D) $19 < A$
(E) $A < 20$

CHARTS AND GRAPHS

Look at any business report and you will find it full of many tables, charts, and diagrams. Humans find it easier to understand data when presented graphically. Questions on the GRE regarding data analysis test whether you can read those diagrams carefully to obtain reasonably precise information. The main types of diagrams used are pie charts, tables, line graphs, and bar graphs.

Data are usually summarized in tables by tallying which data elements belong to each of several categories.

North America Population (in millions)	United States	Canada	Mexico	Guatemala	Cuba	Others
519	300	33	106	15	11	54

An alternative to the table, pie charts can be used to show what percentage of the data belong to each category. In the following chart it is easy to see that the United States has more than half the population of the continent or that Canada and Mexico together do not have as many people as the United States. Notice the title often includes

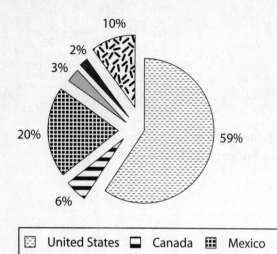

North American Population—519 Milion

important information—in this case the total population. This would allow you (using the percentages) to determine the population of each country. For instance, the population of Mexico is 519 × 20% = 519 × 0.2 = 103.8 million people. (Notice this value is not exactly the same as the figure in the table. Rounding in the pie chart places Mexico at 20% when in actual fact they are 106/519 = 20.42%. This kind of discrepancy can affect all data analysis questions. In most cases, a good estimate is sufficient—exact values may be difficult to provide.)

Pie charts can also just be labeled with the data values though you can estimate the percentages just by looking at the pie. Notice the title indicates the units.

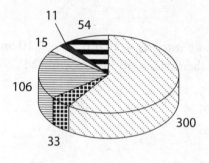

North American Population (in millions)

EXAMPLE 1

Which countries have more than 20% of the North American Population?

   I. United States
  II. Cuba
 III. Mexico

(A) I only
(B) II only
(C) III only
(D) I and II
(E) I and III

Solution: Let's estimate. 25% of the whole would be represented by a quarter pie. The United States has more than a quarter of the pie. The only other country close to a quarter pie is Mexico, so it is the only other country with more than 20% of the North American population. Choose **E**.

Especially when the categories are years, a bar graph is a useful way to compare data from category to category. The following graph shows how the population of all three countries is distributed. It is clear than Mexico has a larger portion of the population in 2000 than 1960, since their blue bar is larger in 2000. Meanwhile, Canada seems to occupy roughly the same percentage of the population in the last 50 years—since their bar is about the same size in all five graphs. Note that this graph does not tell us how the overall population has been growing. The population may even be shrinking!

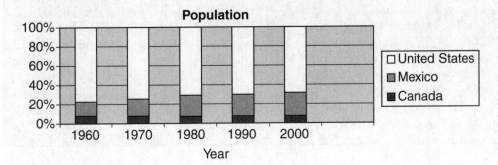

Line graphs provide the information in a way that emphasizes the trends or rates of change. Again this is most often used for categories that are years. First of all we note that population is growing in all three countries. More precisely, the rate of growth in the United States and Mexico is similar, but the rate of growth in Canada is slower. This is clear because the *slope* of the Canada line is less than the slope of the others.

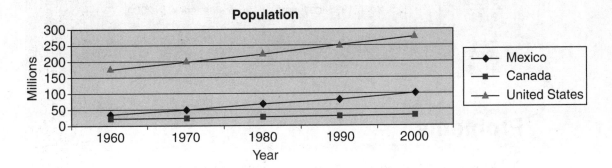

TIP

Watch for totals. In most pie charts it is important to know what the whole pie represents. If it is a pie of U.S. voters, you want to know how many U.S. voters there are. If it is a pie of world countries, you want to know how many countries there are. In some cases, the information is given somewhere on the chart; in other cases, you may need to total the values of each category to get the total. For example on page 146 you would have to total the populations of each country ($300 + 33 + 106 + 15 + 11 + 54 = 519$) to see that the North American population is 519 million.

Watch for percentages as opposed to values. In many charts, you are given percentages not actual values. In "All U.S. Companies Ownership" chart (see problems 5–8 at end of this section) you can see from the right bar that female-owned companies have around 5% of all company revenues. That does not tell you how much revenue they have. To determine actual revenues, you would need to know the total revenue as well. If the total revenue is $22 trillion, then female-owned companies have revenue of $22 \times 5\% = 22 \times 0.05 = \$1.1$ trillion.

Watch for connecting tables. When given multiple tables, information from one table is often connected to information from other tables. Some questions cannot be answered by using just one of the tables but requires information from both tables to find a solution. See problem 12 below.

Estimate, don't calculate. It is impossible to determine precise figures from the given charts. Try to make good estimates and quick calculations. That is usually sufficient to determine the correct answer. Be careful though—a very loose estimate may lead you to an incorrect answer.

In problem 5 below, you might estimate that the percentage of female-owned firms is 30% and calculate 23 million × 0.30 = 6.9 million. If you were to choose the closest answer, 7.1 million, you would be incorrect. If you were to wisely infer the answer must be less than 6.9 million since the percentage is less than 30% and choose (D) 6.4 million, you would be correct. Alternatively a better estimate of 28% leads one to calculate 23 million × 0.28 = 6.64 million and choose the correct answer of D.

Indexes are a commonly used term in economics and other fields. When comparing data from year to year, they use a fixed point in time as the index value (100). All other values are expressed as a percentage of that value (without the percentage symbol).

EXAMPLE 2

In 1990, the Widmaker Company produced 120,000 widgets. If 1990 is the index year and they made 150,000 widgets in 1995, what value would that have on the index? What value on the index would 2000 have when they made only 80,000 widgets?

Solution: The index value is 120,000. So we express 150,000 as a percentage of 120,000.

$$\frac{150,000}{120,000} \times 100 = 125.$$ So in 1995 they were at 125 on the index. In 2000,

$$\frac{80,000}{120,000} \times 100 = 66.6,$$ so they were at 66.6 on the index.

Problems

Problems 1–4 and 9 and 10 concern the following diagram.

Australian Population 2002
21 Million

- ☑ New South Wales
- ☐ Victoria
- ⊞ Queensland
- ☒ Western Australia
- ☐ South Australia
- ◀ Tasmania
- ☰ Australian Capital Territory
- ☐ Northern Territory

	Column A	Column B
1.	Population of Queensland	Population of New South Wales
2.	Population of Victoria	7,000,000
3.	500,000	Population living in Territories

4. If the population of Queensland doubles (while all other regions remain the same), what will be Queensland's percentage of the Australian population?

(A) 20%
(B) 30%
(C) 33%
(D) 40%
(E) 50%

Problems 5–8 concern the following diagrams.

5. If there are 23 million companies in the United States, how many of them have totally female ownership?

   (A) 1.15 million
   (B) 3.8 million
   (C) 5 million
   (D) 6.4 million
   (E) 7.1 million

6. If 17.5 million U.S. companies do not have employees, then how many U.S. firms with employees have totally female ownership?

   (A) 500,000
   (B) 650,000
   (C) 1,000,000
   (D) 3.5 million
   (E) 5 million

	Column A	Column B
7.	Average receipts per female company	Average receipts per male company
8.	Average salary in public company	Average salary in nonpublic company

9. Forecasts predict the population of Australia will grow by 10% in the next 10 years, but the population of Queensland will remain the same. What percentage of the Australian population will reside in Queensland in 2012?

   (A) 10%
   (B) 15%
   (C) 18%
   (D) 20%
   (E) 30%

10. A political restructuring is proposed where 25% of New South Wales citizens will become citizens of Queensland, and South Australia and Victoria will merge to become New Victoria. If the restructuring goes forth, what will be the most populous of the new states?

   (A) Queensland
   (B) New South Wales
   (C) New Victoria
   (D) Western Australia
   (E) South Australia

Problems 11–14 refer to the following charts describing marijuana use among 12 to 17 year olds.

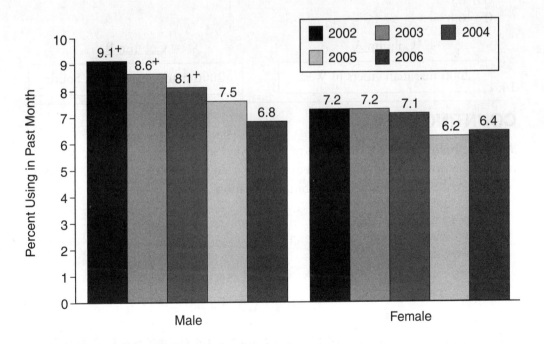

11. Marijuana use is generally decreasing, except in which of the following instances?

(A) 2004–2005 in the West
(B) 2002–2003 among males
(C) 2005–2006 in Midwest
(D) 2005–2006 among females
(E) 2003–2004 in Northeast

12. Male marijuana use in all categories is higher than female marijuana use. In which of the following is the overall marijuana use higher than the national male marijuana use for that year.

(A) 2002 Midwest
(B) 2003 Northeast
(C) 2004 South
(D) 2005 West
(E) 2006 South

For problems 13–14 assume the number of 12 to 17 year olds in 2006 were as follows:

Notheast	Midwest	South	West
7 million	4 million	17 million	13 million

13. *Nationally,* what would be the percentage of 12 to 17 years olds that had tried marijuana in the past month for 2006?

(A) 5.6%
(B) 6.0%
(C) 6.5%
(D) 6.6%
(E) 6.8%

Column A	Column B
2006 marijuana users in West	2006 marijuana users in South

14.

COUNTING

There are many problems that ask how many ways something can happen. Although it's not as simple as what you learned in kindergarten, we call that counting. The most fundamental problems involve combining situations.

> **Basic Counting Principle**
> If there are *m* ways to do *X* and *n* ways to do *Y*, then there are *m* × *n* ways to do *X* and *Y*.

EXAMPLE 1

A combination door lock has a two symbol access code. The first digit is A, B, C, or D. The second is 1, 2, 3, 4, or 5. How many different access codes are there? How many access codes have only consonants and even numbers in them?

(A) 20
(B) 16
(C) 12
(D) 9
(E) 6

Solution: According to the counting principle, since there are four choices for the first symbol (A, B, C, or D) and five choices for the second symbol (1, 2, 3, 4, 5) there are $4 \times 5 = 20$ possible access codes. We list them all in the hopes you see why this principle works.

		2nd Symbol				
		1	**2**	**3**	**4**	**5**
1st Symbol	**A**	A1	A2	A3	A4	A5
	B	B1	B2	B3	B4	B5
	C	C1	C2	C3	C4	C5
	D	D1	D2	D3	D4	D5

If the first symbol has to be a consonant there are only three choices (B, C, or D). The second symbol has to be even so there are two choices (2 or 4). Hence, there are $3 \times 2 = 6$ possible access codes that are made of a consonants and an even number. Choose **E**.

EXAMPLE 2

Column A	Column B
Gary has 4 pairs of pants, 4 ties, and 4 shirts.	
Number of outfits if he loses a tie and a shirt	Number of outfits if he loses 2 pants

Solution: The counting principle applies even to more than two situations. Here Gary has $4 \times 4 \times 4$ outfits to begin with, since he has a choice of 4 pants, 4 ties, and 4 shirts. In both cases he loses two articles of clothing so the result is the same, right? Wrong. If he loses a tie and a shirt he now has $4 \times 3 \times 3 = 36$ outfits. If he loses two pants, he now has $2 \times 4 \times 4 = 32$ outfits. Choose **A**.

EXAMPLE 3

If x and y are integers so that $1 \leq x < 5$ and $2 < y < 7$, how many possible values could xy have?

(A) 30
(B) 25
(C) 20
(D) 16
(E) 13

Solution: Since $1 \leq x < 5$ and x is an integer, there are four choices for x: 1, 2, 3, and 4. Since $2 < y < 7$ and y is in integer, there are 4 choices for y: 3, 4, 5, and 6. So by the counting principle, we expect there are $4 \times 4 = 16$ possible values for xy. Unfortunately, this is wrong. There are 16 possible products, but some of them have the same value. Let's see:

$1 \times 3 = 3$	$2 \times 3 = 6$	$3 \times 3 = 9$	$4 \times 3 = 12$
$1 \times 4 = 4$	$2 \times 4 = 8$	$3 \times 4 = 12$	$4 \times 4 = 16$
$1 \times 5 = 5$	$2 \times 5 = 10$	$3 \times 5 = 15$	$4 \times 5 = 20$
$1 \times 6 = 6$	$2 \times 6 = 12$	$3 \times 6 = 18$	$4 \times 6 = 24$

As you can see from the table, some values are repeated. So we actually have only 13 different possible values for *xy*. You don't actually have to check all these possible values. After determining there were at most 16 possible values and knowing that some of them were repeated, you would know the actual answer was less than 16. Thus the only possible answer is **E**.

Venn Diagrams

There are 100 students at Baltimore High School—60 ride the bus and 60 walk. How is that possible? Wouldn't that make 120 students? No, because 20 do both.

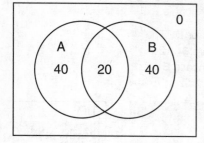

They walk in the morning but take the bus after school.

Often we count objects in groups, instead of individually. When we do so, some groups overlap and we can, unintentionally, over-count the objects. Venn diagrams are a way to avoid this. Each circular region inside the diagram represents the objects with a given trait. In this case we have a region (A) for bus riders and a region (B) for walkers. The overlap of regions represents those who do both. The area outside the regions represents those who do neither, in this case—none.

EXAMPLE 4

Of the 120 students at Regina High School, 70 own a PC, 20 own both a Mac and a PC, and 30 own neither. How many own a Mac but not a PC?

(A) 0
(B) 10
(C) 20
(D) 30
(E) 50

Solution: We use a Venn diagram. As 70 people own a PC and 20 own a PC and a Mac, we conclude that 50 own just a PC. And 30 own neither. Now we can count those distinct groups to see that 30 + 20 + 50 = 100 students are accounted for, of the 120 students at the school. That leaves 120−100 = 20 students who must own a Mac but not a PC. Choose **C**.

Partitions

A common counting problem is to find out how many ways a given positive integer can be represented as the sum of smaller positive integers. For the number 5, there are six different "partitions": $5 = 4 + 1$, $5 = 3 + 2$, $5 = 3 + 1 + 1$, $5 = 2 + 2 + 1$, $5 = 2 + 1 + 1 + 1$, and $5 = 1 + 1 + 1 + 1 + 1$. If you think of a chocolate bar with five pieces, this is asking how you can share the bar with others, if the smallest portion is one piece.

Sometimes you are asked to partition a number into just two parts (share with only one other person). Sometimes you are asked to partition into only certain size parts. All these restrictions can cause wrinkles but the basic principle remains the same. Break the analysis down into small cases and take it one at a time, being sure not to miss any possibilities.

EXAMPLE 5

How many different ways are there to write 11 as the sum of three positive integers? Order does not matter: $x + y + z = 11$ and $y + x + z = 11$ count as just one way.

Solution: I always organize my sums by the largest part. There is no way for the largest part to be 11, $0 + 0 + 11 = 11$ but each part has to be at least 1. Similarly the largest part cannot be 10.

Largest Part Nine: $9 + 1 + 1$
Largest Part Eight: $8 + 2 + 1$
Largest Part Seven: $7 + 3 + 1, 7 + 2 + 2$ Notice that once you fix 7 as the largest part you are really looking at finding all the ways to write $11 - 7 = 4$ as the sum of two parts: $4 = 3 + 1$ and $4 = 2 + 2$.
Largest Part Six: $6 + 4 + 1, 6 + 3 + 2$
Largest Part Five: $5 + 5 + 1, 5 + 4 + 2, 5 + 3 + 3$
Largest Part Four: $4 + 4 + 3$

It's impossible to have three numbers add to 11 if the largest is 3 or less. So there are 10 different ways to write 11 as the sum of three positive integers.

EXAMPLE 6

Column A	Column B
A total of 58¢ in 7¢ and 4¢ stamps	
Number of stamps	11

Solution: This question really asks you to write 58 as the sum of two positive integers, one a multiple of 4 and the other a multiple of 7. Since 58 is odd, we cannot use an odd multiple of 7. For example, we use one 7, then some multiple of 4 would have to be $58 - 7 = 51$, which is impossible. I suggest proceeding according to the number of sevens used.

Zero: There cannot be zero 7's since 58 is not divisible by 4.

Two: If we have two 7's, then we need $58 - (2 \times 7) = 44$ as a multiple of 4. As $44 = 11 \times 4$, take 2 seven-cent stamps and 11 four-cent stamps.

Four: If we have four 7's, then we need $58 - (4 \times 7) = 30$ as a multiple of 4. But 30 is not divisible by 4. No answer in this case.

Six: If we have six 7's, then we need $58 - (6 \times 7) = 16$ as a multiple of 4. As $16 = 4 \times 4$, take 6 seven-cent stamps and 4 four-cent stamps.

Eight: If we have eight 7's, then we need $58 - (8 \times 7) = 2$ as a multiple of 4. Impossible. And clearly more than 8 seven-cent stamps is also impossible.

So there are only two possibilities— $(2 \times 7¢) + (11 \times 4¢) = 58¢$ or $(6 \times 7¢) + (4 \times 4¢) = 58¢$. That is a total of 13 or 10 stamps respectively. In one case this is greater than 11 and in the other less than 11. Choose **D**.

Counting Commas

How many numbers are there from 1 to 10? Anyone would say 10, which is correct. How many numbers are there from 3 to 10? Since $10-3 = 7$, most people say 7 which is incorrect. There are actually 8. Let's investigate carefully.

Number to Count	Number Listed	End-Start	Actual Count	Count of Commas
1 to 10	1, 2, 3, 4, 5, 6, 7, 8, 9, 10	$10-1 = 9$	10	9
3 to 10	3, 4, 5, 6, 7, 8, 9, 10	$10-3 = 7$	8	7

When you subtract the starting number from the ending number you are actually counting the number of commas! If you prefer, think of it as the number of spaces between the numbers. The count of numbers in the list is always one more than the number of commas.

EXAMPLE 7

Column A   Column B

In a 200-page book, photos appear on pages 50 through 150

Number of pages without photos   Number of pages with photos

Solution: At first glance, most people would think that 100 pages have photos and thus $200-100 = 100$ do not. Of course page 50 through 150 means $150-50 + 1 = 101$ pages with photos. Thus there are $200-101 = 99$ pages without photos. Choose **B**.

TIP

- The sum of the first n positive integers is $n(n + 1)/2$. For example, $1 + 2 + 3 + \ldots + 17 = 17(18)/2 = 153$.

- The sum of the first n odd numbers is n^2. For example $1 + 3 + 5 + 7 + 9 = 5^2 = 25$.

EXAMPLE 8

On the first day of his Vegas vacation, Jerry lost $100 gambling. On the second day, he lost $200. On the third day, he lost $300. If the pattern continues for 9 days in total, how much does he need to win on the tenth day to break even for the trip?

(A) $3,000
(B) $3,500
(C) $4,000
(D) $4,500
(E) $5,500

Solution: Jerry lost $100 + $200 + \ldots + $900 = $100(1 + 2 + 3 + \ldots + 9) = $100 \times (9)(10)/2 = $100 \times 45 = $4,500. Choose **D**.

Problems

Basic Problems

	Column A	Column B
1.	Sum of first 25 positive integers	250
2.	Sum of first 25 odd positive integers	600

A lock has a three digit combination from 000 to 999

	Column A	Column B
3.	Combinations with no zeros	Combinations with no ones
4.	Number of partitions of 7	7

5. Theresa's wardrobe has seven blouses, four pairs of pants, and three belts. How many different outfits can she make?

   (A) 14
   (B) 36
   (C) 49
   (D) 84
   (E) 160

6. At Brebeuf College, there are 124 students in the band and 78 students who play rugby. If 12 students do both and 44 students do neither, how many students attend Brebeuf?

   (A) 156
   (B) 200
   (C) 202
   (D) 204
   (E) 234

GRE Problems

	Column A	Column B
7.	Sum of first 50 positive integers	Sum of first 35 odd positive integers

Questions 8–10 concern a book that has pages numbered 1 to 999.

	Column A	Column B
8.	Total number of digits used to number pages	2,800
9.	Number of pages numbered with a zero	Number of pages numbered with a one

10.	Number of pages numbered with a two		Number of pages numbered with a one

11.	Number of integers between -4 and 37 inclusive		Number of integers between 1 and 41 inclusive

12.	Number of ways to make 85¢ from 3¢ and 10¢ stamps		Number of ways to make 85¢ from 4¢ and 15¢ stamps.

13. If $4 < x \leqslant 7$ and $2 \leqslant y < 6$, then how many different values are there for the sum $x + y$?

    (A) 6
    (B) 9
    (C) 12
    (D) 20
    (E) 42

14. In a freshman calculus class of 34, students study in either the library or the math lab. 25 students study in the library and 15 study at the math lab. If all students study, what is the minimum number of students who study in both places?

    (A) 2
    (B) 3
    (C) 6
    (D) 8
    (E) 15

15. Chris is 12th in line and Sara is 27th in line for concert tickets. After Chris purchases his tickets, he informs Sara there are 114 tickets left for sale. If each person buys the maximum of 8 tickets, how many tickets will Sara get?

    (A) 0
    (B) 2
    (C) 4
    (D) 6
    (E) 8

PROBABILITY

Probability is the study of chance or the likelihood of an event occurring. If there are four equally likely outcomes to an experiment, we say each of them has a one in four chance of occurring. We also say the probability of each outcome is $\frac{1}{4}$.

EXAMPLE 1

George buys a raffle ticket from a local charity. They sell only 50 tickets. What is the probability George wins the grand prize?

Solution: Since each ticket is equally likely to be the winner, George has a one in fifty chance of winning. The probability of his winning is 1/50.

In any experiment, if all the possible outcomes are equally likely, the probability of an event, X, occurring is

$$P(X) = \frac{\text{Number of outcomes where } X \text{ occurs}}{\text{Total number of outcomes}}$$

$P(X)$ is 0 exactly when X cannot occur. $P(X)$ is 1 exactly when X always occurs. Otherwise $P(X)$ is between 0 and 1. The probability that an event will not occur is $1-P(X)$. The sum of all probabilities must be 1.

> **TIP**
>
> When experiments are repeated, the probability of getting event X and then event Y is the product of their probabilities.

EXAMPLE 2

A number is drawn randomly from 1 to 100. Find the probability of each of the following: (a) 105 is drawn, (b) an even number is drawn, (c) a number with zero in it is drawn, (d) a number without zero in it is drawn.

Solution:

(a) This is impossible—you can't draw 105 if only the numbers 1 to 100 are used. So the probability is zero.
(b) There are 50 even numbers and 100 possible outcomes so $P(\text{even}) = 50/100 = 1/2$.
(c) There are 10 numbers with a zero in them (10, 20, . . . , 80, 90,100). So the probability is $10/100 = 0.1$.
(d) The answer is one minus the probability of drawing a number with zero in it. That is $1-0.1 = 0.9$. Why? If 10 out of 100 numbers have a zero in them, then 90 have no zero in them. So the probability is $90/100 = 0.9$.

EXAMPLE 3

Roll one six sided die and flip a coin. What is the probability of getting Heads and a number bigger than 3?

(A) $\frac{1}{6}$

(B) $\frac{1}{4}$

(C) $\frac{1}{3}$

(D) $\frac{1}{2}$

(E) $\frac{2}{3}$

Solution: There are six possible die rolls and three of them are bigger than 3, namely 4, 5, and 6. So when rolling the die, three of the outcomes are positive. Thus $P(\text{die} > 3)$ is $\frac{3}{6} = \frac{1}{2}$.

The probability of getting heads when flipping a coin is $\frac{1}{2}$. So the probability of getting heads and a number greater than 3 is the product $\frac{1}{2} \times \frac{1}{2} = \frac{1}{4}$. Alternatively this can be solved by listing all possible outcomes:

1H	2H	3H	4H	5H	6H
1T	2T	3T	4T	5T	6T

Clearly 3 of the possible 12 outcomes are desired (4H, 5H, or 6H). So the probability is $\frac{3}{12} = \frac{1}{4}$. Choose **B**.

EXAMPLE 4

Roll two six sided dice. What is the probability of getting a *total* of 7?

(A) $\frac{1}{7}$

(B) $\frac{1}{6}$

(C) $\frac{7}{36}$

(D) $\frac{1}{3}$

(E) $\frac{5}{12}$

Solution: There are six possible outcomes for the first die and six possible outcomes for the second die, so there are $6 \times 6 = 36$ possible outcomes. We list them below.

Which of these outcomes give a total of seven? Only the shaded ones on the off-diagonal. Thus the probability of rolling a total of seven is $6/36 = \frac{1}{6}$.

1,1	1,2	1,3	1,4	1,5	1,6
2,1	2,2	2,3	2,4	2,5	2,6
3,1	3,2	3,3	3,4	3,5	3,6
4,1	4,2	4,3	4,4	4,5	4,6
5,1	5,2	5,3	5,4	5,5	5,6
6,1	6,2	6,3	6,4	6,5	6,6

Alternatively we could find $P(1,6) + P(2,5) + P(3,4) + P(4,3) + P(5,2) + P(6,1)$. For instance, $P(1,6) = P(1) \times P(6) = \frac{1}{6} \times \frac{1}{6} = \frac{1}{36}$. Similarly $P(2,5) = P(3,4) = P(4,3) = P(5,2) = P(6,1) = \frac{1}{36}$. Thus $P(1,6) + P(2,5) + P(3,4) + P(4,3) + P(5,2) + P(6,1) = 6 \times \frac{1}{36} = \frac{1}{6}$. Choose **B**.

Problems

Column A	Column B

For problems 1–3: In biology class, Mary is assigned a lab partner randomly. The other people in the class are Alice, Fred, Jamal, Sara, Tom, Vera, and Zoe.

1.

Probability her partner is Tom	Probability her partner is Zoe

| Probability her partner has a four-letter name | Probability her partner has a five-letter name |

2.

| Probability her partner is John | Probability her partner is male |

3.

For problems 4 and 5: John rolls a fair six-sided die.

| Probability of rolling an even number | Probability of not rolling 6 |

4.

| Probability of rolling greater than 2 | Probability of rolling a prime |

5.

6. Cole chooses a marble randomly from a jar that contains five white marbles, eight red marbles, and seven blue marbles. What is the probability he chooses a non-white marble?

(A) $\frac{1}{4}$

(B) $\frac{3}{4}$

(C) $\frac{1}{2}$

(D) $\frac{7}{8}$

(E) 1

7. Cole rolls two ten-sided dice (each has numbers 1–10). What is the probability that the sum of his numbers is 18 or better?

(A) $\frac{2}{9}$

(B) $\frac{3}{50}$

(C) 0.04

(D) 0.05

(E) 0.18

8. Veronica is flipping three fair coins. What is the probability that she ends up with more heads than tails?

(A) $\frac{1}{8}$

(B) $\frac{1}{4}$

(C) $\frac{3}{8}$

(D) $\dfrac{1}{2}$

(E) $\dfrac{5}{8}$

9. Marg designed a very unusual spinner for a game she created. What is the probability of spinning a 1 on this spinner?

(A) $\dfrac{1}{2}$

(B) $\dfrac{1}{3}$

(C) $\dfrac{1}{4}$

(D) $\dfrac{7}{24}$

(E) $\dfrac{11}{48}$

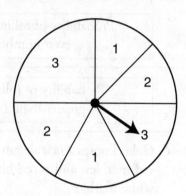

Column A   Column B

For questions 10 and 11: A jar contains eight marbles: two red, two green, and four white.

10. Probability of choosing two white marbles	Probability of choosing two green marbles
11. Probability of choosing white	Probability of choosing red or green

An experiment consists of flipping a fair coin three times. Results are heads (H) or tails (T).

12. Probability of flipping HHH	Probability of flipping HTH

For questions 13 and 14: You pick a number randomly from 1 to 100.

13. Probability of picking an even prime	Probability of picking 77
14. Probability of picking a prime	Probability of picking a multiple of 7

SOLUTIONS

Percentages

1. **(B)** You do not need to solve for x to answer this problem. We know that x % of 100 is always x. And x is less than $2x$ (as long as x is positive, which it is in

this case). If you want to solve for x, ask "35 is what percentage of 50?" So $x\% = 35/50 = 70/100$. Thus $x = 70$. Clearly 70 is less than $2 \times 70 = 140$. Choose **B**.

2. **(C)** 6% of 60 = $0.06 \times 60 = 3.6$ and 60% of 6 = $0.6 \times 6 = 3.6$. See the first tip in this section. Choose **C**.

3. **(A)** 200% of \$35,000 = $200/100 \times \$35,000 = \$70,000$. 35% of \$200,000 would also equal \$70,000 so 35% of \$180,000 must be less than \$70,000. Choose **A**.

4. **(B)** The increase is \$25,000. Compared to her original salary, $\dfrac{\$25,000}{\$50,000} = 0.5 = 50\%$. Choose **B**.

5. **(D)** 150% of \$60,000 = $150/100 \times \$60,000 = \$90,000$. Choose **D**.

6. **(C)** 20% of \$10 is \$2. So \$10 less 20% plus 8% tax is $1.08 \times \$8 = \$8.64$. 10% of \$8 is \$0.80. \$8 less 10% plus 20% tax is $1.20 \times \$7.20 = \$8.64$. This does not follow directly from $a\%$ of $b = b\%$ of a, but it is the same principle. Choose **C**.

7. **(A)** You do not need to solve for x to answer this problem. 84% of x, plus 10% is $(0.84x) \times 1.10 = 0.924x = 92.4\%$ of x, which is clearly less than x (as long as x is positive, which it is since 62% of x is 84.) Choose **A**.

8. **(D)** Ellen earned \$700 compared with an investment of \$5,000. The percentage profit is $\dfrac{\$700}{\$5,000} = 0.14 = 14\%$ Choose **D**.

9. **(C)** Bob earned at most 5 points on the essay question (1/4 of 20%). So he earned between 68 (if he got zero on the essay) and 73 (if he got five on the essay) out of 80 on the multiple-choice questions. Solving $x/50 = 68/80$, we find $x = 42.5$ so he got at least 42.5 multiple-choice questions correct. Solving $x/50 = 73/80$, we find $x = 45.6$ so he got at most 45.6 multiple-choice questions correct. Thus Bob got 43, 44, or 45 multiple-choice questions correct. Choose **C**.

10. **(D)** The cola contributes 1% of 6 oz = 0.01×6 oz = 0.06 oz of caffeine. The coffee contributes 3% of 3 oz = 0.03×3 oz = 0.09 oz of caffeine. The espresso contributes 10% of 1 oz = 0.10×1 oz = 0.1 oz of caffeine. That is a total of $0.06 + 0.09 + 0.1 = 0.25$ oz of caffeine in a 10 oz drink. As $\dfrac{0.25 \text{ oz}}{10 \text{ oz}} = 0.025 = 2.5\%$, the "Wake Me Up" is 2.5% caffeine. Choose **D**.

Averages

1. **(B)** The total in Column B is larger than the total in Column A. Since both have three numbers, the average will be larger in Column B. Alternatively, compute average A $= \dfrac{4 + 7 + 9}{3} = 6\dfrac{2}{3}$ and average B $= \dfrac{4 + 7 + 10}{3} = 7$. Choose **B**.

2. **(C)** The mode is 3 (it appears four times). There are 12 numbers in the list and the sixth and seventh numbers (the middle numbers) are both 3. Thus the median is also 3. Choose **C**.

3. **(A)** The average of A is $\dfrac{1 + 1 + 1 + 2 + 2 + 3 + 3 + 3 + 3 + 5 + 7 + 9}{12} =$

   $\dfrac{40}{12} = 3\dfrac{1}{3}$, which is bigger than 3. Choose **A**.

4. **(B)** Let x be her score on the fifth test, then $\dfrac{82 + 84 + 90 + 88 + x}{5} = 85$.

   So $82 + 84 + 90 + 88 + x = 5 \times 85$. Solving, we find $x = 81$. Alternatively, if we think of averaging as sharing and always share with x, we find x plus 4 must be 85. The fifth test grade must be 81. This technique avoids adding, multiplying, or dividing large numbers. Choose **B**.

$$
\begin{array}{ccccc}
82 & 84 & 90 & 88 & \underline{x} \\
+3 & +1 & -5 & -3 & -3 \\
 & & & & -1 \\
 & & & & +5 \\
 & & & & +3 \\
\\
85 & 85 & 85 & 85 & 85
\end{array}
$$

5. **(C)** First we list them in order: $57K, $85K, $90K, $99K, $104K, and x and y. There are seven sale values so $90K being the median means three were priced above or equal to $90K and three were priced below or equal to $90K. C is the only answer that satisfies this. All other answers have both values below $90K. Also $x = $57K guarantees the unique mode is $57K. Choose **C**.

6. **(C)** By our first tip, we know 21 is the middle integer, or fourth in the list of seven. Counting backwards three odd numbers, the first integer in the list is 15 (the full list must be 15, 17, 19, 21, 23, 25, and 27). Choose **C**.

7. **(D)** 9.5 is the average of the two middle integers, which must be 9 and 10. So the full list is 7, 8, 9, 10, 11, and 12. The largest integer is 12. Choose **D**.

8. **(A)** To earn an 85 average, Mary needs a total of $6 \times 85 = 510$ on her six tests. She already has $82 + 84 + 90 + 88 = 344$. If she gets 100 on her sixth

test, she will have 444 points. That means the fifth test need only be $510 - 444 = 66$. Choose **A**.

9. **(C)** Think of averaging as sharing. That extra 10 points will be shared among five tests raising the score of the first four by 2 points to get the average. That means her first four test scores were 80 and her fifth was 90. Alternatively, assume her first four test scores were each x. Then $\dfrac{x + x + x + x + (x + 10)}{5} = 82$. Hence $5x + 10 = 410$, or $x = 80$. The fifth test score will be $x + 10 = 80 + 10 = 90$. Choose **C**.

10. **(D)** Let the number of students be n. The total of the student scores will be $0 + 0 + 0 + 1 + 1 + 2 + (n-6) \times 9$ at most. This total should equal $7n$. Solving for n, we find $4 + 9n - 54 = 7n$ or $2n = 50$. Hence $n = 25$. If any of the other students were to score less than 9/10, it would take even more students in the class to achieve a 7/10 average. Choose **D**.

11. **(E)** The total of the student scores must be $8.5 \times 10 = 85$. The most anyone could earn was 9/10. If nine of the ten students scored 9/10 ($9 \times 9 = 81$) then the tenth could score 4/10 ($85 - 81 = 4$). If the first nine scored less than 9/10, it would force the tenth student to have a higher score. Choose **E**.

12. **(E)** Since $0 < a < 10$ and $20 < b < 30$, $20 < a + b < 40$ and hence $10 < \dfrac{a + b}{2} < 20$. Thus D is impossible and all of A, B, C could be wrong in certain cases. But E is always true. Choose **E**.

Charts and Graphs

1. **(B)** It's easy to see that New South Wales has a larger piece of the pie and thus the greater population. You do not need to calculate the exact population of each state. Choose **B**.

2. **(B)** Victoria has 24% of the population, which is $21{,}000{,}000 \times 0.24 = 5{,}040{,}000$. Certainly B, 7,000,000, is larger. An easier answer is to estimate Victoria's population at 25% of 20 million which is 5 million. Clearly the actual figure cannot be so different from 5 million to exceed 7 million. Choose **B**.

3. **(B)** The territories account for 3% of the population. Estimating, 3% of 20 million is 600,000. 3% of 21 million will be more than 600,00 and certainly more than A, 500,000. Choose **B**.

4. **(C)** Once Queensland's population doubles, Australia's total population will be 120% of 21 million, and Queensland's will be 40% of 21 million. So Queensland will be $40/120 = 1/3$ of the new total population, or 33%. Choose **C**.

5. **(D)** On the first chart, estimate the female-owned companies at 28% of 23 million $= 23$ million $\times 0.28 = 6.64$ million. This is closest to D. Choose **D**.

6. **(C)** First, there are 23 million −17.5 million = 5.5 million U.S. firms with employees. On the second chart, estimate female-owned companies at 18% of 5.5 million = 5.5 million × 0.18 = 0.99 million or 990,000. Choose **C**.

7. **(B)** Since you are not told the total receipts, it is impossible to calculate values here. We can still tell which is larger though. For female-owned firms the ratio of percentage of total receipts over firms is less than $\frac{1}{3}$ as the bar in the left column is more than three times larger than the bar in the right column. For men it is close to $\frac{1}{2}$. Choose **B**.

8. **(A)** We look at the second graph since we are concerned with salary and compare the total payroll to number of employees which would give the average salary. Again we cannot calculate exact figures but we can compare. For public firms, the ratio of percentage of payroll to percentage of number of employees is greater than one, since the bar in the last column is larger than the bar in the second last column. For private firms it is less than 1. Choose **A**.

9. **(C)** Queensland still has 20% of 21 million while the total population is 110% of 21 million. Since $\dfrac{20\% \text{ of } 21 \text{ million}}{110\% \text{ of } 21 \text{ million}} = \dfrac{20}{110} = 0.18 = 18\%$, Queensland will now have 18% of the population of Australia. Choose **C**.

10. **(C)** New South Wales will lose 25% or ¼ of *its* 34% of the population. That means it will lose $\frac{1}{4} = 34\% = 8.5\%$ of the Australian population. Thus New South Wales now has 25.5% of the Australian population. New Victoria will have 7% + 25% = 32% of the Australian population. This will make it the new most populous state. Choose **C**.

11. **(D)** Clear from examining the charts. D is the only place where the bars get larger (left to right). Choose **D**.

12. **(B)** For each year we compare national male (second chart) to the indicated regional usage (first chart): 2002 Midwest 9.1 > 8.1, 2003 Northeast 8.6 < 8.7, 2004 South 8.1 > 6, 2005 West 7.5 > 6.8, and 2006 South 6.8 > 5.6. Choose **B**.

13. **(D)** Here we have to calculate how many have tried marijuana in each region and then express that as a percentage of the total 12–17 population. In the Northeast, 7.8% of 7 million is 546,000. In the Midwest, 6.8% of 4 million is 272,000. In the South, 5.6% of 17 million is 952,000. In the West 7.3% of 13 million is 949,000. That is a total of 546,000 + 272,000 + 952,000 + 949,000 = 2,719,000 users out of a total of 7 + 4 + 17 + 13 = 41 million, 12 to 17 year olds. So the percentage of users is $\dfrac{2.719 \text{ million}}{41 \text{ million}} = 0.066 = 6.6\%$.

Clearly this answer should be somewhere between the percentage of female users (6.4%) and the percentage of male users (6.8%). Assuming the number of males and females to be equal, we would expect the answer to be the average of 6.4% and 6.8%, which it is. One should be careful however, if the number of females was significantly larger than the number of males, the answer might have been (C) 6.5%. Choose **D**.

14. **(B)** We calculated in the last answer that there were 949,000 users in the West and 952,000 users in the South. Even though the percentage in the South was lower, the number of users is higher because of a greater population base. Choose **B**.

Counting

1. **(A)** The sum of the first 25 positive integers is $25(26)/2 = 25 \times 13 = 325$. Choose **A**.

2. **(A)** The sum of the first 25 odd positive integers is $25^2 = 625$. Choose **A**.

3. **(C)** For combinations with no zeros there are nine choices (1–9) for each digit. By the counting principle, that makes $9 \times 9 \times 9 = 729$ combinations. For combinations with no ones, there are nine choices (0,2–9) for each digit. By the Basic Counting Principle that also makes $9 \times 9 \times 9 = 729$ combinations. Choose **C**.

4. **(A)** There are 14 partitions of 7: $7 = 6 + 1, 7 = 5 + 2, 7 = 5 + 1 + 1, 7 = 4 + 3, 7 = 4 + 2 + 1, 7 = 4 + 1 + 1 + 1, 7 = 3 + 3 + 1, 7 = 3 + 2 + 2, 7 = 3 + 2 + 1 + 1, 7 = 3 + 1 + 1 + 1 + 1, 7 = 2 + 2 + 2 + 1, 7 = 2 + 2 + 1 + 1 + 1, 7 = 2 + 1 + 1 + 1 + 1 + 1, 7 = 1 + 1 + 1 + 1 + 1 + 1 + 1$. Once you have found eight of them you could quit and choose **A**.

5. **(D)** By the counting principle she can make $7 \times 4 \times 3 = 84$ outfits. Choose **D**.

6. **(E)** We'll make a Venn diagram to help. As 124 are in the band and 12 do both, $124 - 12 = 112$ who just play in the band. Since 78 play rugby and 12 do both, $78 - 12 = 66$ who just play rugby. Thus, there are $112 + 12 + 66 + 44 = 234$ students in the school. Choose **E**.

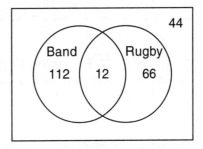

7. **(A)** The sum of the first 50 positive integers is $50(51)/2 = 25 \times 51 = 1,275$. The sum of the first 35 odd numbers is $35^2 = 1,225$. Choose **A**.

8. **(A)** Pages 1–9 use 9 digits in total. From page 10 to 99 there are 90 ($99 - 10 + 1$) pages that each use two digits. That's 180 digits. From page 100 to 999 there are 900 ($999 - 100 + 1$) pages that each use three digits. That's 2,700 digits. So in total $270 + 180 + 9 = 2,889$ digits are used. Choose **A**.

9. **(B)** If a zero is in the units digit place we have pages 10, 20, 30, . . . 990, a total of 99 pages. We also count pages with a zero in the tens place, but not the ones we counted already, 101–109, 201–209, 901–909 a total of 9 × 9 = 81 pages. Zero is never in the hundreds place. Thus, there are at 180 pages with a zero in the page number. A one, unlike a zero, can be in the hundreds place. In fact every page from 100 to 199 has a one in it, a total of 100 pages. When in the tens place we have pages 10–19, 210–219, . . . and 910–919, a total of 9 × 10 = 90 pages. That is already more pages with a one than a zero. But that is not all. If we add in 1, 201, 301, . . . 901, (8 pages) we now have all pages that have a one on them. That totals 198 pages that have a one in the page number. Choose **B**.

10. **(C)** Since ones and twos play identical roles in the numbers from 1 to 999, these values are equal (in fact both are 198). Choose **C**.

11. **(A)** There are 37−(−4) + 1 = 42 integers from −4 to 37 inclusive. There are 41 integers from 1 to 41 inclusive. Choose **A**.

    An alternate answer would be to say that −4 to 37 is comprised of 1 to 37 (37 integers), 0, (1 integer) and −1 to −4 (4 integers) for a total of 37 + 1 + 4 = 42 integers.

12. **(A)** Since 85 is not a multiple of 10 or 3, there must be some 3¢ and some 10¢ stamps included. As no multiple of 10 ends in 5, the 3¢ stamps must produce the 5 ending. So, there are 5 stamps at 3¢, or 15 stamps at 3¢ or 25 stamps at 3¢. Hence the only possibilities are:

3¢ Stamps		10¢ Stamps		
Amount	Value	Amount	Value	Total
5	15¢	7	70¢	85¢
15	45¢	4	40¢	85¢
25	75¢	1	10¢	85¢

To make 85¢ from 4¢ and 15¢ stamps, for similar reasons we must have some of each type of stamp. And there must be 1, 3, or 5 of the 15¢ stamps to produce the 5 ending.

15¢ Stamps		4¢ Stamps		
Amount	Value	Amount	Value	Total
1	15¢	Not possible to make 70¢ from 4¢ stamps.		
3	45¢	10	40¢	85¢
5	75¢	Not possible to make 10¢ from 4¢ stamps.		

Hence there is only one way to make 85¢ from 4¢ and 15¢ stamps, while there are three ways to make 85¢ from 3¢ and 10¢ stamps. Choose **A**.

13. **(A)** We see that x has three possible values (5, 6, or 7), while y has four possible values (2, 3, 4, 5) so we expect at most $3 \times 4 = 12$ values. Some of them might be duplicated so we make a table to check.

+	2	3	4	5
5	7	8	9	10
6	8	9	10	11
7	9	10	11	12

As you can see, there are exactly six different values: 7, 8, 9, 10, 11, and 12. Choose **A**.

14. **(C)** A Venn diagram will help with this question. Let x be the number of students who study in both places. Then $25-x$ students study only in the library, and $15-x$ students study only in the math lab. We don't know how many students study somewhere else entirely—call it y.

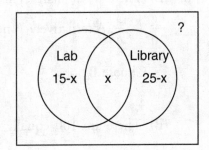

But the total number of students in the class is 34, so $(15 - x) + x + (25 - x) + y = 34$. We solve for x:
$$40-x + y = 34 = 40 + y - 34 = x = x = 6 + y.$$
So x will have a smallest value of 6, when $y = 0$. Choose **C**.

15. **(B)** Counting Chris and Sara there are $27-12 + 1 = 16$ people in line between them. Not counting Chris and Sara, there are 14 people between them. If each of those 14 people buys eight tickets, there will be $114-(8 \times 14) = 114-112 = 2$ tickets left when Sara gets to the booth. Choose **B**.

Probability

1. **(C)** There are seven possible partners and Tom is one of them—so the probability of having Tom as a partner is $\frac{1}{7}$. Likewise Zoe is one of seven possible partners so the probability of having Zoe as a partner is also $\frac{1}{7}$. Choose **C**.

2. **(A)** Three of her classmates (Fred, Sara, and Vera) have four letter names. Only two of them have five letter names (Alice and Jamal). So Column A is $\frac{3}{7}$, which is bigger than Column B, which is $\frac{2}{7}$. Choose **A**.

3. **(B)** John is not in her class so the probability of John being her partner is zero. There are three boys in her class (Fred, Jamal, Tom) so zero is less than the probability of her having a male partner $\frac{3}{7}$. Choose **B**.

4. **(B)** There are six equally likely outcomes (1 through 6). Three of them are even (2, 4, and 6) so $P(\text{even}) = \frac{3}{6} = \frac{1}{2}$. The probability of not rolling 6 is $P(\text{not } 6) = 1 - P(6) = 1 - \frac{1}{6} = \frac{5}{6}$. Choose **B**.

5. **(A)** Four outcomes are greater than 2 (3, 4, 5, and 6). Three outcomes are prime numbers (2, 3, and 5). So $P(>2) = \frac{4}{6} = \frac{2}{3}$ while $P(\text{prime}) = \frac{3}{6} = \frac{1}{2}$. Choose **A**.

6. **(B)** There are 20 marbles in total and 15 of them are not white. $P(\text{not white}) = \frac{15}{20} = \frac{3}{4}$. Alternatively $P(\text{not white}) = 1 - P(\text{white}) = 1 - \frac{5}{20} = 1 - \frac{1}{4} = \frac{3}{4}$. Choose **B**.

7. **(B)** There are 100 equally likely outcomes for this experiment: $\{(x, y) | 1 \leq x \leq 10 \text{ and } 1 \leq y \leq 10\}$. The only outcomes that give a total of 18 or more are (8,10), (9,9), (9,10), (10, 8), (10,9), and (10,10). So the $P(\text{total} \geq 18) = \frac{6}{100} = \frac{3}{50} = 0.06$. Choose **B**.

8. **(D)** There are 8 equally likely outcomes for this experiment : {HHH, HHT, HTH, THH, TTH, THT, HTT, TTT}. The first four have more heads than tails. So the probability of flipping more heads than tails is $\frac{4}{8} = \frac{1}{2} = 0.5$. Choose **D**.

9. **(D)** There are two regions that have 1 in them. The top region is $\frac{1}{8}$ of the circle (it's half of a quarter circle), so the probability of spinning that 1 is $\frac{1}{8}$. The bottom region is $\frac{1}{6}$ of the circle (it's one third of a half circle) so the probability of spinning that 1 is $\frac{1}{6}$. Adding these together we get $\frac{1}{8} + \frac{1}{6} = \frac{3}{24} + \frac{4}{24} = \frac{7}{24}$. So the probability of spinning a 1 is $\frac{7}{24}$. Choose **D**.

10. (**A**) Since there are more white marbles than green marbles, common sense tells us it is more likely to choose two white than two green. Calculating the actual probabilities here is complicated and not worth the time involved. Choose **A**.

11. (**C**) Since there are four white and four "red or green" marbles, both probabilities are $\frac{4}{8} = \frac{1}{2}$. Choose **C**.

12. (**C**) Each result in such an experiment is equally likely, $\frac{1}{2} \times \frac{1}{2} \times \frac{1}{2} = \frac{1}{8}$. As we saw in problem 8, there are eight equally likely outcomes. Choose **C**.

13. (**C**) There is only one even prime (2) so that probability is 1/100. Likewise the probability of picking any single number, like 77, is 1/100. Choose **C**.

14. (**A**) There are 25 primes under 100: 2, 3, 5, 7, 11, 13, 17, 19, 23, 29, 31, 37, 41, 43, 47, 53, 59, 61, 67, 71, 73, 79, 83, 89, and 97. There are only 14 multiples of seven under 100 since $7 \times 14 = 98$. So the probability of picking a prime is 25/100 = 1/4, which is much larger than the probability of picking a multiple of seven 14/100 = 7/50. Even if you didn't know all the primes less than 100, it should have been clear there were more primes than multiples of seven. Choose **A**.

Geometry

Geometry questions occur on the GRE with more regularity than any other type of question. Perhaps this is because using just the basics of high school geometry you can ask a very large number of creative and interesting problems.

As you work through this chapter, remember that diagrams are not drawn to scale, nor are they accurate. What appears as a small angle in the diagram may be much larger. Reviewing strategy tips for diagrams in Chapter 2 can help in this regard.

In geometry it is convenient to use special notations. We give a brief explanation of the notation you are likely to encounter in this book. Some of this notation may not appear in the GRE, as they try very hard to minimize the use of special notation.

Notation	Meaning	Figure
A	A point in space. Although it has no size, we may emphasize it with a black dot.	
AB	The line segment joining point A to point B. Also could mean the length of this segment.	
$\overset{\frown}{AB}$	The arc of the circle from point A to point B. Could also refer to the length of that arc.	
$\angle A$ or $\angle BAC$	The angle at vertex A, or the angle formed at vertex A between lines BA and AC.	
$\triangle ABC$	The triangle formed by the line segments AB, BC, and CA.	
$ABCD$	The quadrilateral formed from line segments AB, BD, CD, and CA.	
	Equal angles can be indicated with matching arcs or symbols. In this example $\angle B = \angle C$ as indicated by the matching double arcs.	
	Equal lengths can be indicated by matching dashes. The top and bottom of the figure have equal lengths as indicated by the matching double hash lines (‖). The sides are also equal as indicated by the matching single lines (|).	

PERIMETER

Perimeter is the distance around the outside of an object. For a square of side length *s*, the perimeter is just $s + s + s + s = 4s$. For a rectangle with side lengths *l* and *w*, the perimeter is just $l + w + l + w = 2l + 2w$.

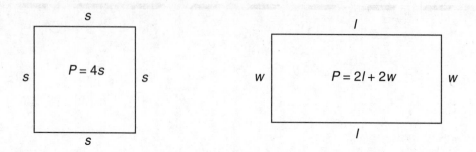

For other shapes with straight line segments on the boundary, simply add the lengths of all these segments.

EXAMPLE 1

All lines shown meet at right angles. Determine the perimeter of the object.

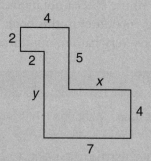

(A) 22
(B) 34
(C) 36
(D) 38
(E) 40

Solution: Two of the side lengths are not given, *x* and *y*. We need to determine their values. By looking at the horizontal segments on the bottom we see that the total horizontal length of the object is $2 + 7 = 9$. That means that $4 + x = 9$, and thus $x = 5$. By looking at the vertical segments on the right, we see that the total vertical height of the object is $5 + 4 = 9$. That means that $2 + y = 9$, and thus $y = 7$. So, starting at the top and working clockwise, the perimeter of the object is $4 + 5 + x + 4 + 7 + y + 2 + 2 = 24 + x + y = 24 + 5 + 7 = 36$. Hence the total perimeter is 36 units. Choose **C**.

The perimeter of a circle is called the circumference, *C*. If the radius of the circle is *r*, its circumference is $2\pi r$; equivalently, if the diameter is *d*, the circumference is πd.

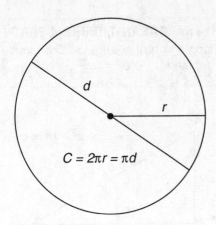

Once you know the circumference of a circle, you can find the length of any arc of a circle. For example, the arclength for $\frac{1}{3}$ of a circle (120° is $\frac{1}{3}$ of 360°) is $\frac{1}{3}$ of the circumference of a circle, or $(\frac{1}{3})2\pi r = \frac{2\pi r}{3}$.

EXAMPLE 2

Find the circumference of the figure below. Each circular arc has center and radius as shown. This figure is drawn to scale.

(A) 16 cm
(B) $(16 + 5\pi)$ cm
(C) $(16 + 9\pi)$ cm
(D) $(12 + 3\pi)$ cm
(E) 12 cm

Solution: We can see the perimeter is given by the lengths of the line segments *FG*, *FJ*, and *JI* plus the arc lengths $\overset{\frown}{GH}$ and $\overset{\frown}{HI}$. $\overset{\frown}{HI}$ is a quarter circle, as the angle $\angle HJI$ is a right angle, with radius 6 cm. So the length of $\overset{\frown}{HI}$ is $(\frac{1}{4})2\pi r = (\frac{1}{4})2\pi(6$ cm$) = 3\pi$ cm. $\overset{\frown}{GH}$ is a semicircle with radius 2 cm so its length is $(\frac{1}{2})2\pi r = (\frac{1}{2})2\pi(2$ cm$) = 2\pi$ cm. *JI* is a radius of the arc $\overset{\frown}{HI}$ so it is 6 cm. *JH* is also a radius of $\overset{\frown}{HI}$, and *JH* has the same length as *FG*. So *FG* is 6 cm in length. Finally, the line *GH* is a diameter of the semicircle $\overset{\frown}{GH}$, so line *GH* has length 4 cm, which is the same as the length of *FJ*. Thus *FJ* has length 4 cm. We conclude the perimeter is $FG + FJ + JI + \overset{\frown}{GH} + \overset{\frown}{HI}$ = 6 cm + 4 cm + 6 cm + 2π cm + 3π cm = $(16 + 5\pi)$ cm. Choose **B**.

The Pythagorean Theorem, at least one part of it, is commonly needed to find perimeters of triangles.

> ## PYTHAGOREAN THEOREM PART I
>
> If *ABC* is a right triangle with right angle at *C* and side lengths *CA* = *b*, *AB* = *c*, and *BC* = *a*, then $a^2 + b^2 = c^2$.

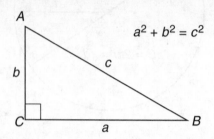

$$a^2 + b^2 = c^2$$

Note the largest value, *c*, called the *hypotenuse,* is always on the side opposite the right angle. This theorem is particularly useful when you know two sides and wish to find the third. You can determine that $c = \sqrt{a^2 + b^2}$, $b = \sqrt{c^2 - a^2}$, and $a = \sqrt{c^2 - b^2}$.

EXAMPLE 3

Column A   Column B

Perimeter of △*ABD*   Perimeter of △*BCD*

Solution: Let *AB* be *x* and *DC* be *y*. Since △*ABD* is a right triangle with right angle at *D*, $5^2 + 3^2 = x^2$. Thus $25 + 9 = x^2$ or $x^2 = 34$. So $x = \sqrt{34}$. Then the perimeter of △*ABD* is $5 + 3 + \sqrt{34}$, which is $8 + \sqrt{34}$. As $\sqrt{36} = 6$, $8 + \sqrt{34}$ is a little less than 14. Since △*BCD* is a right triangle with right angle at *D*, $3^2 + y^2 = 5^2$. So $y^2 = 5^2 - 3^2$, or $y^2 = 16$. Thus $y = 4$. So the perimeter of △*BCD* is $3 + 4 + 5 = 12$. Choose **A**.

TIP

- Some right triangles appear frequently. Knowing their dimensions can save a lot of time. See the Appendix for suggested facts to memorize.

- There are a number of other formulas for the perimeter of certain shapes. They are not really necessary to memorize. Just remember to divide the perimeter of the object into pieces whose length is easy to calculate.

Problems

Basic Problems

<table>
<tr><td align="center"><u>Column A</u></td><td align="center"><u>Column B</u></td></tr>
<tr><td align="center">Circumference of circle
of radius 10</td><td align="center">Circumference of circle
of diameter 20</td></tr>
</table>

1.

<table>
<tr><td>Perimeter of square of side 4</td><td>Perimeter of circle of radius 4</td></tr>
</table>

2.

<table>
<tr><td align="center">Perimeter of triangle</td><td align="center">Perimeter of triangle</td></tr>
</table>

3.

<table>
<tr><td align="center">Perimeter of circle</td><td align="center">Perimeter of semicircle</td></tr>
</table>

4.

<table>
<tr><td align="center">Perimeter of rectangle</td><td align="center">Perimeter of rectangle</td></tr>
</table>

5.

6. In the following diagram, grid points are separated vertically and horizontally by one unit. Find the perimeter of the given shape.

(A) $5 + 2\sqrt{2}$
(B) 5
(C) 6
(D) $5 + \sqrt{2} + \sqrt{5}$
(E) 8

GRE Problems

7. Find the perimeter of the given shape. Each arc is half of a circle. This figure is drawn to scale.

(A) 8 cm
(B) 6 + π cm
(C) 6 + 2π cm
(D) 8 + π cm
(E) 8 + 2π cm

8. Assume all lines meet at right angles. Find the perimeter of the object.

(A) 18
(B) 20
(C) 24
(D) 26
(E) 28

9. Find the perimeter of these stairs. All lines meet at right angles.

(A) 28
(B) 30
(C) 34
(D) 36
(E) 38

Column A	Column B

All arcs shown are semicircles. *B* is the midpoint of *AC*

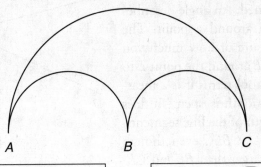

10. | Length of $\overset{\frown}{AC}$ | Length of $\overset{\frown}{AB} + \overset{\frown}{BC}$ |

AB is the diameter of the semicircle

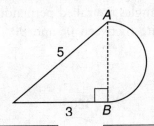

11. | Perimeter of the figure shown | $8 + 2\pi$ |

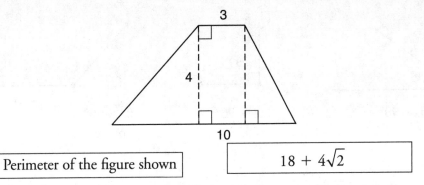

12. | Perimeter of the figure shown | $18 + 4\sqrt{2}$ |

13. The circles are centered at *A* and *B*, respectively, and both have radius 1. What is the perimeter of the object (solid line)?

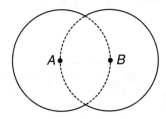

(A) 4π
(B) $4\pi\sqrt{3}$
(C) $8\pi\sqrt{3}$
(D) 8π
(E) 12π

ANGLES

Whenever two lines (or line segments) meet at a point, angles are formed. An angle describes the rotation of a line around a point. The angle ∠*BEC* is a measure of how much you would have to rotate *EB* around the point *E* to get to *EC*. In grade school terms it is a measure of "how wide the mouth is open." It does not depend on the length of the line segments. For instance ∠*AED* = ∠*BEC* even though *AE* and *DE* are much larger than *BE* and *CE*.

We usually measure angles in degrees. An angle of 360° is a full rotation, 180° is a half rotation, usually called a straight angle, and a 90° is a quarter turn, called a right angle. We denote a right angle with a half a square ⌐ instead of an arc. Two lines, *EF* and *EG*, that meet at right angles are called perpendicular, and we write *EF* ⊥ *EG*. Angles are classified as acute (between 0° and 90°), right (90°), and obtuse (more than 90°).

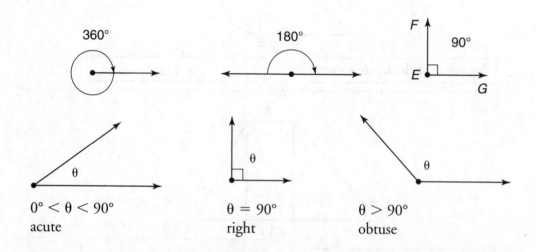

EXAMPLE 1

Find *x*.

(A) 40
(B) 50
(C) 60
(D) 70
(E) 80

Solution: Since these two angles together form a straight angle, $(2x + y)° + (x - y)° = 180°$ ⇒ $3x = 180$ ⇒ $x = 60$. Choose **C**.

Sometimes an angle $\angle ABC$ is cut into two other angles by a line BD. If the new angles $\angle ABD$ and $\angle DBC$ are equal we say BD bisects $\angle ABC$, and call BD an angle *bisector*.

EXAMPLE 2

Lines *AB* and *CD* meet at right angles at *O*. Which of the following is not true?

   (A) $\angle AOD$ and $\angle BOC$ are vertical angles.
   (B) $\angle AOC$ and $\angle BOD$ are vertical angles.
   (C) *BO* bisects $\angle COD$.
   (D) *AO* bisects $\angle DOC$.
   (E) *BD* bisects $\angle AOD$.

Solution: A and B are clearly true. Since the lines meet at right angles, $\angle COB$ and $\angle BOD$ are both 90°. So *BO* does bisect $\angle COD$. Thus C and similarly D are true. *BD* does not appear in the diagram. Even if we draw it in, *BD* does not intersect *O*, the vertex of the angle. So it can't possibly bisect $\angle AOD$. Choose **E**.

When two lines cross at a point they form four angles. The angles opposite each other are called *vertical angles*. Vertical angles are always equal. For example, $\angle AEB$ and $\angle DEC$ are vertical angles. Also $\angle AED$ and $\angle BED$ are vertical angles.

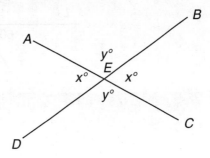

EXAMPLE 3

If lines L_1 and L_2 cross at *O*, what is *y*?

   (A) 40
   (B) 50
   (C) 60
   (D) 70
   (E) 80

Solution: Because of vertical angles, $80° = 2x°$. Divide by 2 to see that $x = 40$. We also see that 80° and $(x + y)°$ together form a straight angle. So $80° + (x + y)° = 180°$. Hence $80 + 40 + y = 180 \Rightarrow y = 60$. Choose **C**.

Two lines in the plane that never meet are called *parallel lines*. We write $L_1 \| L_2$. In effect, parallel lines remain a fixed distance apart, like railroad tracks. Any two lines that are not parallel must meet. When a third line crosses a set of parallel lines, we call it a *transversal*. A transversal crosses each of the parallel lines at the same angles.

> **PARALLEL LINES THEOREM**
> If lines $L_1 \parallel L_2$ and are crossed by a transversal L_3, then the following angles are equal: ① = ④ = ⑤ = ⑧ and ② = ③ = ⑥ = ⑦.

TIP

Although the word *transversal* may not appear on the GRE, this theorem appears very frequently.

Put another way, every time a transversal meets parallel lines there are only two numerical values for the angles created.

$L_1 \parallel L_2$

EXAMPLE 4

Column A	Column B

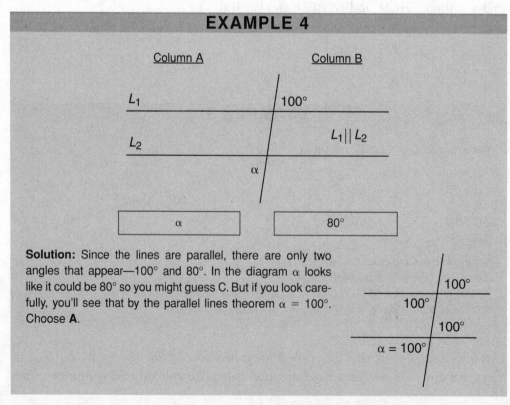

α	$80°$

Solution: Since the lines are parallel, there are only two angles that appear—100° and 80°. In the diagram α looks like it could be 80° so you might guess C. But if you look carefully, you'll see that by the parallel lines theorem $\alpha = 100°$. Choose **A**.

Problems

Basic Problems

<u>Column A</u>   <u>Column B</u>

1.

x	60

2.

$x + y$	120

3.

$4x$	40

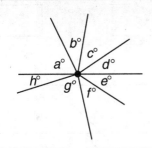

4.

$(a + b + c + d + e + f + g + h)/2$	$a + b + c + d$

5.

$x + 10$	90

6. One angle is incorrect. Which one?

(A) ①
(B) ②
(C) ③
(D) ④
(E) ⑤

7. Which of the following are true?

    I.   *OC* bisects $\angle AOB$
   II. *AO* bisects $\angle DOB$
  III. *OB* bisects $\angle AOC$

(A) I only
(B) III only
(C) I and III
(D) II and III
(E) I and II

GRE Problems

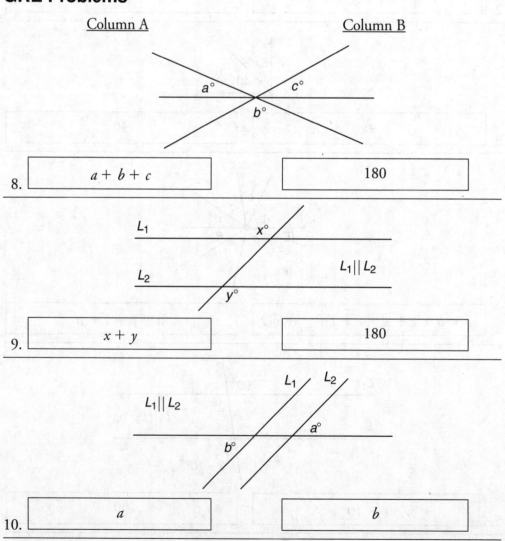

Column A   Column B

8. $a + b + c$ 180

9. $x + y$ 180

10. a b

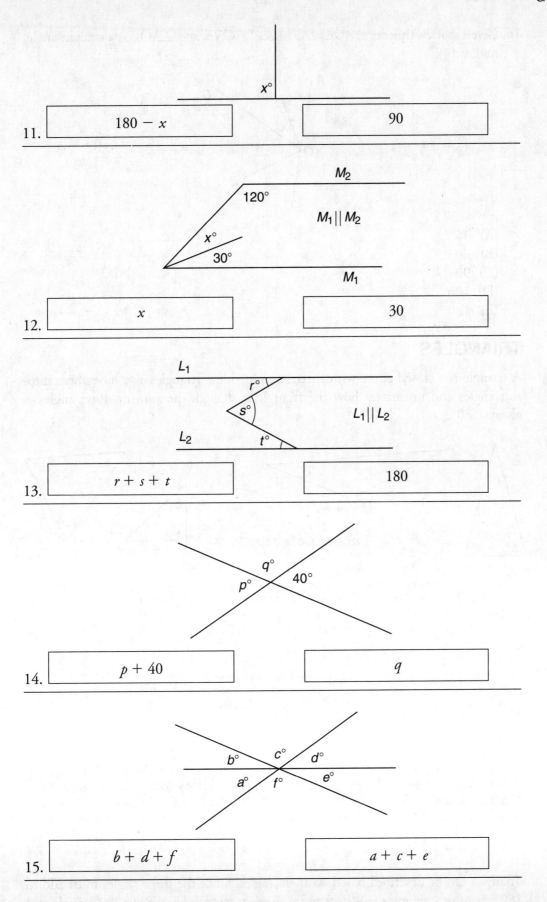

11.

180 − x	90

12.

x	30

13.

r + s + t	180

14.

p + 40	q

15.

b + d + f	a + c + e

16. Given that *BO* bisects ∠*AOC*, *DO* bisects ∠*COE*, and ∠*AOE* is a straight angle, find *x* + *y*.

(A) 45
(B) 60
(C) 90
(D) 100
(E) 180

TRIANGLES

A triangle is a closed curve with three straight sides. Triangles also have three interior angles and no matter how the triangle is shaped, the sum of those angles is always 180°.

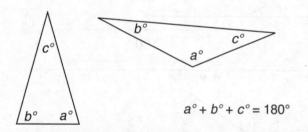

$$a° + b° + c° = 180°$$

EXAMPLE 1

Column A   Column B

| x | 30 |

Solution: Since the sum of angles in a triangle is 180°, (2*x*) + (3*x* − 5) + 60 = 180. Simplifying 5*x* + 55 = 180 ⇒ 5*x* = 125 ⇒ *x* = 25. Choose **B**. An alternate answer would be to plug 30 into the expressions given: 2*x* = 2(30) = 60 and 3*x* − 5 = 3(30) − 5 = 85. Since 60 + 60 + 85 = 205, which is more than the sum of angles in a triangle should be, you know that 30 is larger than *x*.

Triangles can be described based on their angles. Since the three angles must add to 180°, at most one angle is 90° or more. A *right triangle* has a right (90°) angle and two acute angles. An *obtuse triangle* has one obtuse (>90°) angle and two acute angles. An *acute triangle* has three angles less than 90°.

acute triangle	right triangle	obtuse triangle
$0 < a < 90$	$a = 90$	$90 < a < 180$
$0 < b < 90$	$0 < b < 90$	$0 < b < 90$
$0 < c < 90$	$0 < c < 90$	$0 < c < 90$

When one side of a triangle is extended it creates an exterior angle.

> ### EXTERIOR ANGLE THEOREM
> The exterior angle at A, of triangle $\triangle ABC$, is equal to the sum of the two opposite interior angles (at B and at C).

$$z° = x° + y°$$

It's not hard to see why this is true. AB is a straight line so $z° + \angle CAB = 180°$. By the sum of angles in a triangle, $x° + y° + \angle CAB = 180°$. So $z° + \angle CAB = x° + y° + \angle CAB \Rightarrow z° = x° + y°$. Even if you don't remember this, you should be able to refigure it out on the test.

EXAMPLE 2

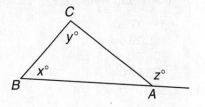

Column A   Column B

| u | $w - 40$ |

Solution: By the exterior angle theorem, $w = 40 + u$. So solving for u we find $u = w - 40$. Choose **C**. Alternatively, if you forget the External Angle Theorem you can still solve the problem. Label the third angle inside the triangle x. Then the sum of interior angles of the triangle is 180° so $x + u + 40 = 180$ (①). But w and x together form a straight angle so $w + x = 180$, and $x = 180 - w$. Substitute $x = 180 - w$ into ①, and we have $(180 - w) + u + 40 = 180$. This implies $-w + u + 40 = 0$, or $u = w - 40$.

Triangles can also be described based on the lengths of their sides. An *equilateral triangle* has three equal length sides and three equal angles. Since the sum of the angles is 180°, each angle must be 60°.

- If you know a triangle has three equal sides, then it has three equal angles.

- If you know a triangle has three equal angles, then it has three equal sides.

An *isosceles triangle* has two equal sides, and the angles opposite those sides are also equal.

- If you know a triangle has two equal angles, the sides opposite those angles are equal.

- If you know a triangle has two equal sides, the angles opposite those sides are equal.

EXAMPLE 3

If *ABDE* is a square find the perimeter of the given hexagon *ABCDEF*.

(A) 17 cm
(B) 20 cm
(C) $20 + \sqrt{3}$ cm
(D) 23 cm
(E) $31 + \sqrt{3}$ cm

Solution: As *ABDE* is a square, all sides have the same length of 4 cm. Consider △*AFE*. It has two angles of 60° so the third angle is 180° − 60° − 60° = 60°. So △*AFE* is equilateral and *AF* = *FE* = *AE* = 4 cm. Now consider △*BCD*. As ∠*BCD* = ∠*BDC*, the triangle is isosceles, and *BC* = *BD*. As *BD* is a side of the square, *BC* = *BD* = 4 cm. Then the perimeter of *ABCDEF* is *AB* + *BC* + *CD* + *DE* + *EF* + *FA* = 4 + 4 + 3 + 4 + 4 + 4 = 23 cm. Choose **D**.

Isosceles right triangle

Obtuse isosceles triangle

Triangle Inequality

Not just any three numbers can represent the side lengths of a triangle. For instance try to make a triangle with one side 10 cm and each of the other sides 3 cm. It's impossible! It won't close. This illustrates an obvious but important fact.

> **TRIANGLE INEQUALITY**
>
> In any triangle, the length of any one side is less that the sum of the lengths of the other two sides.

Put another way, if the lengths of the triangle are a, b and c, then $c < a + b$, $a < b + c$, and $b < a + c$. If even one of these three inequalities is not true, there cannot be a triangle with those side lengths.

EXAMPLE 4

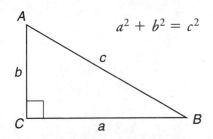

Column A   Column B

| $3 + x$ | 7 |

Solution: Most people will begin by using the Pythagorean Theorem to solve for x. This is totally unnecessary. According to the triangle inequality, the length of any one side (7) is less than the sum of the other two sides ($3 + x$). Choose **A**.

Pythagorean Theorem

As we saw earlier, right triangles have a special property called the Pythagorean Theorem.

$$a^2 + b^2 = c^2$$

> **PYTHAGOREAN THEOREM PART I**
>
> If $\triangle ABC$ is a right triangle with right angle at C and side lengths $CA = b$, $AB = c$, and $BC = a$, then $a^2 + b^2 = c^2$.

The converse to this theorem is also true and very useful for finding right angles.

> **PYTHAGOREAN THEOREM PART II**
>
> If $\triangle ABC$ has side lengths a, b, and c (where $a = BC$, $b = AC$, $c = AB$) and $a^2 + b^2 = c^2$, then $\triangle ABC$ is a right triangle with right angle $\angle ACB$.

Solution: Don't be fooled by appearances. Although $3x°$ looks like it's about 75°, it's not. As $3^2 + 4^2 = 5^2$ this is a right triangle with right angle opposite the side of length 5. That is, $3x = 90$ and hence $x = 30$. Choose **A**.

Because right triangles are so important in mathematics and appear so often on the GRE, it is worth memorizing the side lengths for the most common right triangles. Any multiple of the side lengths of a right triangle are also the side lengths of a right triangle. Since (3, 4, 5) forms a right triangle so does $(2 \times 3, 2 \times 4, 2 \times 5) = $ (6, 8, 10). Similarly as (5, 12, 13) forms a right triangle so does (5/2, 12/2, 13/2) = (2.5, 6, 6.5).

Common Right Triangles

Side Lengths (a, b, c)	$a^2 + b^2 = c^2$	Common Multiples
(3, 4, 5)	$3^2 + 4^2 = 5^2$ $9 + 16 = 25$	(6, 8, 10) (9, 12, 15) (12, 16, 20) (1.5, 2, 2.5) $\left(\dfrac{3}{10}, \dfrac{2}{5}, \dfrac{1}{2}\right)$
(5, 12, 13)	$5^2 + 12^2 = 13^2$ $25 + 144 = 169$	(10, 24, 26) (1, 2.4, 2.6)
$(1, 1, \sqrt{2})$	$1^2 + 1^2 = (\sqrt{2})^2$ $1 + 1 = 2$	$(\sqrt{2}, \sqrt{2}, \sqrt{2})$ $\left(\dfrac{1}{\sqrt{2}}, \dfrac{1}{\sqrt{2}}, 1\right)$
$(1, \sqrt{3}, 2)$	$1^2 + (\sqrt{3})^2 = 2^2$ $1 + 3 = 4$	$\left(\dfrac{1}{2}, \dfrac{\sqrt{3}}{2}, 1\right)$

EXAMPLE 6

Find *z*.

(A) 13
(B) $12\sqrt{3}$
(C) 26
(D) 39
(E) 52

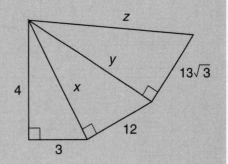

Solution: This question is surprisingly easy if you know your right triangles. First of all, $x = 5$, as (3, 4, 5) is a right triangle. Second, $y = 13$ as (5, 12, 13) is also a right triangle. Finally we have 13,

$13\sqrt{3}$, and *z* in a right triangle. We notice that this must be 13 times the $(1, \sqrt{3}, 2)$ right triangle. So $z = 2 \times 13 = 26$. Choose **C**.

Problems

Basic Problems

Column A   Column B

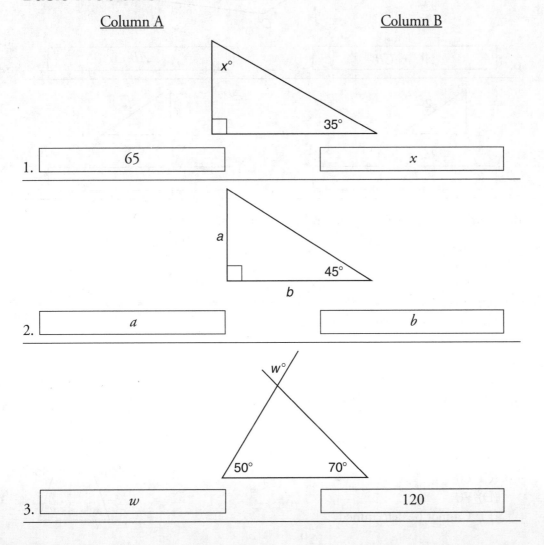

1.

65	*x*

2.

a	*b*

3.

w	120

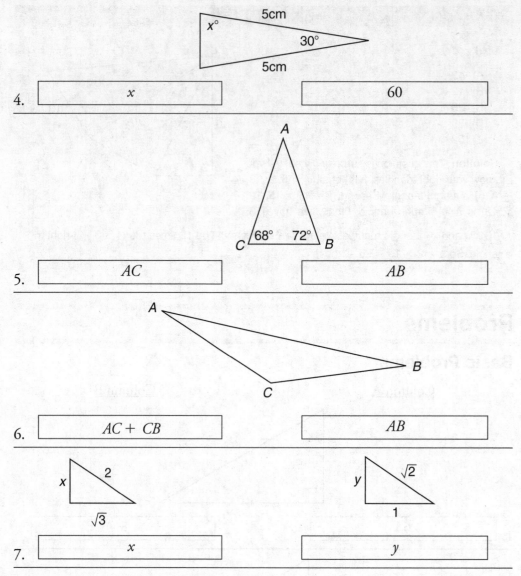

4.

x	60

5.

AC	AB

6.

$AC + CB$	AB

7.

x	y

8. If $AB = AC$ in $\triangle ABC$, then find $(x + y + z)/2$.

(A) 30
(B) 40
(C) 45
(D) 60
(E) 90

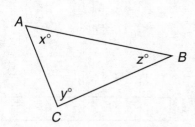

GRE Problems

9. Find. $\frac{2}{3}x + \frac{1}{3}z$.

(A) 40
(B) 50
(C) 60
(D) 70
(E) Cannot be determined

10. △*ABC* is isosceles with *AB = AC* and △*BCD* is equilateral. Find *y* (∠*ABD*).

    (A) 10
    (B) 15
    (C) 25
    (D) 30
    (E) 45

11. In △*ACD*, ∠*ADC* is bisected by *BD*. Determine *y*.

    (A) 40
    (B) 60
    (C) 75
    (D) 80
    (E) 100

12. Find the perimeter of quadrilateral *ACDF*.

    (A) $28 + 4\sqrt{2}$ cm
    (B) $25 + 3\sqrt{2}$ cm
    (C) 32 cm
    (D) 33 cm
    (E) 34 cm

Column A	Column B

13. | *x* | | *y* |

14. | *x* | | 50 |

Problems 15–17 concern $\triangle ABC$ where $AD = AC$.

15.	x		z

16.	w		x

17.	w		y

POLYGONS

A polygon is a closed figure with straight sides. There are usually classified by the number of sides they have. On the GRE we primarily see three-sided and four-sided polygons though with some regularity we see five-, six-, or eight-sided polygons. Others are rare.

Number of Sides	Name	Examples
3	Triangle	
4	Quadrilateral	
5	Pentagon	
6	Hexagon	
8	Octagon	

As long as the polygon is convex, has no indentation, the sum of its interior angles is determined by the number of sides it has. For a triangle its interior angles sum to 180°, for a quadrilateral 360°, and for a pentagon 540°. There is a formula to describe this:

> The sum of the interior angles of a convex n-sided polygon is $(n-2)180°$. It's not really necessary to memorize this. You can always figure it out by dividing the shape into triangles.

EXAMPLE 1

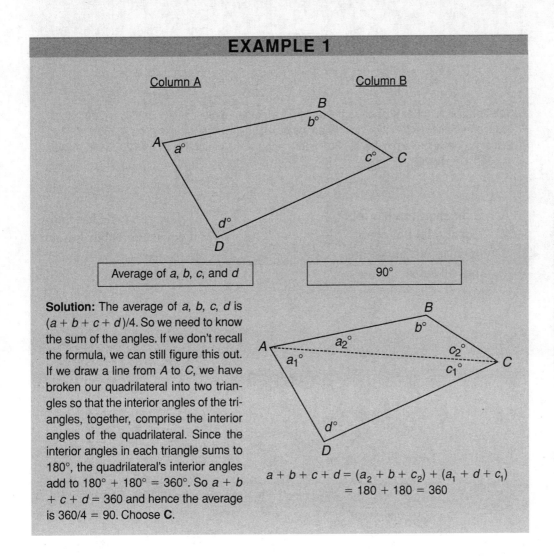

Column A

Column B

Average of a, b, c, and d

90°

Solution: The average of a, b, c, d is $(a+b+c+d)/4$. So we need to know the sum of the angles. If we don't recall the formula, we can still figure this out. If we draw a line from A to C, we have broken our quadrilateral into two triangles so that the interior angles of the triangles, together, comprise the interior angles of the quadrilateral. Since the interior angles in each triangle sums to 180°, the quadrilateral's interior angles add to 180° + 180° = 360°. So $a + b + c + d = 360$ and hence the average is 360/4 = 90. Choose **C**.

$$a + b + c + d = (a_2 + b + c_2) + (a_1 + d + c_1)$$
$$= 180 + 180 = 360$$

Regular Polygons

Regular polygons have all sides equal and all interior angles equal. An equilateral triangle is a regular triangle. A square is a regular quadrilateral. In the previous table, the bold figures are regular polygons.

This makes it very easy to determine their interior angles. As the interior angles of a quadrilateral sum to 360°, in a regular quadrilateral (a square) each of those angles is 360°/4 = 90°. In a regular pentagon each interior angle is 540°/5 = 108°.

EXAMPLE 2

Column A   Column B

This is a regular hexagon.

| *y* | | 120 |

Solution: Since it has six sides, the sum of the interior angles is (6 − 2)180° = 720°. If you don't remember that formula, just divide the hexagon into four triangles and 4(180°) = 720°. Since the hexagon is regular all the interior angles are equal. So 6*y* = 720 which implies *y* = 120. Choose **C**.

This rhombus has four equal sides but is not regular—its angles are not all equal.

This rectangle has four equal angles but is not regular—its sides are not equal

EXAMPLE 3

Column A   Column B

| *a* | | *b* |

Solution: At first glance you might assume the figure at left is just a square rotated. It's not. As the tip above noted having four equal sides does not make it a square. It could be a tall skinny rhombus where *a* > 90 or a flat wide rhombus where *a* < 90 or even possibly a square where *a* = 90. In the figure at right, *b* must be 90 as the sum of the interior angles is 360° and the other three are 90°. Choose **D**.

TIP

• Although the sum of the interior angles changes with the number of sides, the sum of the exterior angles of any convex polygon is the same, 360°. I like to remember this by looking at a square; it has four external angles of 90°.

• For a regular polygon with *n* sides, each exterior angle is 360°/*n*.

EXAMPLE 4

In the diagram, *ABCDE* is a regular pentagon, and *AB* and *DC* extend to meet at *F*. Find *w*.

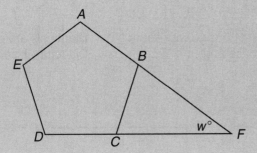

(A) 108
(B) 72
(C) 45
(D) 36
(E) 30

Solution: As *ABCDE* is a regular pentagon, each of its exterior angles is 360°/5 = 72°. Note that ∠*BCF* and ∠*CBF* are exterior angles. Then the angles in △*BCF* sum to 180°, so 72° + 72° + *w*° = 180°, That means *w* = 36. Choose **D**.

Quadrilaterals

There are many special four-sided polygons, and each of them has special properties. We cannot hope to inform you of all the properties of these figures (nor would you want to study that much material), but we will try to hit the highlights and the ideas most likely to appear on the GRE. In most cases, knowledge from this section will help you solve problems faster, though there may be other ways to solve the problem using basic geometric knowledge that you have.

We describe six types of quadrilaterals. There is significant overlap in these groups. For instance, a square belongs to all of them!

Name	Definition	Properties to Note
Square	A regular quadrilateral	Four equal sides Four equal right interior angles Diagonals are equal in length Diagonals bisect each other
Rectangle	A quadrilateral with four interior right angles	Opposite sides parallel and equal Diagonals are equal in length Diagonals bisect each other
Parallelogram	A quadrilateral with two pairs of opposite parallel sides	Opposite sides equal Diagonals bisect each other Opposite interior angles equal
Rhombus	A quadrilateral with four equal sides	Opposite sides parallel and equal Diagonals bisect each other Diagonals are perpendicular
Trapezoid	A quadrilateral with at least one pair of parallel sides	
Isosceles trapezoid	A trapezoid with equal base angles	Diagonals are equal in length Diagonals bisect each other

Examples 5 and 6 are concerned with parallelogram *ABCD*

EXAMPLE 5

Column A	Column B
w	*u*

Solution: As ∠*A* and ∠*C* are opposite angles in a parallelogram, they are equal. Choose **C**.

EXAMPLE 6

Column A	Column B
x	y

Solution: As *ABCD* is a parallelogram, *AB*∥*CD*. Then *BD* is a transversal for parallel lines *AB* and *CD*. By the Parallel Lines Theorem, *x* = *y*. Choose **C**.

Problems

Basic Problems

Column A   Column B

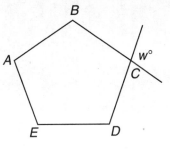

1.
$a + b + c + d + e$	$360°$

ABCDE is a regular pentagon

2.
w	$72°$

ABCD is a rectangle

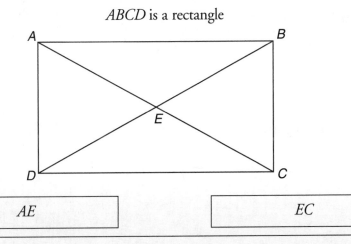

3.
AE	EC

Column A   Column B

A regular octagon has interior angle of $x°$ and exterior angle of $y°$

4.
| x | | $180 - y$ |

A regular hexagon has interior angle of $h°$ and an equilateral triangle has exterior angle of $t°$

5.
| h | | t |

ABCDEF is a regular hexagon with perimeter 24 cm

6.
| AC | | 8 cm |

7. *ABCD* is a parallelogram. Find x.

(A) 35
(B) 30
(C) 25
(D) 20
(E) 15

GRE Problems

8. Mary formed a new shape by gluing together four regular polygons. Find the perimeter of this figure.

(A) 45 cm
(B) 50 cm
(C) 53 cm
(D) 57 cm
(E) 60 cm

9. Find x in Mary's figure.

(A) 24°
(B) 30°
(C) 42°
(D) 48°
(E) 60°

Column A	Column B

In quadrilateral *ABCD*, *AB* = *BC* and *CD* = *DA*

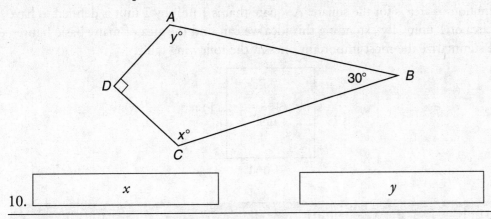

10.

x	y

This is a convex pentagon

11.

$a + b + c + d$	$360°$

ABCD is a rectangle

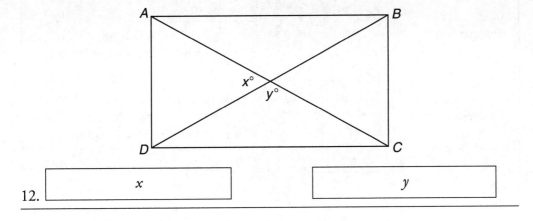

12.

x	y

13. A regular polygon has exterior angles of $x°$ and interior angles of $3x°$. How many sides does the polygon have?

(A) 6
(B) 8
(C) 9
(D) 10
(E) 12

AREA

Area is a measure of the two-dimensional space an object occupies. The most basic definition of area is for the square. A square that is 1 unit by 1 unit is defined to have an area of 1 unit^2. By extending this idea we can find the area of many basic figures. We summarize the most important ones in the following table.

Shape	Diagram	Area Formula
Square		$A = s^2$ (side squared)
Rectangle		$A = lw$ (length times width)
Circle		$A = \pi r^2$ (pi times radius squared)
Triangle		$A = \frac{1}{2} bh$ (one-half base times height)
Parallelogram		$A = bh$ (base times height)
Trapezoid		$A = \frac{1}{2} (b_1 + b_2)h$ (one-half the height times the sum of the bases)

The height is always perpendicular to the base and is usually different from the slant height. Don't make the mistake of using the slant height (side length) when the height is needed.

Incorrect Area	Correct Area
$A = \frac{1}{2} bh$	$A = \frac{1}{2} bh$
$= \frac{1}{2}(6)(5)$	$= \frac{1}{2}(4)(5)$
$= 15$	$= 10$

It is essential to know the area formulas for a rectangle, circle, and triangle—often the others may be determined from them.

EXAMPLE 1

Find the area of parallelogram *ABCD*.

(A) 25 cm²
(B) 30 cm²
(C) 37.5 cm²
(D) 40 cm²
(E) 42.5 cm²

Solution: If you know the formula for area of a parallelogram this is very easy, $A = bh = (8 \text{ cm})(5 \text{ cm}) = 40 \text{ cm}^2$. If you don't, you can still solve the problem. Add a line from *A* to *C*. Now the area of $\triangle ACD$ is $\frac{1}{2} bh = \frac{1}{2}(8 \text{ cm})$ $(5 \text{ cm}) = 20 \text{ cm}^2$. Since this is a parallelogram, the height from *C* to *AB* is also 5 cm and *AB* is also 8 cm. So for $\triangle CAB$ with base *AB*, the area is $\frac{1}{2} bh = \frac{1}{2}(8 \text{ cm})(5 \text{ cm}) = 20 \text{ cm}^2$. Adding the areas together, $20 \text{ cm}^2 + 20 \text{ cm}^2 = 40 \text{ cm}^2$. Choose **D**.

EXAMPLE 2

Find the area of the trapezoid *ABCD*.

(A) 29
(B) 36
(C) 40
(D) 42
(E) 68

Solution: If you know the formula for area of a trapezoid, this is very easy: $A = \frac{1}{2}(b_1 + b_2)h = \frac{1}{2}(6 + 14)(4) = 40$. If you don't, you can still solve the problem. Drop a line at B to intersect CD at right angles. Call this new point E. Also use F to denote the point where the original height meets CD. Now the area of the trapezoid is the area of the central rectangle, $ABEF$ plus the area of the two triangles $\triangle BEC$ and $\triangle AFD$. Since $\triangle AFD$ is a right angle triangle with hypotenuse 5 and side length 4, the other side length, DF, must be 3. So the area of $\triangle ADF$ is $\frac{1}{2}bh = \frac{1}{2}(3)(4) = 6$. Now the area of $ABEF$ is $lw = 6 \times 4 = 24$. Finally, as $DF = 3$ and $FE = 6$, $EC = 14 - 3 - 6 = 5$. Then the area of $\triangle BEC = \frac{1}{2}bh = \frac{1}{2}(5 \times 4) = 10$. So the total area of the trapezoid is $6 + 24 + 10 = 40$. Choose **C**.

Of course, most often you need to find the area of a more complicated figure. In this case it is usually best to break the figure up into smaller pieces whose areas are easier to find. Some people call this the addition method.

EXAMPLE 3

If the grid has 1 inch between each dot horizontally and vertically, find the area of the given figure.

(A) 3 in²
(B) 3.25 in²
(C) 3.5 in²
(D) 4 in²
(E) $2 + \sqrt{2} + \sqrt{5}$ in²

Solution: We divide the shape into regions whose area is easily recognized. Region ① is half, diagonally, of a 1 inch square so it has area ½ in². (If you prefer the formula its area is ½ bh = ½ (1 in)(1 in) = ½ in². Region ② is a 2 × 1 rectangle so it has area 2 in². Region ③ is half , diagonally, of a 2 × 1 rectangle so it has area $\frac{1}{2}$ (2 in²) = 1 in². If you prefer formulas, its area is ½ bh = $\frac{1}{2}$ (2 in)(1 in) = 1 in². In total we have Area ① + Area ② + Area ③ = ½ + 2 + 1 = 3.5 in². Choose **C**.

Sometimes it is easier to find areas with subtraction than with addition—that is, subtracting excess area from a larger region to leave the area of the region you want.

EXAMPLE 4

Find the area of the shaded region.

(A) $8 - 4\pi$ cm²
(B) $8 - 2\pi$ cm²
(C) 4 cm²
(D) π cm²
(E) $4 - \pi$ cm²

2cm

Solution: The shaded area can be found as
the area of the rectangle minus the area of a semicircle. Since the radius is 2 cm, the diameter is 4 cm, and thus the rectangle is 2 cm × 4 cm = 8 cm² in area. The semicircle is 1/2 πr^2 = 1/2 π (2 cm)² = 2π cm². So the shaded area is $8 - 2\pi$ cm². Choose **B**.

EXAMPLE 5

<u>Column A</u>   <u>Column B</u>

ABCD is a parallelogram

| Area of △*ACD* | Area of △*BCD* |

Solution: These two triangles share the same base *CD*. And as *AB*∥*DC*, they have the same height too. So their areas are equal.

Connecting Area and Perimeter

For some figures, like a square and circle as the perimeter increase so does the area. For other shapes like a rectangle this may not be the case. Because this connection between perimeter and area is such an interesting relationship, it is the subject of many GRE problems.

EXAMPLE 6

<u>Column A</u>   <u>Column B</u>

A rectangle with area 28 has side lengths that are integers

| Perimeter of the rectangle | 22 |

Solution: We must find integer values for length and width so that $28 = lw$. We could have $l = 7$ and $w = 4$, and then the perimeter would be $4 + 7 + 4 + 7 = 22$. But we could also have $l = 14$ and $w = 2$ and then the perimeter would be $14 + 2 + 14 + 2 = 32$. Since we can't tell which, choose **D**.

This TIP is well worth memorizing. We can illustrate why it is true with an equilateral triangle of side length l. Drop a perpendicular from A to meet BC at D. Then D bisects BC, so $BD = CD = \dfrac{1}{2}$. Now, using the Pythagorean Theorem in

$\triangle ABD$, we have $\left(\dfrac{1}{2}\right)^2 + h^2 = l^2$. So $h^2 = 1 -$

$\dfrac{1}{4} = \dfrac{3}{4}$. Then $h = \dfrac{\sqrt{3}}{2}$. As the height of an equi-

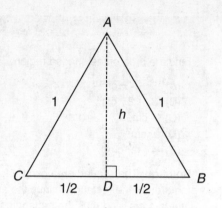

lateral triangle of side length 1 is $\dfrac{\sqrt{3}}{2}$, by scaling the

height of an equilateral triangle of side length x is $\dfrac{\sqrt{3}}{2}x$.

EXAMPLE 7

Column A	Column B

A square with side s and an equilateral triangle with side x have the same area

x	s

Solution: The area of the square is s^2. To find the area of the triangle, we need to know the

height—from above we know it will be $\dfrac{\sqrt{3}}{2}x$. So the area of the triangle is $\left(\dfrac{1}{2}\right)x$

$\left(\dfrac{\sqrt{3}}{2}x\right) = \dfrac{\sqrt{3}}{4}x^2$. Setting them equal, $s^2 = \dfrac{\sqrt{3}}{4}x^2$, which implies $s = \sqrt{\dfrac{\sqrt{3}}{4}}x$. We know

that $0 < \dfrac{\sqrt{3}}{4} < 1$ and so $0 < \sqrt{\dfrac{\sqrt{3}}{4}} < 1$. Thus s is less than x. Choose **A**.

TIP

- For a fixed area, the circle has the smallest perimeter.

- For a fixed perimeter, the circle encloses the most area.

Problems

Basic Problems

Column A	Column B

5cm

5cm

	Column A	Column B
1.	Area of (nonsquare) parallelogram	25 cm²

A given square has area 16 meters²

	Column A	Column B
2.	Perimeter of the square	16 meters

A given rectangle has area 16 in²

	Column A	Column B
3.	Perimeter of the rectangle	16 in

<u>Column A</u>   <u>Column B</u>

The following hexagon is drawn on a 1 cm grid

4. | Area inside the hexagon | 3.5 cm^2 |

ABCD is a rectangle, *EBFD* is a parallelogram, and *EB = FC*

5. | The shaded area | The white area |

6. Find the area of the shaded figure. The semicircular regions have radius 3 cm.

(A) 60 cm^2
(B) $60 - 2\pi$ cm^2
(C) $96 - 36\pi$ cm^2
(D) $96 - 9\pi$ cm^2
(E) $132 - 18\pi$ cm^2

GRE Problems

7. A regular hexagonal nut just fits into a circular hole, 2 inches in diameter. How much area, in square inches, surrounds the nut?

(A) $4\pi - \dfrac{3\sqrt{3}}{2}$

(B) $\pi - \dfrac{3\sqrt{3}}{2}$

(C) $4\pi - 3$
(D) $\pi - 3$
(E) $4\pi - 6\sqrt{2}$

8. A square of area 4 m^2 fits snugly inside a circle. What is the circumference of the circle?

(A) $2\sqrt{2}\pi$ m
(B) 2π m
(C) π m
(D) $2(\pi - 1)$ m
(E) $2\sqrt{2}$ m

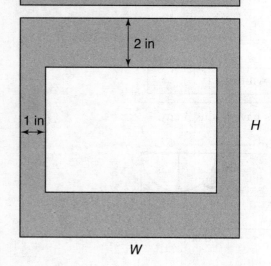

9. An ice hockey rink is formed from a rectangle with a semicircle attached at each end. If the width of the rink is 50 feet and the length is 200 feet, which of the following best approximates the area of the rink?

(A) 8,000 ft²
(B) 9,000 ft²
(C) 9,500 ft²
(D) 10,000 ft²
(E) 12,000 ft²

10. A 10-inch by 14-inch picture is framed with a rectangular mat 2 inches wide. What is the area of the mat?

(A) 52 in²
(B) 96 in²
(C) 112 in²
(D) 128 in²
(E) 192 in²

11. A rectangular framed picture measures H inches by W inches. If the width of the frame is 2 inches on top and bottom and 1 inch on each side, which of the following is NOT a correct expression for the area of the frame?

(A) $2H + 4(W - 2)$
(B) $2(H - 4) + 4W$
(C) $WH - (W - 2)(H - 4)$
(D) $2(H - 4) + 4(W - 2) + 4(2)$
(E) $(W + 1)(H + 2) - WH$

<u>Column A</u>   <u>Column B</u>

In parallelogram $ABCD$, $4 < h < w$

12. | Area of $ABCD$ | | Perimeter of $ABCD$ |

The circles are concentric. The smaller one has diameter 6 cm and the larger has radius 9 cm.

13. | Eight times the white area | | The shaded area |

<u>Column A</u>   <u>Column B</u>

A rectangle is inscribed in a circle of area 4π

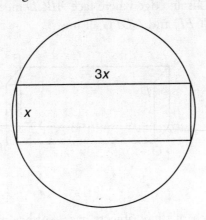

14.

x	1

Problems 15 and 16 concern the following boomerang designs. All arcs shown are semicircles. $AC = DG = 12$ cm. B is the midpoint of AC and $DE = EF = FG$.

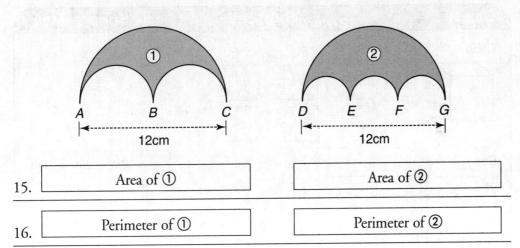

15.

Area of ①	Area of ②

16.

Perimeter of ①	Perimeter of ②

SURFACE AREA AND VOLUME

On the GRE the three-dimensional objects you are most likely to encounter are a sphere, cube, box, and cylinder. You also might see combinations or pieces of these objects or even a right prism. A right prism is a two dimensional polygon joined to a copy of itself by rectangles that are perpendicular to the polygons. Here is a pentagonal prism. A box is a rectangular prism.

The polygons on the surface of a solid are called *faces*. Two faces meet in a line that we call an *edge*. Three (or more) faces meet at a point we call a *vertex*. In the box below *ABCD* is the top face. *BC* is an edge where face *ABCD* meets face *BCEF*. *C* is a vertex where faces *ABCD*, *BCEF*, and *CDFG* all meet.

Surface Area

Except for the sphere, each of these objects has a surface made of two-dimensional objects—polygons and circles. It seems reasonable to ask about the total area of these shapes—that is called surface area. In most cases, you can find surface area by looking at each part of the surface, finding its area and adding up all those areas.

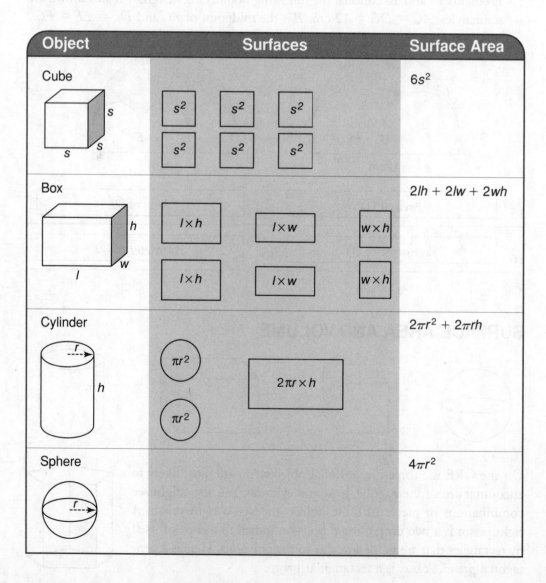

Object	Surfaces	Surface Area
Cube	s^2 s^2 s^2 s^2 s^2 s^2	$6s^2$
Box	$l \times h$ $l \times w$ $w \times h$ $l \times h$ $l \times w$ $w \times h$	$2lh + 2lw + 2wh$
Cylinder	πr^2 $2\pi r \times h$ πr^2	$2\pi r^2 + 2\pi rh$
Sphere		$4\pi r^2$

In the case of a sphere, we use a formula derived from calculus. You should not need to memorize this formula—it is unlikely to appear on the test and if needed it should be given to you in the question.

EXAMPLE 1

Find the surface area of the right triangular prism pictured here.

(A) 48 cm^2
(B) 96 cm^2
(C) 100 cm^2
(D) 108 cm^2
(E) 132 cm^2

Solution: We recognize the bottom as a 3, 4, 5 right triangle. It has area 1/2 (3)(4) = 6 cm^2. The top has the same area of 6 cm^2. There are three rectangular faces. One is 3 × 8, one is 4 × 8, and the last is 5 × 8. Their areas are 24 cm^2, 32 cm^2, and 40 cm^2. So the total surface area is 6 + 6 + 24 + 32 + 40 = 108 cm^2. Choose **D**.

8cm

4cm

3cm

EXAMPLE 2

Column A	Column B
Surface area of cube of side length 1	Surface area of sphere of diameter 1

Solution: A cube of side length 1, has surface area of $6s^2 = 6(1)^2 = 6$. A sphere of diameter 1 has radius 1/2 so its surface area is $4\pi r^2 = 4\pi(1/2)^2 = 4\pi/4 = \pi$. As $6 > \pi$, choose **A**. You may not know the formula for surface area of a sphere and still be able to solve this problem. In this case, it is apparent the sphere would fit entirely inside the cube and thus have smaller surface area.

> **TIP**
>
> For objects like a sphere, cube, box, or cylinder, if one fits inside another, the inner solid has lesser surface area. This is not true for all solid objects.

EXAMPLE 3

Two red cubes and two blue cubes are placed together to form a single rectangular prism. The order of their placement is not known. If each cube has side length 1 cm, which of the following could be the blue surface area?

I. 8 cm^2
II. 10 cm^2
III. 12 cm^2

(A) I only
(B) II only
(C) III only
(D) I and II only
(E) II and III only

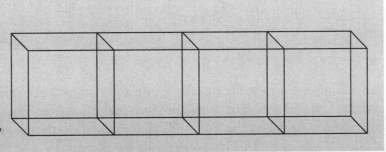

Solution: Notice each face of a cube has area 1 cm². A cube on the end has five faces on the surface. The other face is pressed against its neighbor and thus is not part of the surface area. A cube in the middle has four faces on the surface. If the blue cubes are both in the middle there will be 8 blue faces on the surface and thus 8 cm² of blue surface area. If the blue cubes are on the ends there will be 10 blue faces on the surface and thus 10 cm² of blue surface area. If one is on the end and the other in the middle, there will be 9 blue faces on the surface and thus 9 cm² of blue surface area. Only I and II are possible. Choose **D**.

Volume

Volume is the space inside an object. A basic unit of volume is the cubic centimeter defined as the space occupied by a cube with side length of 1 cm. This definition generalizes to give the formulas in the table below.

Object	Volume
Cube	s^3
Box	lwh
Cylinder	$\pi r^2 h$
Sphere	$4\pi r^3/3$

You will not need to memorize the formula for volume of a sphere. In the unlikely case that you will need it, it should be given in the question. You should note that the volume formulas for a cube, box, and cylinder all follow the pattern: Volume = (Area of base) × (Height). This is a general rule for all prisms.

EXAMPLE 4

Two boxes of cereal have the same volume. One has dimensions 4 in × 9 in × x in, while the other has dimensions x in × x in × 6 in. What is x?

(A) 2 in
(B) 4 in
(C) 6 in
(D) 8 in
(E) 14 in

Solution: The volume of a box is length × width × height so the volume of the first box is $(4)(9)(x) = 36x$. The volume of the second box is $(x)(x)(6) = 6x^2$. As their volumes are equal $36x = 6x^2$. Divide both sides by $6x$, and we have $6 = x$. Choose **C**.

EXAMPLE 5

Column A	Column B

A cube and a cylinder have the same volume

Side length of the cube	Height of the cylinder

Solution: As their volumes are equal, $s^3 = \pi r^2 h$. Solving for height, $h = \dfrac{s^3}{\pi r^2}$. The value of r will greatly affect the relationship between h and s. If $r = s$, then $h = s/\pi$ and so $h < s$. If $r = s/\pi$, then $h = \dfrac{s^3}{\pi r^2} = \dfrac{s^3}{\pi \left(\dfrac{s}{\pi}\right)^2} = \dfrac{s^3}{\dfrac{s^2}{\pi}} = \pi s$. So $h > s$. Choose **D**. In simpler terms, a tall skinny cylinder could have the same volume as the cube, but the height will be greater than cube's side length. A very flat wide cylinder could also have the same volume as the cube, but the height would be smaller than the side length.

EXAMPLE 6

What is the maximum length of a straw that could fit inside a can with radius 2 inches and height 10 inches?

(A) $2\sqrt{39}$
(B) $2\sqrt{21}$
(C) 10.3
(D) $\sqrt{96}$
(E) 11

Solution: The key to solving this problem is noting the longest straw will be the hypotenuse of a right triangle formed by the diameter of the base and a perpendicular to the base on the side of the can. In this right triangle, $x^2 = (4)^2 + (10)^2$ and so $x^2 = 116$. Hence x is $\sqrt{116} = \sqrt{4 \times 39} = 2\sqrt{39}$. Choose **A**.

TIP

- The maximum length line segment inside a box is a diagonal with length $\sqrt{l^2 + w^2 + h^2}$.

- The maximum length line segment inside a sphere is the diameter.

- The maximum length line segment inside a cylinder is $\sqrt{(2r)^2 + h^2}$.

Problems

Basic Problems

Problems 1–2 concern the following box.

Column A   Column B

1. | Length of diagonal *AC* | 15 cm |

2. | 144 cm² | Surface area of the box |

A cube has side length $\sqrt{2}$

3. | Volume of the cube | 12 |

A cube has diagonal 4 cm

4. | 24 cm² | Surface area of the cube |

A cube has surface area equal in magnitude to its volume

5. | Side length of the cube | 6 |

6. Which of the following have a volume equal in magnitude to its surface area?

   I.   Cube of side length 6
   II. Box with dimensions 4 × 8 × 8
   III. Box with dimensions 1 × 2 × 3

   (A) I only
   (B) II only
   (C) III only
   (D) I and II only
   (E) II and III only

GRE Problems

Column A   Column B

Problems 7–9 concern the L-shaped figure below, which is composed of four cubes each with side length 2 cm.

7.	Surface area of L shape	Surface area of $2 \times 4 \times 6$ box

One cube is added to the figure; cubes must touch exactly face to face

8.	Minimum increase in surface area	Increase in volume

One cube is added to the figure; cubes must touch exactly face to face

9.	Maximum increase in surface area	16

A cube and a sphere have the same volume

10.	Surface area of cube	Surface area of sphere

Problems 11 and 12 concern the diagram below. Four cubes are stacked as shown. Two are red and two are blue.

11.	Fraction of surface area that is blue	$\dfrac{1}{2}$

12.	Maximum percentage of surface area that is red	60%

Marg wants to replace her cylindrical spaghetti can, of radius 2 in and height 8 in, with a tin box of dimensions 4 in $\times$ 4 in $\times$ 7 in

13.	Max. length that can fit into the cylindrical spaghetti can	Max. length that can fit into the tin box

14. Find the volume of the triangular prism.

   (A) 60 cm³
   (B) 96 cm³
   (C) 104 cm³
   (D) 108 cm³
   (E) 120 cm³

15. How many 2 × 2 × 2 ice cubes can fit into an ice tray of dimensions 4 × 6 × 8?

    (A) 9
    (B) 18
    (C) 24
    (D) 36
    (E) 192

16. A cube just fits inside a sphere. If the surface area of the cube is 36, what is the diameter of the sphere?

    (A) $2\sqrt{3}$
    (B) $3\sqrt{2}$
    (C) $\sqrt{22}$
    (D) 6
    (E) 9

SOLUTIONS

Perimeter

1. **(C)** A circle of diameter 20 has radius 10, as diameter is twice the radius. Thus these circles are identical and hence their circumference is equal. Choose **C**.

2. **(B)** The square has perimeter $P = 4s = 4(4) = 16$. The circle has circumference $C = 2\pi r = 2\pi(4) = 8\pi$. As $\pi > 3$, $8\pi > 24$. Choose **B**.

3. **(A)** In A, the third side can be found from the Pythagorean theorem. As $3^2 + 4^2 = x^2$, we find $x^2 = 25$ and thus $x = 5$. So the perimeter is $3 + 4 + 5 = 12$.

   In B, $3^2 + y^2 = 4^2$ implies $y^2 = 16 - 9 = 7$ and thus $y = \sqrt{7}$. So the perimeter is $3 + 4 + \sqrt{7} = 7 + \sqrt{7} < 7 + 3 = 10$. Choose **A**. An easier answer would be to notice that the hypotenuse is always larger than the other sides in a right triangle. Hence the missing side is larger than 4 in A and less than 4 in B. Hence the perimeter in A is larger.

4. **(A)** In A the circumference is $2\pi r$. In B the perimeter of the shape is composed of the circular part and the diameter; hence, it is $1/2\ (2\pi r) + 2r = \pi r + 2r$. Since $2 < \pi$, $\pi r + 2r < \pi r + \pi r = 2\pi r$. Choose **A**. If you notice they both have the same radius then the question boils down to "Which is longer, half the circumference of the circle, or the length of *XY*?" The shortest path between two points is a straight line so the length of *XY* is less than the arc from *X* to *Y*. The answer follows.

   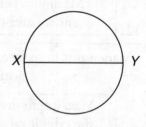

5. **(D)** Although the rectangle in B looks larger, you can't trust appearances. In A the perimeter is $x + y + x + y = 2x + 2y$. In B the perimeter is $x + z + x + z = 2x + 2z$. Since we don't know what z and y are, there is no way to know which is larger. Choose **D**.

6. **(D)** There are two diagonals in this diagram. The smaller one, call it *x*, is the diagonal of a 1 × 1 square, and thus we should recall it has length $\sqrt{2}$ (you can find this using the Pythagorean theorem $1^2 + 1^2 = x^2$). The larger diagonal, call it *y*, is part of a right triangle with other sides 1 and 2. Thus $y^2 = 1^2 +$

2^2, which implies $y^2 = 5$ and hence $y = \sqrt{5}$. Hence the perimeter is $\sqrt{2} +$

$1 + 1 + \sqrt{5} + 1 + 1 + 1 = 5 + \sqrt{2} + \sqrt{5}$. Choose **D**.

7. **(E)** We can see that the diameter of the semicircles is half of 4 cm or 2 cm. Thus the radius of each semicircle is 1 cm. The circumference of two semicircles is the same as the circumference of one circle, $2\pi r = 2\pi(1) = 2\pi$. To complete the perimeter, we add the three other sides $2\pi + 2 + 4 + 2 = 8 + 2\pi$ cm. Choose **E**.

8. **(D)** Call the missing side lengths *x* and *y*. We can find *y* by equating the horizontal sides: $8 = 1 + 3 + y$, and hence $y = 4$. We can find *x* by equating the vertical sides: $1 + x = 2 + 3$ and hence $x = 4$. Finally the perimeter is $8 + 3 + y + 2 + 3 + x + 1 + 1 = 8 + 3 + (4) + 2 + 3 + (4) + 1 + 1 = 26$. Choose **D**.

There is also a quick and tricky answer for this question. By moving the dotted lines to the solid lines, we can change the shape into a rectangle with the same perimeter. And the perimeter of the rectangle is $2(8 + 5) = 26$.

9. **(E)** We could do a lot or reasoning to determine the lengths of all the sides shown. It is much easier to look at horizontal and vertical pieces separately. The five small horizontal pieces must add up to the width of the figure, which is 10. The five smaller vertical pieces must add to the height of the figure which is 9. Hence the perimeter of the object is $9 + 10 + 9 + 10 = 38$.

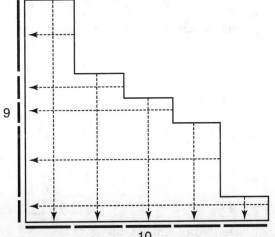

In general, such a figure always has the same perimeter as the corresponding rectangle. Choose **E**.

10. **(C)** No measurements are given in the question. So let's assume that $AC = 8$. Then $AB = 4$ and $BC = 4$. So the radius for the semicircle AC is 4 and for AB (or BC) is 2. Hence the length of arc $\overarc{AC} = \dfrac{1}{2}(2\pi 4) = 4\pi$. Meanwhile the length of $\overarc{AB} + \overarc{BC}$ is $\dfrac{1}{2}(2\pi 2) + \dfrac{1}{2}(2\pi 2) = 4\pi$. Hence the path from A to C has the same length as the path from A to B to C. Choose **C**.

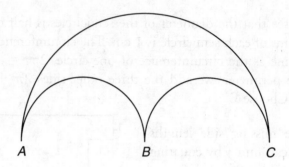

11. **(C)** First we find, d, the diameter of the circle, which is also the third side of the triangle. So $3^2 + d^2 = 5^2$ and solving we find $d = 4$ (you might have recognized the 3, 4, 5 triangle). So the circumference of the semicircle is $\dfrac{1}{2}(\pi d) = 1/2\,(\pi 4) = 2\pi$. Finally the perimeter of the figure is $3 + 5 + \pi = 8 + 2\pi$. Choose **C**.

12. **(D)** The base of this figure can be broken into three pieces, call them x, y and z. If we knew these values, we could find the sloped sides and thus the perimeter. It is immediately clear that $y = 3$ since the central piece of the figure is a rectangle. It is not clear that x and z can be determined—but does that affect the perimeter? It should. In the triangle

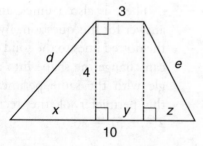

on the left, $x^2 + 4^2 = d^2$ and hence $d = \sqrt{x^2 + 4^2}$. In the triangle on the right, $z^2 + 4^2 = e^2$ and hence $e = \sqrt{z^2 + 4^2}$. So the perimeter is $P = 3 + e + 10 + d = 13 + \sqrt{x^2 + 4^2} + \sqrt{z^2 + 4^2}$. When $x = 3$ and $z = 4$, this is $13 + \sqrt{3^2 + 4^2} + \sqrt{4^2 + 4^2} = 13 + 5 + 4\sqrt{2} = 18 + 4\sqrt{2}$. When $x = 1$ and $z = 6$, this is $13 + \sqrt{1^2 + 4^2} + \sqrt{6^2 + 4^2} = 13 + \sqrt{17} + \sqrt{52} = 13 + \sqrt{17} + 2\sqrt{13}$. I can't easily tell which is bigger, but they are clearly not equal! Choose **D**.

13. **(C)** First we note that *AC*, *AB*, and *BC* are all radii and hence length l. That makes *ABC* an equilateral triangle with three 60° angles. Similarly *ABD* is equilateral with three 60° angles. As $\angle CAD = 60° + 60° = 120°$, and 120° is one-third of 360°, the arc from *C* to *B* to *D* is one-third of the circumference of the circle centered at *A*. Hence the remaining portion of the circumference is $\frac{2}{3}(2\pi r) = \frac{2}{3}(2\pi 1) = 4\pi/3$. The dark portion

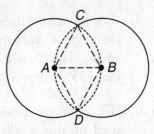

of the circle centered at B has the same length. So the total circumference of the figure is $4\pi/3 + 4\pi/3 = 8\pi/3$. Choose **C**.

Angles

1. **(B)** Since a straight angle is 180°, $2x + (x + 10) = 180$. Solving we find $3x + 10 = 180 \Rightarrow 3x = 170 \Rightarrow x = 56\frac{2}{3}$. Choose **B**.

2. **(A)** By vertical angles $2x = 70$, and so $x = 35$. Also $2x° + (y + 10)°$ forms a straight angle or 180°. Then $2x + y + 10 = 180$ or $x + x + y + 10 = 180$. Substitute 35 for one of the *x*'s, $35 + x + y + 10 = 180$ and hence $x + y = 180 - 10 - 35 = 135$. Choose **A**.

3. **(C)** The two angles form a right angle so $5x + 40 = 90$. This implies $5x = 50$ and hence $x = 10$. So $4x = 40$. Choose **C**.

4. **(C)** Since there are 360° in a circle $(a + b + c + d + e + f + g + h) = 360$. So $(a + b + c + d + e + f + g + h)/2 = 180$. Also $a + b + c + d = 180$ since those four angles form a straight angle. Choose **C**.

5. **(A)** Since the lines are parallel $90° = (x - 10)°$. Hence $x = 100$. Certainly $x + 10 > 90$. Choose **A**.

6. **(D)** When a transversal crosses parallel lines only two angles appear. If the 70° or 110° angles were incorrect then more than one angle would be incorrect. The 120° ④ angle is incorrect. You would also note that $120° + 70° = 190°$, not 180° as it should be for a straight angle. Choose **D**.

7. **(B)** Since $\angle AOD = 90°$ and $\angle AOD + \angle AOC = 180°$, then $\angle AOC = 90°$. As $\angle AOC = \angle AOB + \angle BOC$, $90° = \angle AOB + 45°$ and hence $\angle AOB = 45°$. Now *OC* is not in $\angle AOB$ so it cannot bisect it. I is false. *AO* is in $\angle DOB$ but does not divide it into two equal angles as $\angle AOB = 45°$ and $\angle DOB = 90°$. II is false. *OB* is in $\angle AOC$ and divides it into two equal angles as $\angle AOB = 45°$ and $\angle BOC = 45°$. III is true. Choose **B**.

8. **(C)** Label the angle vertical to $b°$ as $y°$. Then $a°$, $y°$, and $c°$ together form a straight angle, so $a + y + c = 180$. But $y = b$ by vertical angles so $a + b + c = 180$. Choose **C**.

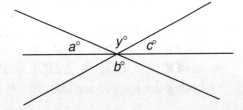

9. **(D)** By parallel lines we know that $x = y$. But what about their sum? Although the angle $x°$ appears large, we cannot trust the diagram. The angle could be small, like 80°, where $x + y = 80 + 80 = 160 < 180$. It could also be large like 135°, where $x + y = 135 + 135 = 270 > 180$. Choose **D**.

10. **(C)** Although the diagram has been turned sideways compared to what we are used to, this is still just an application of the Parallel Lines Theorem. Here $a = b$, so choose **C**.

11. **(D)** Although it appears like a right angle, we cannot trust the diagram to be accurate. So $x°$ could be more or less than 90°. Hence $180 - x$ could be more or less than 90. Choose **D**.

12. **(C)** We extended the transversal to form an angle of $y°$. Since a straight angle is 180°, $y + 120 = 180$ and hence $y = 60$. Now by parallel lines $60° = x° + 30°$, so $x = 30°$. Choose **C**.

13. **(D)** A good way to solve this problem is to exaggerate the diagram. If the vertex at s is moved far to the left, then it is clear that r, s, and t are all very small angles and hence their sum is less than 180. If the vertex at s is moved to the right, we can have s nearly 180°, while r and s are clearly not small. So their sum is more than 180°. Choose **D**.

14. **(B)** Because of vertical angles, we know that $p = 40$. Because they form a straight angle $p + q = 180$. So $40 + q = 180$, or $q = 140$. Then $p + 40 = 40 + 40 = 80$. Hence A < B. Choose **B**.

15. **(C)** By vertical angles, $a = d$, $c = f$, and $e = b$. So $a + c + e = d + f + b$ and rearranging $a + c + e = b + d + f$. Choose **C**. Alternatively, by the argument in problem 8, each is 180° and thus equal.

16. **(C)** Since BO bisects $\angle AOC$, $\angle AOB = \angle BOC = x°$. As DO bisects $\angle COE$, $\angle COD = \angle DOE = y°$. As a straight angle $180° = \angle AOE = \angle AOB + \angle BOC + \angle COD + \angle DOE = x° + x° + y° + y° = 2x° + 2y°$. Then divide both sides by 2 to see that $90° = x° + y°$. Choose **C**.

Triangles

1. **(A)** The sum of angles in a triangle is 180°, so $x + 35 + 90 = 180$. Hence $x = 180 - 35 - 90 = 55$. Choose **A**.

2. **(C)** Call the missing angle x. Since the sum of angles in a triangle is 180°, $x + 45 + 90 = 180$. Solving we find $x = 45$. That means that the triangle is isosceles and the two sides opposite the 45° angles are equal. That is $a = b$. Choose **C**.

3. **(B)** Assume the unnamed angle inside the triangle is x°. As the sum of interior angles of a triangle is 180°, we have $50 + 70 + x = 180$. Hence $x = 60$. Finally, by vertical angles $w = x$. So $w = 60$. Choose **B**.

4. **(A)** As two sides are equal, this is an isosceles triangle. So the angles opposite those sides must also be equal. Hence they are both x°. Finally the sum of interior angles of a triangle is 180° so $x + x + 30 = 180$. This simplifies to $2x = 150$, which implies $x = 75$. Choose **A**.

5. **(A)** Sides opposite larger angles are larger. As $72 > 68$, $AC > AB$. Choose **A**.

6. **(A)** By the Triangle Inequality Theorem, the sum of any two sides must be larger than the third. Choose **A**.

7. **(C)** In A we use the Pythagorean Theorem to solve for x: $2^2 = x^2 + \left(\sqrt{3}\right)^2$.

   Then $4 = x^2 + 3$ or $x^2 = 1$. Hence $x = 1$. In B we again use the Pythagorean Theorem: $\left(\sqrt{2}\right)^2 = y^2 + 1^2$. Then $2 = y^2 + 1$ or $y^2 = 1$. Hence $y = 1$, also.

   Choose **C**. If you have memorized your common right triangles, you could have recognized both of these and saved considerable time.

8. **(E)** Knowing $AB = AC$ proves to be irrelevant. As the sum of interior angles of a triangle is 180°, $x + y + z = 180$. Hence $(x + y + z)/2 = 90$. Choose **E**.

9. **(C)** First note that the triangle is isosceles and hence $x = y$. Then $\frac{2}{3}x + \frac{1}{3}z = \frac{2x + z}{3} = \frac{x + x + z}{3}$. As $x = y$, we can replace one of the x's with a y. So $\frac{2}{3}x + \frac{1}{3}z = \frac{x + y + z}{3}$. And $x + y + z = 180$ as the sum of interior angles in a triangle is 180°. Finally $\frac{2}{3}x + \frac{1}{3}z = \frac{x + y + z}{3} = \frac{180}{3} = 60$.

   Choose **C**.

10. **(B)** As $AB = AC$, we know that $\angle ABC = \angle ACB$. Then summing angles in $\triangle ABC$ we have $180° = \angle ABC + \angle ACB + 30° = 2\angle ABC + 30°$. Solving we find $\angle ABC = 75°$. Now $\triangle BDC$ is equilateral so each angle is $60°$. In particular $\angle DBC = 60°$. Then $\angle DBC + y° = \angle ABC$. So $60° + y° = 75°$, where $y = 15$. Choose **B**.

11. **(D)** Summing angles in $\triangle ACD$, we find that $180° = 40° + 60° + \angle ADC$. Hence $\angle ADC = 80°$. As BD bisects $\angle ADC$, which is $80°$, $\angle ADB = \angle CDB = 40°$. Then, summing angles in $\triangle BDC$, we find that $40° + 60° + y° = 180°$ and hence $y° = 80°$. Choose **D**.

12. **(A)** We recognize $\triangle CBD$ as a 3, 4, 5 triangle so $CD = 5$ cm. $ABDE$ is a rectangle (because of the right angles) and hence $DE = AB = 8$ cm. Also $AE = BD = 4$ cm. Then AEF is a (4 cm, 4 cm, AF) right triangle, which is a multiple of the $(1, 1, \sqrt{2})$ triangle. Hence $AF = 4\sqrt{2}$ cm. Then the perimeter of $ACDF$ is $AB + BC + DE + EF + FA = 8$ cm $+ 3$ cm $+ 5$ cm $+ 8$ cm $+ 4$ cm $+ 4\sqrt{2}$ cm $= 28 + 4\sqrt{2}$ cm. Choose **A**.

13. **(C)** We recognize $\left(1, 1, \sqrt{2}\right)$ as a right-angled triangle, so $y° = 90°$. Also $\left(\dfrac{1}{2}, \dfrac{\sqrt{3}}{2}, 1\right)$ is a multiple (one-half) of the $(1, \sqrt{3}, 2)$ right triangle. Hence $x° = 90°$. Choose **C**.

14. **(A)** By the External Angle Theorem $y = x + 40$. As $y > 90$, this implies $x + 40 > 90$ or $x > 50$. Choose **A**.

15. **(B)** By the External Angle Theorem, $z = x + y$, hence $z > x$. Choose **B**.

16. **(B)** As $AC = AD$, $\angle ADC = x°$. By the external angle theorem in $\triangle ADB$, $\angle ADC = \angle DAB + w°$, so $x° = \angle DAB + w°$. As $\angle DAB > 0$, this implies that $w < x$. Choose **B**.

17. **(D)** This is a really interesting question. The answer depends on what y is. First notice that summing angles in $\triangle ABC$, $180° = x° + y° + \angle DAB + w°$. If y is larger than $90°$, w must be smaller than y or the sum of angles in $\triangle ABC$ would be greater than $180°$. If y is small, say $20°$, then $x° = 80°$. Taking B very close to D would make $w°$ close in value to $x°$, certainly more than $20°$. Choose **D**.

$\angle ABD = w°$ is close to $80°$

Polygons

1. **(A)** This is a pentagon (five sides) so the sum of its interior angles is $(5 - 2)$ $180° = 540°$. So $a + b + c + d + e = 540$. Choose **A**.

2. **(A)** As *ABCDE* is a pentagon, the interior angles sum to $(5 - 2)180° = 540°$. As it is regular, each interior angle is $540°/5 = 108°$. By vertical angles at *C*, $w = 108$. Choose **A**. Each exterior angle of a pentagon is $72°$ $(= 360°/5)$, but w is not an exterior angle. The other two angles at *C* are exterior angles—they are formed by extending a side of the polygon.

3. **(C)** In a rectangle, diagonals bisect each other. So $AE = EC$. Choose **C**.

4. **(C)** In an octagon the interior angles sum to $(8 - 2)$ $180° = 1{,}080°$. As it is regular, each of the interior angles is $1{,}080°/8 = 135°$. So $x = 135$. The exterior angles sum to $360°$, and as it is regular, each exterior angle is $360°/8 = 45°$. So $y = 45$ and $180 - y = 135$. Choose **C**. The short answer to this question is that an interior and the corresponding exterior angle always form a straight angle so $x + y = 180$, and hence $x = 180 - y$.

5. **(C)** A regular hexagon has six sides so its interior angles sum to $(6 - 2)$ $180° = 720°$ and each interior angle is $720°/6 = 120°$. Each exterior angle of the equilateral triangle is $360°/3 = 120°$. Choose **C**.

6. **(B)** A hexagon has six sides and since it is regular each side has the same length. So each side is $24 \text{ cm}/6 = 4$ cm. But *AC* is not a side! It is the line joining vertex *A* and *C*. Of course, $\triangle ABC$ is a triangle and obeys the Triangle Law. So $AC < AB + BC = 4 \text{ cm} + 4 \text{ cm} = 8$ cm. Choose **B**.

7. **(B)** Opposite interior angles in a parallelogram are equal. So $2x + 15 = 3x - 15$. Add 15 to both sides to get $2x + 30 = 3x$, then subtract $2x$ from both sides, and we have $30 = x$. Choose **B**.

8. **(E)** As the hexagon is regular, each of its sides is 5 cm. But it shares one side with the pentagon, so each of its sides is also 5 cm. But the pentagon shares a side with the square so each side of the square is also 5 cm. Finally the equilateral triangle shares a side with the square so each of it sides is also 5 cm. Counting sides, Mary's figure has 12 sides each 5 cm long so its perimeter is $12 \times 5 \text{ cm} = 60$ cm. Choose **E**.

9. **(C)** At the vertex along with $x°$ we have the interior angle of a regular hexagon, a regular pentagon and a square. A regular hexagon has interior angles sum $(6 - 2)180° = 720°$; hence, each interior angle is $720°/6 = 120°$. A regular pentagon has interior angles that sum $(5 - 2)180° = 540°$; hence, each interior angle is $540°/5 = 108°$. Each interior angle in a square is $90°$. These four angles form a full rotation so $120° + 108° + 90° + x° = 360°$. Then $x = 360 - 120 - 108 - 90 = 42$. Choose **C**.

10. **(C)** First draw line segment *AC*. As *AB* = *BC*, △*ABC* is isosceles and ∠*BAC* = ∠*BCA* = $z°$. As *CD* = *DA*, △*DAC* is isosceles and ∠*DAC* = ∠*DCA* = $w°$. Then $y° = z° + w° = x°$. Choose **C**. Notice we could have found the values of z and w, but it was not necessary to solve the problem.

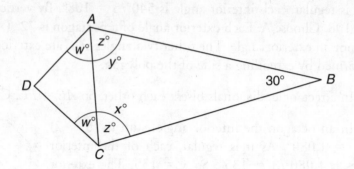

11. **(A)** As this is a convex pentagon, we know the interior angles sum to $(5 - 2)180° = 540°$. So $a + b + c + d + e = 540$, and $a + b + c + d = 540 - e$. How big could e be? Since it is convex, $e°$ must be less than 180° and hence $540 - x > 360$. Choose **A**.

12. **(D)** First note that $x° + y° = 180°$ since together they form a straight angle. In the given diagram, it appears that x is much less than y. But this may not always be the case. If *ABCD* is a square, x will equal y, and if *ABCD* is a tall skinny rectangle, x will be greater than y. Choose **D**.

13. **(B)** We know that in any polygon at a vertex the exterior and interior angles add to 180°. So $x + 3x = 180$, which implies that $4x = 180$ and thus $x = 45°$. In a regular polygon with n sides, each exterior angle is $360°/n$. If $360°/n = 45°$ then $n = 360/45 = 8$. Choose **B**.

Area

1. **(B)** The height of a parallelogram (or triangle) must be measured along a perpendicular to the base. Unless this parallelogram is a square, the height must be less than 5 cm. As the area of a parallelogram is base times height, $A = bh = (5)h < (5)5 = 25$. Choose **B**.

2. **(C)** For a square, $A = s^2$. So $16 = s^2$, and solving we find $s = 4$. The perimeter of a square is given by $P = 4s$ and thus $P = 4(4) = 16$. Choose **C**.

3. **(D)** For a rectangle $A = lw$, so $16 = lw$. We cannot solve for l and w, they could be $l = 4$ and $w = 4$, $l = 2$ and $w = 8$, or even $l = 16$ and $w = 1$. If $l = 4$ and $w = 4$, then the perimeter is $P = 2(l + w) = 2(4 + 4) = 16$, but if $l = 2$ and $w = 8$, then the perimeter is $P = 2(l + w) = 2(2 + 8) = 20$. Choose **D**.

4. **(B)** We find the area be dividing the region into simple shapes. Region ① has area 1. Region ② is half of a 2 × 1 rectangle, so it has area 1/2 (2 × 1) = 1. Region ③ and ④ together would form a 1 × 1 square—an area of 1. So the total area is 1 + 1 + 1 = 3. Choose **B**.

5. **(C)** If we draw in a line from E to F, it should be apparent that $\triangle ADE$, $\triangle DFE$, $\triangle EBF$, and $\triangle CFB$ all have the same area, call it x. So the shaded area is $2x$ and the white area is also $2x$. Choose **C**. Alternatively, let the height of the rectangle be h and the width w. Then $EB = DF$ (opposite sides of a parallelogram are equal) and $EB = FC$ (given) so $DF = FC = w/2$. It follows that $AE = EB = w/2$ as well. Then the area of $\triangle AED$ is $1/2\,bh = \frac{1}{2}(w/2)h$. The area of $\triangle FCB$ is also $\frac{1}{2}(w/2)h$. So the white area is $\frac{1}{2}(w/2)h + \frac{1}{2}(w/2)h = wh/2$. The area of the shaded parallelogram is $bh = (w/2)h = wh/2$. So the shaded and white areas are equal.

6. **(D)** The shaded area equals the area of the rectangle minus the area of the semicircles. Since the semicircles have radius 3, they have diameter 6 and thus the width of the rectangle is 10 + 6 = 16 cm. The area of the rectangle is 6 × 16 = 96 cm². Two semicircles make one full circle so the white area is $\pi r^2 = \pi(3)^2 = 9\pi$ cm². So the shaded area is $96 - 9\pi$ cm². Choose **D**.

7. **(B)** The radius of the circle is 1 inch since the diameter of the circle is 2 inches. The area inside the circle is $\pi r^2 = \pi(1)^2 = \pi$ in². By connecting opposite vertices of the hexagon, you can see the hexagon is made of six equilateral triangles. (Why are they equilateral? The six angles at the center of the circle are equal and together add to 360°. As two sides of each triangle are radii, and the angle between them is 60°, the other two angles are equal and add to 180 − 60 = 120° and thus are also 60°). The height of an equilateral triangle is $\frac{\sqrt{3}}{2}$ times the side length. In this case, the side length is 1 in. So each of those equilateral triangles has area $\frac{1}{2}(1)\left(\frac{\sqrt{3}}{2}\right) = \frac{\sqrt{3}}{4}$ in². Finally the shaded area is

$$\pi - 6\left(\frac{\sqrt{3}}{4}\right) = \pi - \frac{3\sqrt{3}}{2}\ \text{in}^2.\ \text{Choose } \mathbf{B}.$$

8. **(A)** The key to this question is to notice that the diagonal of the square must be the diameter of the circle. As the area of the square is 4 m², each side is 2 m. The diameter of any square is $\sqrt{2}$ times its side length. That means the diagonal of the square (and the diameter of the circle) is $2\sqrt{2}$ m. Hence the circumference of the circle is $\pi d = \pi(2\sqrt{2}) = 2\sqrt{2}\,\pi$ m. Choose **A**.

9. **(C)** As the width of the rink is 50, the diameter of the circles is 50 and thus the radius is 25. The two circular ends together make a circle of area $\pi r^2 = \pi(25)^2 = 625\pi$ ft^2. Roughly approximating π as 3, this is $625 \times 3 = 1,875$ ft^2. Since π is greater than 3, maybe the area is closer to 2,000 ft^2. The remaining rectangle has height 50 ft and length 150 ft (because it is $200 - $ two radii). So its area is $50 \times 150 = 7,500$ ft^2. Added together the area of the rink is at least $7,500 + 1,875 = 9,375$ and maybe about $7,500 + 2,000 = 9,500$ ft^2. 9,500 seems to be the best approximation. Choose **C**.

10. **(C)** The picture and mat together has a width of $14 + 2 + 2 = 18$ inches and height of $10 + 2 + 2 = 14$ inches. So that total area is $14 \times 18 = 252$ in^2. The area of the picture is $10 \times 14 = 140$ in^2. Thus the area of the mat is $252 - 140 = 112$ in^2. Choose **C**.

11. **(E)** This is a good problem to try substituting numbers into the given answers. Let's use $H = W = 10$. Then A is $2H + 4(W - 2) = 2(10) + 4(8) = 20 + 32 = 52$, B is $2(H - 4) + 4W = 2(6) + 4(10) = 52$, C is $WH - (W - 2)(H - 4) = (10)(10) - (8)(6) = 100 - 48 = 52$, D is $2(H - 4) + 4(W - 2) + 4(2) = 2(6) + 4(8) + 4(2) = 12 + 32 + 8 = 52$, and E is $(W + 1)(H + 2) - WH = (11)(12) - 10^2 = 132 - 100 = 32$. Since only E has a different value, it must be the case that it is the incorrect formula. Choose **E**.

   Alternate approach: Although it would seem strange to use $H = W = 0$ (since the width has to be greater than 2 and the height greater than 4), it would be a valid and much simpler way to find which formula is not equal to the others.

12. **(D)** No matter what $\angle ADC$ is, the area of the parallelogram is hw. When $\angle ADC$ is a very small angle (like 1°), the sides AD and BC become very large, and thus the perimeter can be incredibly large, certainly more than the area. When $\angle ADC$ is 90°, the perimeter of $ABCD$ is smallest with a value of $2(h + w)$. Is that smaller than the area? As $h < w$, $2(h + w) < 2(w + w) = 4w$. But $4 < h$ so $4w < hw$. Yes, the perimeter can be smaller than the area. Choose **D**.

13. **(C)** The small white circle has diameter 6 cm and thus radius 3 cm. So eight times its area is $8\pi r^2 = 8\pi(3)^2 = 72\pi$. The large circle has radius 9 cm so its area is $\pi(9)^2 = 81\pi$. We subtract the area of the white circle to find the shaded area $81\pi - \pi(3)^2 = 81\pi - 9\pi = 72\pi$. Choose **C**.

14. **(A)** The area of the circle is πr^2, which equals 4π. So $4 = r^2$ and hence $r = 2$ and the diameter of the circle is 4. The key to this question is to note that a diagonal of the rectangle is a diameter of the circle. Now using Pythagoras's Theorem $x^2 + (3x)^2 = 4^2$. We simplify to see $x^2 + 9x^2 = 16 \Rightarrow 10x^2 = 16 \Rightarrow x^2 = 1.6$. Then as $1 < x^2$ and x is positive, we can conclude that $1 < x$. Alternatively, if $x < 1$, it is clear that x^2 would be less than 1, but it's not. So $x > 1$. Choose **A**.

15. **(B)** In ① the large semicircle has radius 6, which is the diameter of the small semicircle. So the small semicircle has radius 3. To find the area of ①, we find the area of the large semicircle and subtract the area of a small circle (the two semicircles = 1 small circle). So the area of ① is $1/2\pi(6)^2 - \pi(3)^2 = \frac{1}{2}(36\pi) - 9\pi = 18\pi - 9\pi = 9\pi$. In ② the three small semicircles share the diameter of the large semicircle. So the diameter of each small semicircle is $12/3 = 4$. Then the radius of a small semicircle is 2. To find the area of ② we find the area of the large semicircle minus the area of three small semicircles. The area of ② is $\frac{1}{2}\pi(6)^2 - 3(\frac{1}{2}\pi(2^2)) = 18\pi - \frac{3}{2}(4\pi) = 18\pi - 6\pi = 12\pi$. Choose **B**.

16. **(C)** The perimeter of the large semicircle (in ① and ②) is $\frac{1}{2}\pi d = \frac{1}{2}\pi(12) = 6\pi$. The perimeter of the two semicircles is like the perimeter of one small circle, $\pi d = \pi(6) = 6\pi$. The total perimeter of ① is 12π. In ② each small semicircle has perimeter $\frac{1}{2}(2\pi r) = \frac{1}{2}(2\pi(2)) = 2\pi$. So the total perimeter of ② is $6\pi + 2\pi + 2\pi + 2\pi = 12\pi$. Remarkably, both figures have the same perimeter. Choose **C**.

Surface Area and Volume

1. **(B)** To find the diagonal, we first find the length of *AD*. We can see that it is the hypotenuse of a (3, 4, 5) triangle so *AD* is 5. Now $\triangle ADC$ is also a right triangle. So $AD^2 + DC^2 = AC^2$. But $AD = 5$ and $DC = 12$, so $5^2 + 12^2 = AC^2$, and thus $169 = AC^2$ or $AC = 13$. A quicker answer is to notice that $\triangle ADC$ is a (5, 12, 13) triangle. As $13 < 15$ choose **B**. If you noted the tips, you would know the shortest way to find the diagonal of the box is $\sqrt{3^2 + 4^2 + 12^2} = 13$.

2. **(B)** The surface area of the box is given by $SA = 2lw + 2wh + 2lh = 2(12)(3) + 2(3)(4) + 2(12)(4) = 72 + 24 + 96 = 192$ cm². Choose **B**.

3. **(B)** The volume is given by $V = s^3 = \left(\sqrt{2}\right)^3 = 2\sqrt{2}$. Choose **B**.

4. **(B)** The diagonal of a cube is always $\sqrt{3}\,s$. If $4 = \sqrt{3}\,s$ then $s = \dfrac{4}{\sqrt{3}}$. The surface area is $SA = 6s^2 = 6\left(\dfrac{4}{\sqrt{3}}\right)^2 = \dfrac{6 \times 16}{3} = 32$. Choose **B**.

5. **(C)** Since surface area equals volume in magnitude, we have $6s^2 = s^3$. Divide both sides by s^2, and we see that $s = 6$. Choose **C**.

6. **(D)** For a cube of side length 6, $V = s^3 = (6)^3 = 216$ while $SA = 6s^2 = 6(6)^2 = 216$. I is true. For a box with dimensions $4 \times 8 \times 8$, $V = lwh = (4)(8)(8) = 256$, while $SA = 2lw + 2hw + 2lh = 2(4)(8) + 2(8)(8) + 2(4)(8) = 64 + 128 + 64 = 256$. So II is true. For a box with dimensions $1 \times 2 \times 3$, $V = lwh = (1)(2)(3) = 6$, while $SA = 2lw + 2hw + 2lh = 2(1)(2) + 2(3)(2) + 2(1)(3) = 4 + 12 + 6 = 22$. III is not true. Choose **D**.

7. **(B)** We label the cubes to aid our discussion. The surface area of this shape includes five faces from ①, four faces from ①, four faces from ③, and five faces from ①. Each face is 2×2 so it has area 4. That makes a total of $18 \times 4 = 72$ square units of surface area. The box with dimensions $2 \times 4 \times 6$ has surface area $2lw + 2wh + 2lh = 2(2)(4) + 2(4)(6) + 2(2)(6) = 16 + 48 + 24 = 88$. As $88 > 72$, choose **B**.

8. **(C)** The least (or minimum) increase in surface area occurs when the new cube covers as many existing faces as possible. In this case that would be two when the new cube is placed under ③. Then it covers two faces and adds four more in surface area. That's a net change of 2 faces or $2(2)(2) = 8$ square units increase in surface area. Adding one cube, the increase in volume is the volume of the new cube or $V = s^3 = (2)^3 = 8$. Ignoring units, the values are equal. Choose **C**.

9. **(C)** To have a maximum increase in surface area, we want to cover as little as possible of the existing surface area. If the new cube touches the existing figure in just one face, say if it was placed on top of ②, then it covers one face and adds five more in surface area. That's a net change of 4 faces or $4(2)(2) = 16$ square units increase in surface area. Choose **C**.

10. **(A)** The volume of the cube is $V = s^3$ while the sphere has volume $V = 4\pi r^3/3$. If they are equal then $s^3 = 4\pi r^3/3$ so $s = \sqrt[3]{\dfrac{4\pi r^3}{3}} = \left(\sqrt[3]{\dfrac{4\pi}{3}}\right) r$.

Notice some estimation shows us that $\sqrt[3]{\dfrac{4\pi}{3}} \cong \sqrt[3]{4} = \sqrt[3]{2}\sqrt[3]{2} \cong (1.7)$

$(1.7) = 2.89$. Then the surface area of the sphere is $4\pi r^2$ while the surface area of the cube is $6s^2 = 6\left(\sqrt[3]{\dfrac{4\pi}{3}}\right)^2 r^2$ which is approximately $6(2.89)^2 r^2$, which is certainly more than $4\pi r^2$. Choose **A**. This is a terribly tricky estimation—perhaps too much to expect on the GRE. But if you remember the tip that for a fixed volume the sphere has the smallest surface area, this and any related problems become very simple.

11. **(D)** Boxes ①, ②, and ④ each contribute five faces of surface area. Box ② only contributes three faces of surface area (the other three are hidden). In total the object has $3 \times 5 + 3 = 18$ faces of equal size for surface area. If the blue boxes are two of ①, ②, and ④, then there will be 10 blue faces and thus

10/18 = 5/9 of the surface area will be blue. If the blue boxes are ③ and one of the other boxes, then there will be 8 blue faces, and thus $\frac{8}{18} = \frac{4}{9}$ of the surface area will be blue. As one possible answer is greater than $\frac{1}{2}$ and the other is less than $\frac{1}{2}$, choose **D**.

12. **(B)** Red surface area is maximized when the red cubes are some two of boxes ①, ②, and ④, In which case they have 10/18 faces of surface area. As a percentage 10/18 × 100% = 5/9 × 100% = 500/9%, which is approximately 55.6%. Choose **B**.

13. **(B)** From our tips, the largest distance inside the cylindrical can is $\sqrt{(2r)^2 + h^2} = \sqrt{(2 \times 2)^2 + (8)^2} = \sqrt{16 + 64} = \sqrt{80}$. The largest distance inside the box is the diagonal, which is $\sqrt{l^2 + w^2 + h^2} = \sqrt{4^2 + 4^2 + 7^2} = \sqrt{81} = 9$. Choose **B**.

14. **(A)** Volume can be found by area of the base times height. In this case that is $\frac{1}{2}(3)(5)(8) = 60$ cm³. If you don't remember that formula, you could think of it as one-half of a 3 × 5 × 8 box. Choose **A**.

15. **(C)** The tray has volume $V = lwh = (4)(6)(8) = 192$. Each cube has volume $V = s^3 = (2)^3 = 8$. Based strictly on volume, there could be 192 ÷ 8 = 24 cubes in the tray. Do they actually fit? Since all the dimensions are multiples of 2, the side length of the cube, they will indeed fit. Choose **C**.

16. **(B)** As the cube just fits, the longest length in the cube, the diagonal, must be the diameter of the sphere. The surface area of the cube is given by $6s^2$. Since that must equal 36, we conclude that $s^2 = 6$ and thus $s = \sqrt{6}$. The diagonal of the cube will be $\sqrt{3}s = \sqrt{3}\sqrt{6} = \sqrt{18} = 3\sqrt{2}$. Thus the diameter of the sphere is $3\sqrt{2}$. Choose **B**.

Sample Exams and Solutions

When trying one of these sample tests, try to simulate the actual circumstances of your GRE test as best as possible.

- Take this test in a quiet room.
- Turn off all cell phones, pagers, music players, and other possible disturbances.
- Keep a clock handy and give yourself exactly 45 minutes to complete the test.
- Use the given answer sheet to record your answers.
- Your only aids should be a pencil and several sheets of blank paper.

As you take the sample test, take it seriously.

- Focus on the test and each problem, but try to stay calm and relaxed.
- Record your answers on the answer sheet.
- Keep a careful watch of the time left.
- Try to average 90 seconds per question.
- Guess if you cannot complete all 28 questions in the time allotted.

Good Luck!

Answer Sheet 1

SAMPLE TEST 1

Quantitative Ability

1 Ⓐ Ⓑ Ⓒ Ⓓ Ⓔ	7 Ⓐ Ⓑ Ⓒ Ⓓ Ⓔ	13 Ⓐ Ⓑ Ⓒ Ⓓ Ⓔ	19 Ⓐ Ⓑ Ⓒ Ⓓ Ⓔ	24 Ⓐ Ⓑ Ⓒ Ⓓ Ⓔ
2 Ⓐ Ⓑ Ⓒ Ⓓ Ⓔ	8 Ⓐ Ⓑ Ⓒ Ⓓ Ⓔ	14 Ⓐ Ⓑ Ⓒ Ⓓ Ⓔ	20 Ⓐ Ⓑ Ⓒ Ⓓ Ⓔ	25 Ⓐ Ⓑ Ⓒ Ⓓ Ⓔ
3 Ⓐ Ⓑ Ⓒ Ⓓ Ⓔ	9 Ⓐ Ⓑ Ⓒ Ⓓ Ⓔ	15 Ⓐ Ⓑ Ⓒ Ⓓ Ⓔ	21 Ⓐ Ⓑ Ⓒ Ⓓ Ⓔ	26 Ⓐ Ⓑ Ⓒ Ⓓ Ⓔ
4 Ⓐ Ⓑ Ⓒ Ⓓ Ⓔ	10 Ⓐ Ⓑ Ⓒ Ⓓ Ⓔ	16 Ⓐ Ⓑ Ⓒ Ⓓ Ⓔ		27 Ⓐ Ⓑ Ⓒ Ⓓ Ⓔ
5 Ⓐ Ⓑ Ⓒ Ⓓ Ⓔ	11 Ⓐ Ⓑ Ⓒ Ⓓ Ⓔ	17 Ⓐ Ⓑ Ⓒ Ⓓ Ⓔ	22 ———————	28 Ⓐ Ⓑ Ⓒ Ⓓ Ⓔ
6 Ⓐ Ⓑ Ⓒ Ⓓ Ⓔ	12 Ⓐ Ⓑ Ⓒ Ⓓ Ⓔ	18 Ⓐ Ⓑ Ⓒ Ⓓ Ⓔ	23 Ⓐ Ⓑ Ⓒ Ⓓ Ⓔ	

Sample Test 1

QUANTITATIVE ABILITY

In this section use scrap paper to solve each problem. Then decide which is the best of the choices given and fill in the corresponding oval on the Answer Sheet.

Directions: In the following type of question, two quantities appear, one in Column A and one in Column B. You must compare them. The correct answer to the question is

A if the quantity in Column A is greater
B if the quantity in Column B is greater
C if the two quantities are equal
D if it is impossible to determine which quantity is greater

Note: Sometimes information about one or both of the quantities is centered above the two columns. If the same symbol appears in both columns, it represents the same thing each time.

Time—45 Minutes, 28 Questions

Column A	Column B
1. $\left(\dfrac{1}{3}\right)^8$	$\left(\dfrac{1}{8}\right)^3$
2. $\dfrac{4}{5}$ of $\dfrac{6}{7}$	$\dfrac{7}{8}$ of $\dfrac{9}{10}$

p is a prime

Column A	Column B
3. The number of factors of $p + 1$	The number of factors of p.

$$u \, \heartsuit \, v = (v - u)^u (u - v)^v$$

Column A	Column B
4. $9 \, \heartsuit \, 11$	$11 \, \heartsuit \, 9$

63% of a is 72

Column A	Column B
5. $2a$	250
6. $5 \times 5^2 \times 5^3$	$\dfrac{1}{\left(\dfrac{1}{5}\right)^3}$
7. Remainder when 1,003 is divided by 4	Remainder when 1,004 is divided by 3

<u>Column A</u>   <u>Column B</u>

$$0 < a < b < c$$

8.
| $\dfrac{abc}{cab}$ | $\dfrac{abc}{b^3}$ |

$$x + 2y = 4$$
$$2x + y = 5$$

9.
| Average (arithmetic mean) of x and y | 4.5 |

A jar contains four red and four green marbles

10.
| Probability of choosing two red | Probability of choosing two green |

A cylinder of gas has height 48 inches, and the base has radius 2 feet

11.
| Volume of the cylinder | Surface area of the cylinder |

12.
| $a + b + c$ | $x + y + z$ |

$$x^2 < 1$$

13.
| $\dfrac{1}{1-x}$ | $\dfrac{x+1}{x^2-1}$ |

The midpoints of a square are joined to form another square

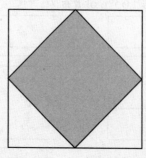

14.
| Shaded area | Unshaded area |

Directions: In the following questions, choose the best answer from the five choices listed.

Questions 15 and 16 are concerned with the tables below.*

Data from the Internet Hockey database; salaries from HockeyZone Plus.

15. In which season did Jagr earn the most money per game?

(A) 1994–1995
(B) 1995–1996
(C) 1996–1997
(D) 1997–1998
(E) 1998–1999

16. In which season did Jagr average the most points per game?

(A) 1990–1991
(B) 1995–1996
(C) 1996–1997
(D) 1997–1998
(E) 1998–1999

Questions 17 and 18 are concerned with the following chart.*

U.S. Census 2000 for St. Lawrence County, New York

Place	Population	Under 18	18-24	25-44	45-64	65+	Males per 100 females
Brasher Falls-Winthrop	1,140	23.4	7.7	24.9	23.9	20.1	89.4
Canton	5,882	12.3	45.8	16.7	13.6	11.7	101.2
Edwards	465	29.5	7.3	27.5	19.1	16.6	90.6
Gouverneur	4,263	29.8	9.5	27.3	19.7	13.7	90.6
Hammond	302	30.5	4.3	26.2	20.5	18.5	85.3
Hermon	402	26.4	7.2	26.6	24.8	15.2	103.0
Heuvelton	804	24.3	6.0	28.7	27.0	14.1	86.1
Massena	11,209	24.1	7.0	27.4	22.6	18.9	88.4
Morristown	456	27.9	5.7	27.0	25.9	13.6	92.4
Norfolk	1,334	23.9	8.2	26.5	22.5	18.9	94.2
Norwood	1,685	23.4	8.8	28.4	25.6	13.7	97.5
Ogdensburg	12,364	21.3	9.5	35.3	21.3	12.4	127.6
Potsdam	9,425	11.3	56.2	14.1	9.4	9.1	110.1
Rensselaer	337	28.5	8.6	29.4	20.2	13.4	93.7
Richville	274	23.7	9.5	32.8	21.5	12.4	101.5
Star Lake	860	23.6	6.7	26.3	26.6	16.7	95.9
Waddington	923	18.2	7.2	23.4	30.8	20.5	93.1

*Data from the U.S. Census Bureau.

17. Which place has the largest number of minors (those younger than 18)?

    (A) Massena
    (B) Ogdensburg
    (C) Potsdam
    (D) Hammond
    (E) Gouverneur

18. Which of the following statements can be inferred from the data given?

    I. There are more teenage girls than teenage boys in Star Lake.
    II. The only places with at least 1,000 minors are Potsdam, Massena, Ogdensburg, and Gouverneur.
    III. There are 45 more men than women in Hammond.

    (A) I and II
    (B) II and III
    (C) II and I
    (D) II only
    (E) III only

19. All three circles shown have radius 1 and are tangent to each other. Find the perimeter of the shaded region.

(A) 3

(B) π

(C) $\dfrac{3}{2}\pi$

(D) 2π

(E) 3π

20. The USS *Mathematica* sailed 6 knots north, then 5 knots east, then 2 knots south. How far, in knots, was the ship from her starting point?

(A) 3

(B) $\sqrt{41}$

(C) $\sqrt{61}$

(D) 41

(E) 61

21. You can buy C cans of tennis balls for D dollars. If five balls are in each can then how much does each ball cost?

(A) $\dfrac{5D}{C}$

(B) $\dfrac{C}{D^2}$

(C) $\dfrac{D}{5C}$

(D) $5DC$

(E) $\dfrac{5C}{D}$

22. If $2x + 35 = 9x$, then

$$\frac{3}{5}x = \boxed{}$$

23. If abc is a three digit number define $f(abc) = a \times b - c$. How many three digit numbers, abc, are there so that $f(abc) = 1$?

(A) 0

(B) 5

(C) 10

(D) 15

(E) 25

24. The advertised rate for roaming charges is 0.002 cents per second. What is that in dollars per hour?

   (A) 7.2
   (B) 2
   (C) 0.72
   (D) 0.2
   (E) 0.072

25. What is the average of four consecutive odd numbers starting with $2n + 1$?

   (A) 4
   (B) $2n + 3$
   (C) $2n + 4$
   (D) $2n + 5$
   (E) $n + 4$

26. In 2000 Paul was twice as old as his brother Biko. In 2008 Paul was only four years older than his brother. In what year was Biko born?

   (A) 1990
   (B) 1992
   (C) 1996
   (D) 1998
   (E) 2000

27. Draw all diagonals in a regular eight-sided polygon. What is the largest number of diagonals that meet in a single point?

   (A) 2
   (B) 3
   (C) 4
   (D) 5
   (E) 6

28. Which of the following values is closest to $\sqrt{201}$?

   (A) 13.3
   (B) 13.9
   (C) 14.2
   (D) 14.8
   (E) 15.3

Answer Sheet 2
SAMPLE TEST 2

Quantitative Ability

1 Ⓐ Ⓑ Ⓒ Ⓓ Ⓔ	7 Ⓐ Ⓑ Ⓒ Ⓓ Ⓔ	13 Ⓐ Ⓑ Ⓒ Ⓓ Ⓔ	19 Ⓐ Ⓑ Ⓒ Ⓓ Ⓔ	24 Ⓐ Ⓑ Ⓒ Ⓓ Ⓔ
2 Ⓐ Ⓑ Ⓒ Ⓓ Ⓔ	8 Ⓐ Ⓑ Ⓒ Ⓓ Ⓔ	14 Ⓐ Ⓑ Ⓒ Ⓓ Ⓔ	20 Ⓐ Ⓑ Ⓒ Ⓓ Ⓔ	25 Ⓐ Ⓑ Ⓒ Ⓓ Ⓔ
3 Ⓐ Ⓑ Ⓒ Ⓓ Ⓔ	9 Ⓐ Ⓑ Ⓒ Ⓓ Ⓔ	15 Ⓐ Ⓑ Ⓒ Ⓓ Ⓔ	21 Ⓐ Ⓑ Ⓒ Ⓓ Ⓔ	26 Ⓐ Ⓑ Ⓒ Ⓓ Ⓔ
4 Ⓐ Ⓑ Ⓒ Ⓓ Ⓔ	10 Ⓐ Ⓑ Ⓒ Ⓓ Ⓔ	16 Ⓐ Ⓑ Ⓒ Ⓓ Ⓔ		27 Ⓐ Ⓑ Ⓒ Ⓓ Ⓔ
5 Ⓐ Ⓑ Ⓒ Ⓓ Ⓔ	11 Ⓐ Ⓑ Ⓒ Ⓓ Ⓔ	17 Ⓐ Ⓑ Ⓒ Ⓓ Ⓔ	22 ————	28 Ⓐ Ⓑ Ⓒ Ⓓ Ⓔ
6 Ⓐ Ⓑ Ⓒ Ⓓ Ⓔ	12 Ⓐ Ⓑ Ⓒ Ⓓ Ⓔ	18 Ⓐ Ⓑ Ⓒ Ⓓ Ⓔ	23 Ⓐ Ⓑ Ⓒ Ⓓ Ⓔ	

Sample Test 2

QUANTITATIVE ABILITY

In this section use scrap paper to solve each problem. Then decide which is the best of the choices given and fill in the corresponding oval on the Answer Sheet.

Directions: In the following type of question, two quantities appear, one in Column A and one in Column B. You must compare them. The correct answer to the question is

A if the quantity in Column A is greater
B if the quantity in Column B is greater
C if the two quantities are equal
D if it is impossible to determine which quantity is greater

Note: Sometimes information about one or both of the quantities is centered above the two columns. If the same symbol appears in both columns, it represents the same thing each time.

Time—45 Minutes, 28 Questions

Column A	Column B
1. $\dfrac{-1}{2} \times \dfrac{-2}{3} \times \dfrac{-3}{4} \times \dfrac{-4}{5}$	$\dfrac{-5}{4} \times \dfrac{-4}{3} \times \dfrac{-3}{2}$
2. 64^3	2^{16}

p is an odd prime

3. Number of positive divisors of $p + 1$	p

$$f \blacklozenge g = fg^2 + gf^2$$

4. $4 \blacklozenge 8$	$(1/4) \blacklozenge 16$
5. $a\%$ of $b\%$ of c	$abc \div 10^3$
6. $\dfrac{\dfrac{1}{10} - \dfrac{1}{11}}{11^2 - 10^2}$	$\dfrac{7}{10} - \dfrac{5}{11}$
7. Price of a \$30,000 car after a 10% discount and 10% sales tax	Price of a \$30,000 car after a 7% discount and 7% sales tax

Column A	Column B

$$0 < a < b < c$$

8.

$(abc)^0$	$\dfrac{b^3}{abc}$

$$x > 0$$

9.

$\dfrac{1}{x^2}$	$\dfrac{1}{x}$

A jar contains n red and n green marbles where $n \geq 2$. You pick two marbles from the jar.

10.

Number of ways to pick one of each color	n^2

11.

The volume of a cube of side length 4	The volume of a sphere of radius 2

12.

$a - b + c$	0

This is a unit circle centered at O

13.

x	$\sqrt{2}$

Column A   Column B

Maria's average after three tests was 86. She scored 94 on her fourth
test and has only one test remaining.

14.

| Score Maria needs to score on her fifth test to have a 90 average | 95 |

Directions: In the following questions, choose the best answer from the five choices listed.

Questions 15 and 16 are based on the following data on volunteerism.*

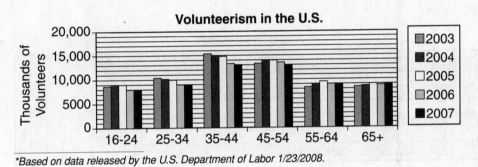

*Based on data released by the U.S. Department of Labor 1/23/2008.

15. Which age group, between which two years, had the greatest decrease in the number of volunteers?

   (A) 16–24 from 2004 to 2005
   (B) 25–34 from 2005 to 2006
   (C) 35–44 from 2005 to 2006
   (D) 45–54 from 2005 to 2006
   (E) 65+ from 2006 to 2007

16. The number of seniors (age 65+) volunteering has remained fairly constant even when the total number of volunteers fluctuates. In which year, 2003–2007, do the seniors have their best proportion of all volunteers?

   (A) 2003
   (B) 2004
   (C) 2005
   (D) 2006
   (E) 2007

Questions 17 and 18 are based on the following data.*

Average U.S. apple prices by consumption	2001	2002	2003	2004
All sales (cents per pound)	15.80	18.90	20.90	15.80
Fresh consumption (cents per pound)	22.90	25.80	29.40	21.70
All processing (dollars per ton)	108.00	130.00	131.00	107.00
Canned (dollars per ton)	139.00	161.00	154.00	149.00
Juice and cider (dollars per ton)	83.40	104.00	103.00	73.00
Frozen (dollars per ton)	139.00	175.00	173.00	172.00
Dried (dollars per ton)	84.70	108.00	107.00	77.30

*Data from U.S. Apple Association www.usapple.org.

Apple Production

1000's of 24 lb units

17. Comparing 2001 to 2003 what is the approximate percentage change in *value* of the apple crop?

(A) increase of 25%
(B) decrease of 25%
(C) increase of 6%
(D) decrease of 6%
(E) increase of 12%

18. Which is worth the most?

(A) 25% of the 2001 crop sold for juice
(B) 10% of the 2002 crop sold for canning
(C) 5% of the 2003 crop sold for freezing
(D) 15% of the 2004 crop sold dried
(E) 1% of the 2001 crop sold fresh

19. Find the perimeter.

    (A) 42 m
    (B) 42 m²
    (C) 51 m
    (D) 60 m
    (E) 63 m

20. What is the area of a regular six-sided polygon where each side has length 2?

    (A) 6
    (B) $3\sqrt{3}$
    (C) $6\sqrt{2}$
    (D) $6\sqrt{3}$
    (E) 12

21. What is the surface area of a cube with side length $\sqrt{2}$?

    (A) $\sqrt{2}$
    (B) $2\sqrt{2}$
    (C) 6
    (D) $6\sqrt{2}$
    (E) 12

22. Martina needs 35 gallons of fuel in each winter month to heat her home. Each spring and fall month she uses 15 gallons of fuel. She uses no fuel during the summer. What part of her annual heating bill is spent during the winter?

    Give your answer as a fraction:

23. Simplify $\dfrac{x^2 - y^2}{y^2 - xy} \div \dfrac{y^2 + xy}{y^2}$.

    (A) $x + y$
    (B) y^2
    (C) $\dfrac{x^2 - y^2}{y^2}$
    (D) $\dfrac{x}{y} + 1$
    (E) -1

24. George earned 80, 85, and 90 on the first three tests in his geography class. Because he didn't have time to study, he decides to guess randomly on the final test. That test has ten true-false questions, each worth 10 points. What is the probability his final average is more than 85?

(A) $\dfrac{12}{2^8}$

(B) $\dfrac{11}{2^8}$

(C) $\dfrac{12}{1,024}$

(D) $\dfrac{11}{1,024}$

(E) 0.5

25. A right triangle has sides 12, 15, and x. How many possible values are there for x?

(A) 0
(B) 1
(C) 2
(D) 3
(E) Infinite

26. If n and m are integers so that $nm = 30$ and $\dfrac{1}{n} - \dfrac{1}{m} = \dfrac{1}{30}$, then what is $n - m$?

(A) −1
(B) 1
(C) −2
(D) 2
(E) 5

27. Not counting zero, what is the forty-ninth digit in the decimal expansion of 1/7? Recall $1/7 = 0.142.\ldots$

(A) 1
(B) 4
(C) 2
(D) 8
(E) 5

28. Which of the following can be expressed as the sum of three consecutive integers?

(A) 278
(B) 49
(C) 11
(D) −1
(E) −6

Answers and Complete Solutions to Sample Exams

SAMPLE TEST 1

Answers

1. B	8. D	15. D	22. 3
2. B	9. B	16. B	23. E
3. D	10. C	17. A	24. E
4. C	11. B	18. D	25. C
5. B	12. A	19. B	26. C
6. A	13. A	20. B	27. C
7. A	14. C	21. C	28. C

Detailed Solutions

1. **(B)** This question really asks which is bigger, $\dfrac{1}{3^8}$ or $\dfrac{1}{8^3}$. A feasible but time-consuming strategy is to multiply out the denominators. Alternatively you can notice that $3^8 = 3^{2 \times 4} = (3^2)^4 = 9^4$, and since $9 > 8$, we conclude that $9^3 > 8^3$. Then clearly $9^4 = 9 \times 9^3 > 8^3$; hence $3^8 > 8^3$ and $\dfrac{1}{3^8} < \dfrac{1}{8^3}$. Choose **B**.

2. **(B)** A computational approach would be to multiply out and then do equal operations to each column until it is clear which is bigger. For instance,

$$\frac{4}{5} \times \frac{6}{7} \qquad\qquad \frac{7}{8} \times \frac{9}{10}$$

   Clear the denominators by multiplying each column by $7 \times 8 \times 10$ canceling where you can.

$$2 \times 8 \times 4 \times 6 \qquad\qquad 7 \times 7 \times 9$$
$$64 \times 6 \qquad\qquad\qquad 49 \times 9$$

   Clearly the second column is larger so choose **B.**
   Alternatively, I prefer to think of each fraction as a difference with one so $\dfrac{4}{5} = 1 - \dfrac{1}{5}, \dfrac{6}{7} = 1 - \dfrac{1}{7}, \dfrac{7}{8} = 1 - \dfrac{1}{8}$, and $\dfrac{9}{10} = 1 - \dfrac{1}{10}$. Since $\dfrac{1}{10}$ and $\dfrac{1}{8}$ are both smaller than $\dfrac{1}{5}$ and $\dfrac{1}{7}$ it should be clear that $\dfrac{7}{8}$ and $\dfrac{9}{10}$ are both larger than $\dfrac{4}{5}$ and $\dfrac{6}{7}$. Hence the product $\dfrac{7}{8} \times \dfrac{9}{10}$ is larger than $\dfrac{4}{5} \times \dfrac{6}{7}$.

3. **(D)** If p is prime, p has precisely two factors—one and itself. If p is an odd prime, then $p + 1$ is even and always has at least three factors (1, 2, and itself).

But when $p = 2$, the only even prime, then $p + 1 = 3$, and it also has two factors. Hence sometimes they have an equal number of factors and sometimes $p + 1$ has more. Choose **D**.

4. **(C)** The quick answer is to notice that the operation is symmetric in u and v, so $u \heartsuit v = v \heartsuit u$. If you were to substitute, you would find $9 \heartsuit 11 = (11 - 9)^9 (9 - 11)^{11} = 2^9 (-2)^{11}$ and $11 \heartsuit 9 = (9 - 11)^{11}(11 - 9)^9 = (-2)^{11}2^9$, which are clearly equal. Choose **C**.

5. **(B)** We solve for a. $\dfrac{63}{100} \times a = 72$; hence, $a = 72 \times \dfrac{100}{63}$ and $2a = 144 \times \dfrac{100}{63}$. I don't know exactly what $100 \div 63$ is, but it is a little more than 1.5 $(100/63 = 1 + 37/63)$. 1.5 times 144 is 216, nowhere near 250, so 250 must be larger than $2a$. Choose **B**. A more precise calculation would lead to the same conclusion, but why work harder when an estimate will do?

6. **(A)** We use rules of exponents to see that Column A is $5 \times 5^2 \times 5^3 = 5^6$. Column B is equal to $\dfrac{1}{\frac{1}{5^3}} = 1 \times \dfrac{5^3}{1} = 5^3$. Choose **A**.

7. **(A)** Since 1,000 is divisible by 4, $1{,}003 \div 4 = 250$ R 3. The remainder when dividing by 3 is always less than 3. Choose **A**. Alternatively just use long division—it shouldn't take too long and leads to the same conclusion.

8. **(D)** Use cancellation to see that Column A is just 1. In Column B, $\dfrac{abc}{b^3} = \dfrac{ac}{b^2} = \dfrac{a}{b} \times \dfrac{c}{b}$. Since $a < b$, $a/b < 1$ and since $c > b$, $c/b > 1$. It's not clear what the product of a number less than one and a number greater than one might be. Maybe the answer is D? Try $a = 1$, $b = 2$, and $c = 3$. Then $\dfrac{1}{2} \times \dfrac{3}{2} = \dfrac{3}{4}$, which is less than 1. Try $a = 1$, $b = 2$, and $c = 8$. Then $\dfrac{1}{2} \times \dfrac{8}{2} = 2$, which is greater than 1. Choose **D**.

9. **(B)** One can solve for x and y and then compute their average, but it's not necessary to do so. Adding both equations together we get $3x + 3y = 9$. Divide both sides by 3 to see that $x + y = 3$. Hence the average of x and y is $\dfrac{3}{2}$ or 1.5. Choose **B**.

10. **(C)** The easy answer here is to notice that the role of red and green is symmetric, so whatever the probabilities are they must be equal. Choose **C**. To compute

the probabilites, note there are $\begin{pmatrix} 4 \\ 2 \end{pmatrix} = 6$ ways to pick two marbles from four.

Only one of these ways is the two red marbles. So Column A is $\frac{1}{6}$. Similarly Column B is $\frac{1}{6}$.

11. **(B)** Just apply the proper formulas and the same units. I chose to use feet and converted 48 inches $\times$ (1 foot/12 inches) = 4 feet. To find volume use $V = \pi r^2 h = \pi(2)^2 4 = 16\pi$. To find surface area use $SA = 2\pi r^2 + 2\pi rh = 2\pi(2)^2 + 2\pi(2)(4) = 8\pi + 16\pi = 24\pi$. The surface area is larger. Choose **B**.

12. **(A)** Label the internal angles of the triangles as A, B, and C. Then by vertical angles, $x = A$, $y = B$, and $z = C$. As the sum of interior angles of a triangle is 180°, $A + B + C = 180°$ and hence $x + y + z = 180°$. If you recall that the sum of the exterior angles of a triangle are 360° and notice that a, b, c are exterior angles, then you will know that $a + b + c = 360°$. Choose **A**.

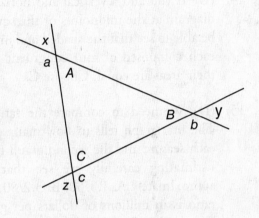

   Alternatively, since a and x are supplementary angles, $a + x = 180°$. Similarly $c + z = 180°$ and $b + y = 180°$. Adding all three equations, we see that $a + z + c + x + b + y = 540°$. Rearranging the left-hand side $(a + b + c) + (x + y + z) = 540°$. But $x + y + z = 180°$, so $(a + b + c) + 180° = 540°$. Hence $a + b + c = 360°$.

13. **(A)** As $x^2 < 1$, we know that $-1 < x < 1$. Most importantly, this means that $x \neq 1$ and $x \neq -1$, so that the denominator of both fractions is never zero. If we consider the fraction in Column B and factor the denominator, we see that

$$\frac{x + 1}{x^2 - 1} = \frac{x + 1}{(x + 1)(x - 1)} = \frac{1}{x - 1}$$

This is very similar to Column A! In fact

$$\frac{1}{x - 1} = (-1) \times \frac{1}{1 - x}$$

This means that if Column A is negative, then Column B is positive and vice versa.

   Since $-1 < x < 1$, adding -1 to all sides, we see that $-2 < x - 1 < 0$. So $x - 1$, and Column B is always negative. Hence Column A is always positive and thus bigger than Column B. Choose **A**.

Alternatively, clear denominators by multiplying both columns by $1 - x$.

$$(1 - x) \times \frac{1}{x - 1} \qquad (1 - x) \times \frac{x + 1}{x^2 - 1}$$

$$= 1 \qquad = \frac{\overset{-1}{\overline{(1 - x)}}\,(x + 1)}{(x - 1)\,(x + 1)}$$

$$= -1$$

Clearly Column A is larger.

14. **(C)** If you add a vertical and horizontal line to the diagram at the midpoints of the square, you should be able to see that the shaded and unshaded areas are each composed of four congruent triangles. Hence their areas are equal. Choose **C**.

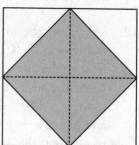

15. **(D)** We need to compare the ratios salary/games. The first graph tells us how many games he played each season, and the second graph tells us his salary. Estimating carefully we see that the ratios are approximately A: 1.5/50, B: 3.2/80, C: 4.1/64, D: 5.1/75, and E: 5/80. Each ratio is in millions of dollars per game. Which of those fractions is largest? Clearly E > B and C > A so A and B are out. Also E has smaller numerator and larger denominator than D, so D > E. E is out. That just leaves C and D to consider. If we approximate 4.1/64 ≈ 4/64 = 1/16, while 5.1/75 ≈ 5/75 = 1/15. As 1/15 > 1/16, choose **D**.

If you are uncomfortable with that approximation (yes, they are very close in value), let's check this precisely. Finding common denominators we see that $\frac{4.1}{64} \times \frac{75}{75} = \frac{307.5}{64 \times 75}$, while $\frac{5.1}{75} \times \frac{64}{64} = \frac{326.4}{64 \times 75}$. Again D is larger.

16. **(B)** We can read both points and games from the first graph and simply compare the length of the dark rectangle (points) to the light rectangle (games) for each season. In 1995–1996, the dark rectangle is much larger than the light rectangle; in fact, it is almost twice as large (150 points/81 games). No other ratio comes close. Choose **B**.

17. **(A)** To find the number of minors we must multiply the percentage of the population younger than 18 by the population. It would be too time consuming to do this for all the places so start with the one with the largest population. Consider Massena and roughly estimate a population of 10,000 with 25% minors or 2,500 minors. Only places with more population than 2,500 could have more minors. This immediately rules out all places except Canton, Gouverneur, Ogdensburg, and Potsdam. Rough estimates show that Canton

has approximately 10% of 5,000 or 500 minors, Gouverneur has 30% of 4,000 or 1,200 minors, Ogdensburg has 20% of 12,000 or 2,400 minors, and Potsdam has 10% of 9,000 or 900 minors. Massena and Ogdensburg are close so we will estimate more precisely.

Massena	11,209 people	Ogdensburg	12,364 people
10%	1,121	10%	1,236
20%	2,242	20%	2,472
1%	112	1%	124
2%	224	21% = 20% + 1%	2,596
4%	448		
24% = 20% + 4%	2,690		

Choose Massena, **A**.

18. **(D)** In Star Lake there are 95.9 males for each 100 females so there are more females than males. But there is no way to infer how that affects a segment of the population like teenagers. In fact we don't know how many teenagers there are—just minors. It cannot be inferred from the data.

We have already seen in question 17 that Massena, Ogdensburg, and Massena have at least 1,000 minors. For Potsdam our rough estimate of 900 suggests we try a more precise estimate.

Potsdam	9,425 people
10%	942
1%	94
11% = 10% + 1%	1,036

Potsdam, with 11.3% minors, will have more than 1036 minors. Yes, II can be inferred from the data

Hammond has 85.3 men for each 100 women. That means Hammond has more women than men. III cannot be inferred from the data because it is false! Choose **D**.

19. **(B)** If you connect the centers of the three circles you will form an equilateral triangle. The shaded region is formed from the triangle by removing the pie-shaped pieces, each with angle 60° as an equilateral triangle has 60° angles. If we reassemble the arcs forming the perimeter of the shaded area we can form a semicircle ($3 \times 60° = 180°$). So the perimeter of the shaded area equals the circumference of the semicircle $P = 1/2 \times 2 \pi r = \pi (1) = \pi$. Choose **B**.

20. **(B)** Draw a diagram.

You can see that the ship is 5 knots east of its starting point and by subtraction we know it is $6 - 2 = 4$ knots north of its starting point. We simply use the Pythagorean Theorem to find d. So $4^2 + 5^2 = d^2$ and thus $d = \sqrt{4^2 + 5^2} = \sqrt{41}$. Choose **B**.

A common error here would be to assume that this is a 3, 4, 5 triangle. It's not. The hypotenuse must be 5 in a (3, 4, 5) triangle.

21. **(C)** For D dollars you get C cans of tennis balls—that is $5 \times C$ balls in total. What is the price per ball? Cost/# balls $= D/5(C)$. Choose **C**.

If this does not seem straightforward, try using numbers instead of letters. Say you get 3 cans of tennis balls for 7 dollars, that is, $D = 7$ and $C = 3$. What does it cost per ball? Well, 3 cans of balls is $3 \times 5 = 15$ balls for a total price of $7. So the price per ball is 7/15. Substitute $D = 7$ and $C = 3$ into the given solutions.

(A) $5D/C = 35/3$
(B) $C/D^2 = 3/49$
(C) $D/(5C) = 7/(5 \times 3) = 7/15$
(D) $5DC = 5 \times 7 \times 3 = 105$
(E) $5C/D = 5 \times 3/7 = 15/7$

Again, **C** is the answer.

22. First we solve for x. If $2x + 35 = 9x$, subtract $2x$ from both sides to get $35 = 7x$. Then divide by 7 to see that $x = 5$. Finally $\frac{3}{5}x = \frac{3}{5} \times 5 = 3$.

$$\frac{3}{5}x = \boxed{3}$$

23. **(E)** Essentially we have to find solutions to $ab - c = 1$ where a, b, c are single digits from 0 to 9 except a cannot equal zero. There is no right or wrong way to proceed, but you need to be careful to check all possibilities. I chose to start by looking at the value of a.

    If $a = 1$, we need to solve $b - c = 1$. That will have solutions $b = 1$ and $c = 0$, $b = 2$ and $c = 1, \ldots$, and $b = 9$ and $c = 8$. That is nine solutions — 110, 121, 132, $\ldots$, 198. But notice that anytime abc is a solution so is bac. Thus, 110, 210, 312, $\ldots$ and 918 are also solutions. That makes at least 17 solutions. Choose **E**.

    To find all solutions it is easiest to use the values of c to determine cases.
    If $c = 0$, solve $ab = 1$. The only solution is 110.
    If $c = 1$, solve $ab = 2$. The solutions are 121 and 211.
    If $c = 2$, solve $ab = 3$. The solutions are 132 and 312.
    If $c = 3$, solve $ab = 4$. The solutions are 143, 413, and 223.
    If $c = 4$, solve $ab = 5$. The solutions are 154, and 514.
    If $c = 5$, solve $ab = 6$. The solutions are 165, 615, 235, and 325.
    If $c = 6$, solve $ab = 7$. The solutions are 176, and 716.
    If $c = 7$, solve $ab = 8$. The solutions are 187, 817, 247, and 427.
    If $c = 8$, solve $ab = 9$. The solutions are 198, 918, and 338.
    If $c = 9$, solve $ab = 10$. The solutions are 259 and 529.
    That is a total of 25 solutions.

24. **(E)** We use simple conversion factors.

$$\frac{0.002¢}{s} \times \frac{1\$}{100¢} \times \frac{60\ s}{1\ min} \times \frac{60\ min}{1\ hr} = \frac{0.002 \times 3600}{100}\frac{\$}{hr} = \frac{7.2}{100}\frac{\$}{hr} = 0.072\frac{\$}{hr}.$$

When multiplying, think $2 \times 3{,}600$, and then move the decimals to find the final answer. Choose **E**.

25. **(C)** Remembering to add 2 to get to the next odd number, the four numbers in question are $2n + 1$, $2n + 3$, $2n + 5$, and $2n + 7$. The average of consecutive (odd) numbers is the middle number (odd amount of numbers) or the average of the two middle numbers (even amount of numbers). In this case (4 is even) the middle numbers $2n + 3$ and $2n + 5$ have an average of $2n + 4$. Choose **C**.

    Alternatively, add and divide by 4.

$$[(2n + 1) + (2n + 3) + (2n + 5) + (2n + 7)] \div 4 =$$
$$[8n + 16] \div 4 = 2n + 4$$

26. **(C)** A table can help here.

	Paul	Biko
2000	$2x$	x
2008	$x + 8 + 4$	$x + 8$

Let Biko's age in 2000 be x. Since Paul is twice Biko's age, Paul is $2x$. In 2008, 8 years have passed so Biko is now $x + 8$. Paul is only four years older so Paul is $x + 8 + 4$. But Paul is also $2x + 8$ since 8 years have passed for him as well. So $2x + 8 = x + 8 + 4$, and solving we find $x = 4$. That means Biko was 4 in 2000 and hence he was born in 1996. Choose **C**.

27. (**C**) Draw a diagram, but yes, it is hard to be completely accurate. Still, it should be clear that four diagonals meet in the center and at most three meet anywhere else. Choose **C**.

28. (**C**) Recall that $14^2 = 196$ and $15^2 = 225$. Hence $\sqrt{201}$ is between 14 and 15. Is it closest to 14.2 or 14.8? Since 201 is much closer to 196 than 225 it seems clear that $\sqrt{201}$ should be closest to 14.2. You can check more carefully by calculating 14.2^2.

$$
\begin{array}{r}
14.2 \\
\times \quad 14.2 \\
\hline
284 \\
5680 \\
14200 \\
\hline
201.64
\end{array}
$$

Clearly $(14.2)^2$ is very close to $\sqrt{201}$. Choose **C**.

SAMPLE TEST 2

Answers

1. A	8. D	15. C	22. 7/13
2. A	9. D	16. E	23. E
3. D	10. C	17. A	24. D
4. A	11. A	18. A	25. C
5. B	12. C	19. D	26. A
6. B	13. B	20. D	27. A
7. B	14. A	21. E	28. E

Detailed Solutions

1. (**A**) Most people will use cancellation.

$$\frac{-1}{\cancel{2}} \times \frac{\cancel{-2}}{\cancel{3}} \times \frac{\cancel{-3}}{\cancel{4}} \times \frac{\cancel{-4}}{5} = \frac{(-1)^4}{5} = \frac{1}{5} \qquad \frac{-5}{\cancel{4}} \times \frac{\cancel{-4}}{\cancel{3}} \times \frac{\cancel{-3}}{2} = \frac{(-1)^3 5}{2} = \frac{-5}{2}$$

Clearly $\frac{1}{5} > -\frac{5}{2}$. Choose **A**.

A quicker answer would be to note that Column A is the product of four negative numbers and hence positive. Column B is the product of three negative numbers and hence negative. Positive is always larger than negative.

2. (**A**) We express 64 as a power of two and use our laws for exponents to simplify: $64^3 = (2^6)^3 = 2^{18}$. Certainly 2^{18} is larger than 2^{16}. Choose **A**.

3. (**D**) For large values of p, we expect that $p + 1$ would have much fewer than p divisors (not every number less than $p + 1$ divides into it). But for small p interesting things happen. When $p = 3$, $p + 1 = 4$, which has three divisors; hence, the two columns are equal. When $p = 5$, $p + 1 = 6$, which has four divisors; hence, Column A is smaller than Column B. Choose **D**.

4. (**A**) A straightforward calculation is best here.

$$\frac{1}{4} \blacklozenge 16 = \frac{1}{4} \times 16^2 + 16 \times (\frac{1}{4})^2 = 4 \times 16 + 1 = 64 + 1 = 65$$

$$4 \blacklozenge 8 = 4 \times 8^2 + 8 \times 4^2 = 4 \times 64 + 8 \times 16 = 256 + 128 = 384$$

If you calculate Column B first, you may not have to complete your calculation of Column A, since part way through it becomes clear that Column A is larger than Column B. Choose **A**.

5. (**B**) $a\%$ of $b\%$ of $c = \frac{a}{100}\left(\frac{b}{100} \times c\right) = \frac{abc}{10,000}$, while $abc \div 10^3 = \frac{abc}{1,000}$. Choose **B**.

6. **(B)** First we factor and simplify Column A.

$$\frac{\dfrac{1}{10} - \dfrac{1}{11}}{11^2 - 10^2} = \frac{\dfrac{\cancel{11-10}}{10 \cdot 11}}{(\cancel{11-10})(11+10)} = \frac{\dfrac{1}{10 \cdot 11}}{21} = \frac{1}{21} \cdot \frac{1}{10 \cdot 11}$$

We do not completely multiply out the answer—it may be better to compare to Column B this way.

$$\frac{7}{10} - \frac{5}{11} = \frac{7 \cdot 11 - 5 \cdot 10}{10 \cdot 11} = \frac{77 - 50}{10 \cdot 11} = 27 \cdot \frac{1}{10 \cdot 11}$$

Yes, since $27 > \dfrac{1}{21}$ Column B is larger. Choose **B**.

Alternatively, try to clear the denominators by multiplying both columns by 10 and 11.

$$10 \cdot 11 \cdot \frac{\dfrac{1}{10} - \dfrac{1}{11}}{11^2 - 10^2} = \frac{10 \cdot 11 \cdot \dfrac{1}{10} - 10 \cdot 11 \cdot \dfrac{1}{11}}{(11 - 10)(11 + 10)} = \frac{\cancel{11 - 10}}{(\cancel{11-10})(11+10)} = \frac{1}{21}$$

$$10 \cdot 11 \cdot \left(\frac{7}{10} - \frac{5}{11} \right) = \frac{7 \cdot 10 \cdot 11}{10} - \frac{5 \cdot 10 \cdot 11}{11} = 77 - 50 = 27$$

As $27 > \dfrac{1}{21}$, Column B is larger.

7. **(B)** Note that a 10% discount is like paying 90% of the price. Then in Column A the price is $30,000 \times (0.9) \times (1.1)$. Don't know why we multiplied by 1.07? See page 137. In Column B the price is $30,000 \times (0.93) \times (1.07)$. It's hard to estimate which is bigger so we compute: $(0.9) \times (1.1) = .99$, while $(0.93) \times (1.07) = 0.9951$. Choose **B**.

8. **(D)** Column A is 1 as anything to the exponent zero is 1. And if we simplify Column B, we get $\dfrac{b^2}{ac} = \dfrac{b}{a} \cdot \dfrac{b}{c}$. Notice that, since $b > a$, b/a is always greater than 1. Similarly b/c is always less than 1. Let's try $a = 1$, $b = 2$, and $c = 3$. Then we get $\dfrac{2}{1} \cdot \dfrac{2}{3} = \dfrac{4}{3}$, which is greater than 1. This will change if we make c much larger. Try $a = 1$, $b = 2$, and $c = 8$. Then $\dfrac{2}{1} \cdot \dfrac{2}{8} = \dfrac{1}{2}$, which is less than 1. Hence Column B is sometimes larger and sometimes smaller. Choose **D**.

9. **(D)** When $0 < x < 1$ we know from our facts to memorize that $x^2 < x$; hence, $\dfrac{1}{x^2} > \dfrac{1}{x}$. When $x > 1$ the opposite is true: $x^2 > x$ and hence $\dfrac{1}{x^2} > \dfrac{1}{x}$. Choose **D**.

Alternatively, just try some values. If $x = 1$, both columns are equal to 1. If $x = 2$, $\frac{1}{x^2} = \frac{1}{4}$, which is less than $\frac{1}{x} = \frac{1}{2}$. Hence it depends on the choice of x.

10. **(C)** There are n choices for which green marble to take and n choices for which red marble to take. That makes $n \times n = n^2$ ways to pick one of each color. Choose **C**.

11. **(A)** For a cube $V = s^3 = 4^3 = 64$. For a sphere $V = 4\pi r^3/3 = 4\pi(2)^3/3 = 32\pi/3$. Since $\pi/3$ is close to 1, $32\pi/3$ is much less than 64. Choose **A**.

Alternatively, as you may not know the formula for the volume of a sphere (it is not commonly used on this exam), try drawing a diagram.

12. **(C)** Label the interior angles of the triangle as having measures $A°$, $B°$, and $C°$.

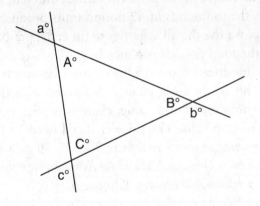

Then $A + B + C = 180$. By supplementary angles $b + B = 180$ (or $B = 180 - b$) and by vertical angles $a = A$ and $c = C$. Substituting we have $a + (180 - b) + c = 180$; hence, $a - b + c = 0$. Choose **C**.

13. **(B)** A full circle has $360°$ so the triangle has an angle at O of $60°$. Also the two sides that extend from O to the circle are both radii, so the triangle is actually isosceles. Furthermore each base angles must be $(180° - 60°)/2 = 60°$. So the triangle is actually equilateral. Since this is a unit circle the two radii have length 1. That means x is also 1. Choose **B**.

14. **(A)** We can assume that each of her first three tests was actually 86. If she scores 95 on her last test her average will be (86 + 86 + 86 + 94 + 95)/5 = 447/5 = 89.4. So she must score more than 95. Choose **A**.

    Alternatively, let's try the sharing technique.

86	86	86	94	____
+4			−4	____
90	86	86	90	____

    To get an average of 90 her fifth test would have to be high enough to give 4 to each of the remaining 86's and still have 90 left. Hence it would have to be 98.

15. **(C)** This question asks for the greatest decrease in *numbers*—not percentage decrease. You cannot just compare the size of the bars. You must look at the scale—but luckily all the bars use the same scale. By inspection you can see the largest drop comes between 2005 and 2006 for age 35–44. Choose **C**.

16. **(E)** We must look at seniors as a portion (or percentage) of all volunteers, that is (65 + volunteers) ÷ (sum all volunteers). We could calculate these values for each year but that is tedious and time consuming. Since the numerator is roughly constant, we just need to find the year where the sum of all volunteers was lowest. Year 2007 is lowest for all groups except 56–64. Even so, the difference there (1,000 thousand volunteers) is much less than the differences in other age groups. 2007 will be the lowest total of volunteers. Hence seniors had their best proportion of all volunteers in 2007. Choose **E**.

17. **(A)** Notice the first table shows price (in various different units), while the second table shows the thousands of 42 pound units produced. To find the value of the total crop, we use the all sales figure (in cents per pound), and we need to multiply by the total pounds produced.

    In 2001 they produced about 15,000 more (thousands of 42 pound units) than in 2003. This is not a big change compared with the total of 210,000. If the crops had been exactly the same, change in price would completely dictate the change in crop value The price changed from 15.80 in 2001 to 20.90 in 2003, as a percentage increase that is 5.10/15.80 or a little less than 33%. The only answer even close to 33% is A. Allowing for the differences in production 25% is a reasonable answer. Choose **A**.

    If you want to calculate more precisely (hard to do without a calculator—even estimates are tricky), here is an answer.

    For 2001, 225,000 thousand units × 42 lb/unit is 9,450 million pounds. At a value of 15.8 cents/lb, we have a total crop value of 15.8 × 9,450 million cents or 149,310 million cents. That's about 1,500 million dollars. For 2003, 210,000 thousand units × 42 lb/unit is 8,820 million lbs of apples. At a value of 20.9 cents/lb, we have a total crop value of 20.9 × 8,820 million cents or 184,338 million cents. That's about 1,840 million dollars.

    Thus the increase in value is about 340 million dollars compared with the 1,500 million dollar value of 2001's crop. We find that 340/1500 × 100% is approximately 23%.

18. **(A)** It is difficult to actually calculate these values but not as hard to compare them. Since canning and freezing have the same price and it is clear that 10% of 2002 production is more than 5% of 2004 production we know that B > C. Now juice sells for more than half the price of canning and 25% of 2001 is more than double 10% of 2002, so A > B. Notice that dried and juice sell for almost the same price, and 15% of 2004 is much less than 25% of 2001, so A > D. That just leaves E to compare with A. The price for juice is $83.40/ton, which equals 8340¢/ 2,000 lb which is approximately 4.1¢/lb. That is only a sixth of the price for fresh consumption but 25% of the 2001 crop is 25 times more than 1% of the 2001 crop. Hence A has the greatest value. Choose **A**.

19. **(D)** It is best to recall the perimeter of such a shape is the same as a rectangle with side lengths 13 m and 17 m. Hence $P = 2(l + w) = 2(13\text{ m} + 17\text{ m}) = 60$ m. Choose **D**.

    Alternatively, label the missing vertical length x and the missing horizontal length y. Equating the vertical sides we have $3x + 1 = 13$; hence, $x = 4$. Equating the horizontal sides we have $2y + 5 + 6 = 17$, hence, $y = 3$. Adding clockwise from 1, the perimeter of the figure is $1 + 17 + 13 + 6 + 4 + 5 + 4 + 3 + 4 + 3 = 60$.

20. **(D)** If you connect each vertex to the center of the hexagon you obtain six congruent equilateral triangles. Convince yourself of why the triangles are equilateral and congruent.

    We recall that the height of an equilateral triangle is $\frac{\sqrt{3}}{2}$ times its side length.

    Hence the area of one of the triangles is $A = \frac{1}{2}bh = \frac{1}{2}(2)\left(\frac{\sqrt{3}}{2}2\right) = \sqrt{3}$.

    So the area of the hexagon is $6\sqrt{3}$. Pick **D**.

21. **(E)** The surface area of a cube of six times the area of one face $SA = 6s^2$. In this case that is $SA = 6\left(\sqrt{2}\right)^2 = 12$. Choose **E**.

22. 7/13. There are three months in each season. She uses $3 \times 35 = 105$ gallons of fuel in winter. She uses $3 \times 15 = 45$ gallons of fuel each spring and fall. Hence the portion used in winter is $\dfrac{105}{105 + 45 + 45 + 0} = \dfrac{105}{195} = \dfrac{21}{39} = \dfrac{7}{13}$.

    Give your answer as a fraction: $\dfrac{7}{13}$

23. **(E)** Division is the same as multiplying by the reciprocal. Then we factor and cancel.

$$\frac{x^2 - y^2}{y^2 - xy} \div \frac{y^2 + xy}{y^2} = \frac{x^2 - y^2}{y^2 - xy} \times \frac{y^2}{y^2 + xy} =$$

$$\frac{\overset{-1}{\cancel{(x - y)}} \cancel{(x + y)}}{y \cancel{(y - x)}} \times \frac{y^2}{y \cancel{(y + x)}} = \frac{-y^2}{y^2} = -1$$

Choose **E**.

24. **(D)** His first three tests already average 85. To have a final average higher than that, he must score higher than 85 (i.e., he must score 90 or 100). There are 2^{10} possible ways he could answer the test as there are two choices, T or F, for each of ten questions. Only one of the ways results in a perfect score of 100. Hence, his chance of scoring 100 is $1/2^{10}$. There are ten ways he could score 90 (ten different questions to get wrong) out of the 2^{10} possible ways he could answer on the test. Hence his chance of scoring 90 is $10/2^{10}$. Adding, his chance of scoring 90 or 100 is $11/2^{10}$. Choose **D**.

25. **(C)** By the Pythagorean Theorem and depending on which side is the hypotenuse, either $12^2 + 15^2 = x^2$ or $12^2 + x^2 = 15^2$ or $15^2 + x^2 = 12^2$. The last case is impossible since the hypotenuse must be the largest side. Each of the other two cases will lead to one answer for x. Choose **C**.

26. **(A)** Start with the equation $\dfrac{1}{n} - \dfrac{1}{m} = \dfrac{1}{30}$ and multiply both sides by nm:

    $nm\left(\dfrac{1}{n} - \dfrac{1}{m}\right) = nm\dfrac{1}{30}$, to clear the denominators. Distribute and cancel,

    remembering that $nm = 30$, $\dfrac{\cancel{n}m}{\cancel{n}} - \dfrac{n\cancel{m}}{\cancel{m}} = \cancel{nm}\dfrac{1}{\cancel{30}}$ to get $m - n = 1$.

    Multiply both sides by negative one and you get $n - m = -1$. Choose **A**.

27. **(A)** Use long division to find that $1/7 = 0.142857142857\ldots$. Because of the repeating pattern every sixth digit after the decimal point is a 7. As 48 is a multiple of 6, the 48th digit is a 7. Hence the next digit is a 1. Choose **A**.

28. **(E)** We try a few examples: $1 + 2 + 3 = 6$, $2 + 3 + 4 = 9$, $3 + 4 + 5 = 12$, and $11 + 12 + 13 = 36$. The sum of three consecutive numbers is always a multiple of three The only answer that is a multiple of three is -6. In fact, $-6 = -3 + -2 + -1$. Choose **E**.

Appendix

Suggested Facts to Memorize

Common fractions and their decimal equivalents

$$\frac{1}{8} = 0.125 \quad \frac{1}{6} \cong 0.16 \quad \frac{1}{5} = 0.2 \quad \frac{1}{4} = 0.25 \quad \frac{1}{3} \cong 0.333$$

Common irrational numbers square roots and their decimal equivalents

$$\sqrt{2} \cong 1.4 \quad \sqrt{3} \cong 1.7 \quad e \cong 2.7 \quad \pi \cong 3.14$$

Perfect squares

$$11^2 = 121, \quad 12^2 = 144, \quad 13^2 = 169, \quad 14^2 = 196, \quad 15^2 = 225,$$
$$16^2 = 256, \quad 17^2 = 289, \quad 18^2 = 324, \quad 19^2 = 361$$

Inequalities

$$\text{If } 0 < a < 1, \text{ then } 0 < a^2 < a < 1$$
$$\text{If } 1 < a, \text{ then } 1 < a < a^2$$

Algebra

$$(x + y)^2 = x^2 + 2xy + y^2 \quad (x - y)^2 = x^2 - 2xy + y^2 \quad x^2 - y^2 = (x - y)(x + y)$$

Common right triangles

Geometrical measurement

Area = πr^2
Circumference = πd

Areas and perimeter

Index